MEDITATIONS ON THE PSALMS

MEDITATIONS
ON THE
PSALMS

by Bernard C. Mischke, O.S.C.

SHEED AND WARD · NEW YORK

© Sheed and Ward, Inc. 1963

Library of Congress Catalog Card Number 63–8549

NIHIL OBSTAT:
ALOYSIUS J. MEHR, O.S.C., J.C.D.
CENSOR LIBRORUM

IMPRIMI POTEST:
VERY REV. BENNO MISCHKE, O.S.C.
PROVINCIAL

NIHIL OBSTAT:
JOHN R. READY
CENSOR LIBRORUM
OCTOBER 1, 1962

IMPRIMATUR:
✠ ROBERT F. JOYCE
BISHOP OF BURLINGTON
OCTOBER 2, 1962

MANUFACTURED IN THE UNITED STATES OF AMERICA

to
my sister, Marie

ACKNOWLEDGMENTS

Grateful acknowledgment is made to the following for the use of quoted material:

Benziger Brothers for quotations from the *Summa Theologica* in English translation, copyright 1947, and quotations from the Roman Breviary in English, 1950.

The Confraternity of Christian Doctrine, for quotations from the Confraternity translation of the New Testament, 1941.

Life magazine, for the article on the Fréjus Dam, © 1959 Time, Inc.

The Macmillan Company, for quotation from *Crime and Punishment,* by Fiodor Dostoyevsky.

Pantheon Books, Inc., for quotations from *Joy,* by Georges Bernanos.

Harcourt, Brace & Company for a quotation from *Murder in the Cathedral,* by T. S. Eliot.

Random House, Inc., for excerpts from St. Augustine's *The City of God,* 1950.

The Liturgical Press, Collegeville, Minn., for quotations from *Masses of Holy Week and the Easter Vigil,* 1956.

Miss Dorothy Collins, for excerpts from the poem "Gloria in Profundis," by G. K. Chesterton, and from "Essay on Laughter" in *The Common Man,* G. K. Chesterton.

His Eminence, the Cardinal Archbishop of Westminster, for excerpts from the Scripture in the translation of Ronald Knox, copyright 1944, 1958 and 1950 Sheed & Ward, Inc., New York.

The author wishes to express his thanks to the editors of *The Messenger of the Sacred Heart,* in whose pages many of these meditations have previously appeared.

ACKNOWLEDGMENTS

CONTENTS

Psalm   *1*   The Real Holiday   3

2   Love or Hate   4

3   My Enemies   7

4   What to Pray For   8

5   Who Shall Pay the Price?   10

6   The House of Death   12

7   My Friends   13

8   Childhood   15

9   The World is Silent   17

10   The Dawn   19

11   True Metal, Like Silver   21

12   Lest I Fall Asleep   23

13   No One is Good   25

14   A Word for Critics   26

15   The Treasure   28

16   Test Me as by Fire   31

17   Do I Love?   32

18   The Day's Secrets   35

19   Divine Generosity   37

20   The Meaning of Life   39

21   The New Cross   40

Psalm 21, b Abandoned in His Victory   42

   21, c The Daily Cross   44

   22 Happiness   47

   23 Who Dares Climb?   48

   24 Perseverance   51

   24, b Fear of the Critics   52

   25 The Beginner   54

   26 Father   56

   27 Rescue   58

   28 The Voice of God   59

   29 The Mystery of Sorrow   62

   30 Into His Hands   64

   31 The Chuck-Holes   66

   32 The Charity of God   67

   33 What is Charity?   69

   34 More than a Human Love   71

   35 Mercy—Divine and Human   73

   36 Christian Patience   76

   37 To Make a Mole-Hill out of a Mountain   78

   38 Choose the Better Part   80

   39 Integrity   83

   40 The Lord Sustains Him   85

   41 Who is God?   87

   42 Up to the Altar   88

   43 Bowed in the Dust   90

   44 Godly Love   93

   44, b Virgin All Fair   96

   45 He Dared to be Different   97

   46 The Search for Christ   99

   47 The Great King   101

Psalm 48   He Came to Rescue   103

49   A Great Fugue   105

50   Miserere   107

50, *b*   True Contrition   110

50, *c*   Resolution and Revolution   112

51   Rooted in Prayer   113

52   The Agony of Charity   115

53   Divine Humor   116

54   The Riddle of Death   118

55   King of Freedom   120

56   The Resurrection   121

57   Psalm of Curses   123

58   Awake, Arise!   125

59   Loving Providence   126

60   Day after Day   128

61   Attentive to God   129

62   Who is This Speaking?   131

63   On One Condition   132

64   A Fearful Joy   134

65   Song of the Unbelievable   135

66   His Saving Power   137

67   The Victory of Life   139

68   The Great Temptations   141

69   It All Depends . . .   143

70   The Sign of Contradiction   145

71   The Forward Look   147

72   Am I in the Way?   149

73   Trowel and Spear   151

74   Of Noble Blood   152

75   Nothing to Live For   154

Psalm 76 Amid the Darkness   156
      77 A Lesson Not Learned   158
      78 The Price of Blood   160
      79 The Purity of Joseph   162
      80 "This Way Out"   165
      81 Cleaned in the Winter   167
      82 False Faith   168
      83 No Other Home   170
      84 Peace with Justice   172
      85 No Answer?   174
      86 City of God   175
      87 Two Lives   177
      88 The Paradox of Happiness   179
      89 Broken Arcs   181
      90 I Cannot Rise   182
      91 No Imagination   184
      92 The Wonders of Water   185
      93 Just for the Record   188
      94 What is Wrong?   190
      95 A Song for Christmas   192
      96 The Spirit of Christmas   194
      97 Balance   196
      98 Through the Door   198
      99 A Good Sport   200
     100 It Doesn't Feel Like Love   202
     101 Power Control   203
     102 Restored Youth   205
     103 Laugh and Live   207
     104 and 105 Of Mercy and Ingratitude   209
     106 Poor Souls that were Thirsty   211

Psalm	*107*	No More Shadows	213
	108	Excuse Me, Not Responsible	216
	109	All Beauty Within	218
	110	Who Ever Loved?	220
	111	Wisdom of the Saints	223
	112	Mightiest in the Mighty	224
	113	Loneliness	226
	114	A Tyrant	228
	115	What Can I Give You?	229
	116	Why Live?	232
	117	The Resurrection Psalm	233
	117, b	Day of Triumph	236
	118	Divine Law	238
	119	Treacherous Tongues	240
	120	At the Summit	242
	121	The Royal Race	244
	122	Waiting for His Mercy	246
	123	Tide and Snare	248
	124	Those Who Trust	250
	125	School of Anguish	251
	126	Unless the Lord . . .	253
	127	My Parting Advice	255
	128	Which is Harder?	257
	129	Penance	259
	130	Black Thread through the Blaze	260
	131	The Secret of Happiness	262
	132	Christian Unity	263
	133	A Song in the Night	265
	134	Idols to Feed	267
	135	Mercy and Wisdom	269

Psalm 136 Pilgrims and Strangers 270

137 Perseverance 272

138 I Cannot Describe It 273

139 The Neglected Commandment 276

140 True Friends 278

141 Challenge and Conquest 280

142 A Thirst Unquenched 282

143 Strong for Battle 284

144 I Get So Bored 286

145 Man-Made Monotony 288

146 Gratitude for Life 290

147 Not Given to All 291

148 A Name as No Other 293

149 Toward Victory 295

150 The Grand Finale 297

INTRODUCTION

THIS BOOK makes the rash presumption that everything you find in this world can lead you to happiness. It takes for granted that almost everything you might lay your hands on—provided you prudently keep hands off thereafter—can be your way to real joy and contentment.

God has scattered happiness for men throughout the world. But it doesn't come to you; you have to go out and collect it. You have to begin paying attention to things you took for granted. You have to take note of the free gifts, the free tickets to happiness that lie all around. These chapters aim to call your attention, over and over, to the obvious.

The Book of Psalms is the best compendium of man's hopes, fears, desires, struggles and emotions—the best guidebook to man's way to happiness—that I know, next to the New Testament. But you will see that the New Testament has worked its way into these psalm-inspired thoughts everywhere.

A very charming and devout Catholic lady once told me the story of her part in a town's jubilee parade some fifty years ago. She was at that time a nurse, and in the parade she was riding a float—little more than a carriage, really—with the doctor whom she assisted, a pious Protestant who revered the Bible. While the doctor sang selections from the psalms, she tried to drown him out with hymns to the Blessed Virgin, hoping thereby to exceed his piety.

Fortunately, this attitude of suspicion toward Old Testament prayer and thought is no longer common among American Catholics. A greater interest in Scripture and the liturgy is making us more fully aware of the Old Testament's meaning—a meaning as strong and as true for us as it was for David or Isaias. We no longer consider it strange for a Catholic to call the Book of Psalms his favorite prayerbook. After all, the Catholic Church herself has done so, centuries ago. Her liturgy is filled with the psalms; no other texts are more frequently used in the Roman Missal or the Roman Breviary—and these are the official Catholic prayerbooks.

Other Christian books of prayer have made equally strong use of the psalms. And why not, since they are God's inspired words, given to us for our use?

Nevertheless, Christians as a whole make too little use of the psalms. Their antiquity and mysteriousness seem to frighten us away. Yet the psalms were modernized and illuminated for all centuries and all people in the person of Christ. It was He Himself who taught us to see them as a poetic biography of Himself, to use them for intimate conversation with Him, for thinking and feeling with Him. After His resurrection, Jesus was walking with two of His disciples to Emmaus, and there He told them, "O foolish and slow to understand when it comes to believing anything the prophets have said!" Then, "going back to Moses and the whole line of prophets," St. Luke tells us, "He began to interpret the words used of Himself by all the Scriptures." And later that night when these two disciples returned to the eleven apostles and their companions, Jesus again appeared, and told the whole group: "This is what I told you, while I still walked in your company; how all that was written of me in the law of Moses, and in the prophets, *and in the psalms,* must be fulfilled."

The psalms deserve far more use than we make of them. They overflow with a fullness of thought, not only for our own personal life, but for that of our family, community, our nation and the world. All these, with their hopes and needs, are singly and carefully and understandingly treated in the psalms; the thoughts can readily be applied to our time, our circumstances, our daily duties. That is what I have tried to illustrate in this book of musings or meditations on the psalms. We have hardly begun to sound the psalms for their poetic beauty, their psychological brilliance, their human warmth, and—since they are surprisingly modern in thought—their therapeutic excellence. What can be said of Chaucer can certainly be said of the psalms: here is God's plenty!

Some apologies may be made for my method of treating the psalms. Since each of us ought to use these scriptural songs for his own meditation, I frequently use the first person in these essays, suggesting a personal conversation between the reader and God. But since the psalms are meant for families, communities, and nations as well, I also use the plural "we" and the third person "he" and "they." I hope this creates an impression of the psalms' fullness of meaning, rather than of the author's confusion.

The psalms were meant to be used by parts, day by day. They were not intended to be read in one sitting. Yet they were intended by God to create a unified view of life. It is natural, then, that the same thoughts keep reappearing, both in the psalms and in these meditations. I have tried to view the repeated thoughts from various angles, anxious to preserve the reader's interest. Really, what is worth saying once, in one way, is worth saying again, in another way; and perhaps in a third and fourth way, too. Thus at length the idea begins to sink in.

If one single theme can be found in the psalms to make them a unit and to make them appeal at once to our modern ears, I think it is the theme of happiness and our search for it. This, in the truest sense, is what God wanted to teach us through the psalms: the way to real happiness. Witness the constantly recurring phrases, "Happy is the man who. . . , blessed are they who. . . , rejoice, my soul, in the Lord. . . ," and so many others. This theme does serve, surely, to make the psalms eternally up-to-date and interesting.

It will appear at times that, to gain a variety of approaches and subject matter, I have pressed and forced meanings out of the psalms. First, I admit having tried to apply the psalms to every crook and corner of a Christian's spiritual life, with emphasis on the essentials. Second, I believe it is well within reasonable and solid traditions, especially when working with poetry, to use any interpretation, from the strictest literal sense to the most accommodated sense. I have made no pretense of scholarship; these are simply meditations for modern Christians, mere suggestions for using the psalms in our own time, using them as the beautiful prayers they are.

I have chosen Monsignor Knox's translation of the psalms, simply because it is the most readable English translation, and in my opinion the only one that in our language keeps the Book of Psalms what it was in the original: a masterpiece of poetry.

—BCM

MEDITATIONS
ON THE PSALMS

Psalm 1

THE REAL HOLIDAY

Blessed is the man who does not guide his steps by ill coun-
sel, / or turn aside where sinners walk, / or, where scornful souls
gather, sit down to rest. . . . He stands firm as a tree planted by
running water, / ready to yield its fruit when the season comes,
not a leaf faded.

I CAN TEST the truth of this psalm by imagining myself as I will
be, not many years from now. I can see myself and read my thoughts
the first time I become aware that I am soon to die. It is then that a
man knows the value of his life. I will understand then, Lord, the
quality of the fruit I have borne.

If I have not followed the counsels of the godless, I will experience
the depth of that promised happiness. There is serene peace in the
words, the looks, the noble face of an aged mother who has fulfilled
her vocation, who has never known corruption. She has borne fruit;
the tree has not withered. Her calm contentment, her silent joy, her
boundless love are the unfaded leaves and fruits of her life.

I have seen venerable, mellowed men, too, at the end of life. Their
genuine loyalty, understanding, kindliness are the fruits of a just,
upright life. I have seen the reward, the maturing of grace in men
who have not turned aside where the godless walk. I have seen how
calmly and confidently they await that day so feared by those who
have wasted their lives.

When I come to the evening of my life, Lord, I want to experience that blessing myself. I want to know the beauty of peace after the worst of the battle is won. This is the happiness of which You spoke in Psalm 1. Far greater than the infirmities, the petty regrets, the fond memories of old age is the sense of success or defeat. Happy the man who has found success in his defeats; who has found Your strength in his weakness, Your wisdom in his stupidity, Your glory in his lowliness. For that alone is true success.

Nowhere, Lord, will I learn to understand better the strong truth of this psalm than in the lives of the Saints. For those who have borne fruit, the harvest is a time of pride, a time of fulfillment, a day of high festival. This is the testing-rod of my success: will I be happy to die? The greatest feast day of my life ought to be the day of my death, the day on which I enter eternal life, my arms filled with the good things I have brought to development.

No greater joy could be mine then, than to be able to say with the psalmist, "It is thou, O God, that hast inspired me ever since the days of my youth, and still I am found telling the tale of thy wonders. O God, do not fail me, now when I am old and grey-headed, till I have made known the proofs of thy power to this, to all the generations that will follow; that faithfulness of thine which reaches up, O God, to the heavens . . ." (Psalm 70).

Psalm 2

LOVE OR HATE

See how the kings of the earth stand in array, / how its rulers make common cause, / against the Lord, and against the King he has anointed, / crying, Let us break away from their bondage, / rid ourselves of the toils!

YOUR ENEMIES never rest, Lord. Why have they not been satisfied to ignore You? Why do they deny that You exist, then immediately muster great forces against You, as against the most powerful of leaders?

You Yourself answered this often enough. "He who is not with me is against me, and he who does not gather with me scatters" (Matt. 12:30). "The prince of this world is coming, and in me he has nothing" (John 14:30). "If the world hates you, be sure that it hated me before it learned to hate you. If you belonged to the world, the world would know you for its own and love you" (John 15:18). "They will treat you thus because you bear my name; they have no knowledge of him who sent me" (John 15:21). Nevertheless, the rulers of the earth are not without guilt, for You said, "If I had not done what no one else ever did in their midst, they would not have been in fault; as it is, they have hated, with open eyes, both me and my Father" (John 15:24).

There is no third choice, Lord. We have been created by You, and You are the one and only way to happiness. Men cannot ignore You; if they will not serve You, they must fight You. Nothing is clearer in all history than this truth: men cannot ignore God. If they will not love You, they must hate You. For Your kingdom stands firm. If they will not work with You, and gather souls with You, they must scatter them, and drive them away from You. Those who defy God know well enough that He is really there. One does not battle against the power of what does not exist.

Lord Jesus, Your truth and Your strength are proved by Your enemies as well as by Your friends. The great tragedy is not that people deny the existence of God or the power of Christ. The tragedy is that by denying and defying You they are rejecting love and life itself. They would destroy Your love with their hate. And since they can never do so, they destroy only their own love.

It must be true, Lord Jesus, that Your love and Your great lovers keep the world from going completely mad. Your infinite charity, and the great devotion of Your lovers—without these, the world would surely collapse, torn apart by the very force of men's hatred for one another. It is only the Saints who have preserved the earth until now. They, recognizing, as Dante did, that their "desire and will were rolled—even as a wheel that runs freely—by the Love that moves the sun and other stars," by their love keep the universe in balance.

Lord Jesus, as a Christian, I have the privilege of belonging to the camp of the saints. It is my high honor to be responsible, with them, for preserving Your blessing on men. May I ever remain small enough to fit through the secret passage of hope in this world. For there is only one hope, and it is beyond the stars. Men who deny You deny all hope.

May it be my vocation to lead them back to hope, through the small channel of humility. Dante, as he sought a way out of the eternal despair of hell, was blessed with a guide, who showed him the way. . . .

> By that hid way my guide and I withal,
> Back to the lit world from the darkened dens
> Toiled upward, caring for no rest at all,
> He first, I following; till my straining sense
> Glimpsed the bright burden of the heavenly cars
> Through a round hole; by this we climbed, and thence
> Came forth, to look once more upon the stars.
>
> (*Inferno*, final lines)

The Church, in speaking of Mary, the Saint of saints, praises her thus from the Book of Judith: "Blessed be the Lord who created heaven and earth, who raised you up to break the head of the Prince of our enemies, for today he has so magnified your Name that your praises will no longer leave the lips of men. You did not spare your soul for them, seeing the anguish and tribulation of your people; on the contrary, you stood up in the presence of our God to oppose yourself to its ruin" (Judith 13:24–25).

In God's own time, Mary will come again, holding before her the Child of whom it was said in Psalm 2: "Thou art my Son; I have begotten thee this day. Ask thy will of me, and thou shalt have the nations for thy patrimony; the very ends of the world for thy domain. Thou shalt herd them like sheep with a crook of iron, break them in pieces like earthenware. Princes, take warning; learn your lesson, you that rule the world. Tremble, and serve the Lord, rejoicing in his presence, but with awe in your hearts."

Psalm 3

MY ENEMIES

See how they surround me, Lord, my adversaries, | how many rise up in arms against me; | everywhere voices taunting me, | His God cannot save him now.

I KNOW well enough, Lord, that all things You created are good. You placed them on earth to help draw me up to Yourself. "If these are so attractive," You wanted me to say, "how much more beautiful must He be who made them."

Yet You know my weakness, and how easily I turn these creatures into myself, and make myself smaller and meaner with them, instead of growing and expanding my understanding of You, their Creator. This is the world and the flesh, of which St. John speaks. Others may not always give me the most inspiring examples; that is the world. My body, my weak will, my misplaced attractions—these are the flesh. They rise up against me, and say, "What help for him in God? God is far away." Satan, the most cunning of adversaries, is pleased. It is the first sign of despair; it may be the first step toward the victory he seeks. If he can make me tired of struggle, tired of asking help, he can make me give up. For no man lives by his own power.

There is a strong weapon against despair. It is divine patience. I must be patient enough with my own weakness and failure to say with the psalmist, "I lay down and slept, and have awoken. . . . Bestir thyself, Lord; my God, save me; thine to smite my enemies on the cheek, thine to break the fangs of malice. From the Lord all deliverance comes." I cannot, should not hope in myself. I can hope in God, and be heard.

In Your divine plan, Lord, it is necessary that I have enemies. I must not forget that I have more friends. In prayer and meditation, I draw on the strength of my friends—You, the All-powerful; Mary, true Mother; all the saints; my own reason and free will working with the grace You have given me.

Many rise up against me; but many also rise up to support me and bring me to victory. "I have but to cry out to the Lord, and my voice reaches his mountain sanctuary, and there finds hearing. Safe in God's hand I lay down . . . and now, though thousands of the people set upon me from every side, I will not be afraid of them." As You strengthened King David in his trials, You will not fail to strengthen me in mine.

Psalm 4

WHAT TO PRAY FOR

To the souls he loves, be sure the Lord shows wondrous favor; / whenever I call on his name, the Lord will hear me. / Tremble, and sin no more; / take thought, as you lie awake, in the silence of your hearts.

THIS is the prayer, Lord, of one who truly meditates. He does not forget Your favors; yet he knows that You are the God of *salvation,* and You will *not* hear his prayer when he asks for things that would only ruin him.

How often I am demanding of You, my Lord, as though I had forgotten Your wisdom. I pray for what I should not have. I am impatient with You, too thoughtless and proud to realize that You know my needs better than I do. If I would ask You for but one favor—that I would "sin no more," that I would "take thought," that I would keep silence in my heart—then I would learn the happiness of living by a wisdom higher than my own.

Must this always be above my power, Lord? Will I forever continue insisting and demanding until You give me the material things that will only bring me spiritual destruction? Or will I become wise with the wisdom of God and pray that You will send me the Holy Spirit who will teach me what to pray for?

The humble King David knew better than I, Lord. For in Psalm 4 he assured You that no earthly thing could substitute for the happiness You Yourself give: "Even as I lie down, sleep comes," he wrote, "and with sleep tranquillity; what need, Lord, of aught but thyself to bring me confidence?"

So I ought to pray. You alone are my security; not my stocks or insurance or friends or talents. These things must pass: but You remain forever. Happier I would be, if all my prayers came from that Spirit of whom St. Paul writes, "We do not know what we should pray for as we ought, but the Spirit himself pleads for us with unutterable groanings. And he who searches the heart knows what the Spirit desires, that he pleads for the saints according to God. Now we know that for those who love God all things work together unto good, for those who, according to his purpose, are saints through his call.

"What, then, shall we say to these things? If God is for us, who is against us? He who has not spared even his own Son but has delivered him for all, how can he fail to grant us also all things with him?" (Rom. 8:26–32). Lord, show me how to pray for what is truly right and good. Teach me to value all things at their true worth. For if I learn the real excellence and purpose of creatures, I will surely come to You. And then I shall have every desire filled.

Psalm 5

WHO SHALL PAY THE PRICE?

Lord, do thou lead me with faithful care; | clear show the path, while I walk beset by enemies. | In their speech no truth can be found; | their hearts are all treachery, their mouths gaping tombs; | flattering is ever on their lips.

IT IS as though the psalmist says, "Lord, let Your grace make me one of those truly honest men of whom You find too few. The world would surely collapse and be destroyed, were there not a few men and women who truly serve God. For these—however many or few they may be, Lord—You have spared the world until now."

It is evident enough from Your Holy Scripture, Lord, and from man's history that the power of a few saints is tremendous. Their spiritual fervor has prevented catastrophes.

You saved the people of Nineveh from destruction because they did penance.

You had promised Abraham to save Sodom and Gomorrah from ruin for only five just men.

You saved Bethulia through the holiness of one woman, Judith.

You saved the Jews in captivity through the penance of Mardochai and Esther.

You saved the doomed city of Rome and restored it through the holy lives of the martyrs and the faith of Your Church.

You saved Europe at the Battle of Lepanto because of the prayers of Christians.

How many times did You not save Your people by the power of a saint, a Joan of Arc, a John of Capistrano, by holy kings and saintly preachers.

You have saved and brought new life to Your Church in our own time through the holy work of our modern saintly pontiffs.

You have promised salvation and resurrection to our threatened world, if again enough just men can be found.

Lord, have we not seen the fulfillment of Your prophecies which warn us what evils will come because the charity of the saints has cooled in a heedless world? "Many false prophets will arise," You said, "and many will be deceived by them; and the charity of most men will grow cold, as they see wickedness abound everywhere; but that man will be saved who endures to the last. This gospel of the kingdom must first be preached all over the world, so that all nations may hear the truth . . ." (Matt. 24:11–14).

I know, Jesus, that we are in desperate need of saints to restore true love to nations filled with hate, suspicion, injustice, selfishness. Is it possible that the price of peace, the ransom from chaos must be paid by me as well as by others? Is it right for me to complain bitterly about leaders who are not sincere in their peace talks, whose "hearts are all treachery," and whose mouths are "gaping tombs," as David observed; and yet I never ask You, "Lord, do thou lead me with faithful care; clear show the path, while I walk beset by enemies"?

Lord, teach me a sense of responsibility toward my neighbor, which is the world. How often do I truly pray for those who suffer injustice, or for the millions who have forgotten You, or know so little of You? Like the psalmist, eager to win God's mercy on erring men, can I truthfully say, "To thee, Lord, my prayer goes up, early to win thy audience"?

Psalm 6

THE HOUSE OF DEATH

Lord, turn back, and grant a wretched soul relief; | as thou art ever merciful, save me. | When death comes, there is no more remembering thee; | none can praise thee in the tomb.

FOR WHAT HAS DEATH to do with You, my God? You are the torrent of joy, the fountain of life. You are the conqueror of death; You are everything that dispels and destroys death. Of You, St. John said most truthfully, "In Him was life, and the life was the light of men. And the light shines in the darkness; and the darkness grasped it not."

What is death? Death is all that is not filled with the breath of God. Death is the rebellion of darkness against the light of life. When Nathan the prophet came to King David to accuse him of his sin, he veiled his message in a parable, the story of a rich man who had stolen from the poor. When David had heard the story of the crime, he exclaimed, "The man who has done this is a child of death!" And Nathan answered, "Thou art the man! . . . Why hast thou despised the word of the Lord? . . . The sword shall never depart from thy house. . . . because thou hast given occasion to the enemies of God to blaspheme . . ." (II Kings 12).

Sin had made this holy king a child of death, and the sword of death would never leave his palace. All who turn away from God become children of death. Thus in Psalm 6 the repentant king begged the Lord to save him from the death he deserved, for he knew not what was beyond death. He only knew that his God was a living God, who would never die.

At length You Yourself came, Lord Jesus, to dispel the darkness of death. You were the new Adam, "for if by reason of the one man's offense death reigned through the one man, much more will they who receive the abundance of the grace . . . reign in life through the one Jesus Christ" (Romans 5:15).

Lord Jesus, by Your resurrection You have restored life, and we have no more reason to fear any death but the immortal, undying death of turning away from You.

How anxious we are to restore our bodily health, to avoid physical death, which must inevitably come, and which is in truth the Christian's day of birth! How helpless we seem to be, when it comes to restoring the health that really matters, to avoid a death that is final!

Forgive me my blindness, Lord. You have opened for me a death which is the door to life. The death of sin and selfishness in me, this is the blessed death of which St. John speaks: "Blessed are the dead who die in the Lord. Yes, forever henceforward, the Spirit says; they are to have rest from their labours; but the deeds they did in life go with them now" (Apoc. 14:13).

You Yourself, Jesus, assured us that we have nothing to fear from those who can kill only the body; we need fear only that which kills both body and soul in hell. Lord, if my sins have made of my soul a house of death like that of David, and if in that death I have forgotten You, Lord, "turn back, and grant a wretched soul relief." Like the sorrowing psalmist, "I have no strength left; Lord, heal me; my limbs tremble; my spirits are altogether broken." You have shown me the way of life; let me abandon the house of death.

Psalm 7

MY FRIENDS

O Lord my God, if I too have been at fault, | if these hands are stained with guilt; | if I have been a false friend, | and not rather spared even those that wronged me, / then indeed let some enemy overtake me with his relentless pursuit, / trample me to earth, and level my pride with the dust!

Is IT NOT TRUE, Lord, that my most uncharitable deeds are done to my friends—or at least to those who by all standards of right reason ought to be my friends? Have I not been "a false friend," instead of being not only a true, unselfish friend, but also sparing "even those that wronged me"?

It is not that I would refuse to pray for my enemies, Lord, provided they are far enough away. It is rather that I am too willing to make enemies out of my friends. It is that I do not love with a genuine charity. My love is spoiled and plagued by the small human vices: petty criticism, harsh tongue-lashing, needless quarrels, proud insistence on my rights, hasty judgments, unwarranted suspicions.

There are many sides to a friend, Lord. Truth requires not only that I think of others, but that I think of how thoughtful they are of me! How much I take them for granted is clear in my unconscious demands of them, my feeling of superiority, by which I expect their services as a king does his servants'. "It's about time he thinks of me!" I tell myself. "Of course she owes me as much!" "Naturally they should offer me their help!" No thought of the price they are paying. Nobody else's time is worth half as much as my own.

Yes, Lord, it is all "natural" and "expected" and "civil" when others work for me, but let them dare to ask my service, and they are soon "trying" and "burdensome" and "overbearing." These may be small incidents, but they add up to an important attitude. When I examine myself on the way I treat my dearest friends, I may well discover how I would have treated You, my Lord, when You walked on earth—and indeed, how I treat You now. "Whatever you did to the least of these, my brethren, you did it to Me."

Your saints were far from demanding, Lord. They had never done enough for others. They never said, "This is the last straw." They never felt "persecuted" by others, even when they really were! They thought the small reverses of life all too little recompense for their own failings. And they thought the demands of others all too few for the charity which urged them on.

David in this psalm begged You to punish him, Lord, if he had been so thoughtless as to do evil to his friends, and that after his great-hearted act of saving Saul, his enemy, when he had Saul in his power. "Do not touch the Lord's anointed," David had warned his men. He stood, fully armed, at the side of Saul, his great persecutor, as Saul slept in his tent; but David would not harm him.

Shall I think less of my friends, Lord, than that they are Your anointed ones? Is there a limit to Your love for them? Can I set bounds to the graces You pour on them? Have you not said to each one of them, "I have loved thee with an everlasting love"? Could it be that I have reason to be less patient with them than You are? I might at least confess, Lord, that I have too little charity, and every reason for repenting of the petty evil I do my friends.

Strange follower of Christ I would be, if I could not love them like Christ. If I profess Your teaching that we should "love our enemies, do good to those who hate" us, what ought I to be doing for my friends, those who have done good to me!

Psalm 8

CHILDHOOD

O Lord, our Master, how the majesty of thy name fills all the earth! / Thy greatness is high above heaven itself. / Thou hast made the lips of children, of infants at the breast, / vocal with praise, to confound thy enemies; / to silence malicious and revengeful tongues.

YOUR BEAUTY, Lord, is mirrored in all that You made. If I am delighted by the glories of a summer sunset, the majestic calm of a winter's night, the gigantic power symbolized by a mountain range, the colors and shades of a pine forest—if all this speaks of You, my Creator, it has still said very little. How much more can I learn of Your goodness, of Your heavenly delights, from the spontaneous laughter of a little child! Poets have written world-famous lines inspired by the happy song of a fresh, untainted child. Not all the beauties of the mountains, skies, rivers, valleys and forests, nor the marvels produced by the handiwork of man can be compared with the loveliness of an innocent soul.

As we grow older, we grow familiar with the cynical distrust of the godless, the bitter selfishness of the materialist, the nervous anxiety of money-makers, the cut-throat battles for power and influence —and we forget. Who shall save us from these falsehoods and the temptation of despair they inevitably bring? Lord, if we should try, we would not be believed, though we are professed Christians. With good reason we would be suspect, for our own records are not unblemished, our own deeds are no favorable witness.

But the honesty, the blameless joy, the guileless confidence of a child has the power to return us to the simple truths of life. The most hardened of men, the most vicious, hateful, cynical of human beings cannot reject the love of a little child.

You said it was Your delight to be with the children of men. Truly, Lord, when in this psalm You reminded us of Your great works, You could not have forgotten the children of men. No doubt it was so because, of all creatures on earth, they are most like You. You assure us that these innocent ones truly praise You, to the shame of Your enemies.

Has my conscience never stirred at the honesty and goodness of a small child? Have I never understood that I could not outgrow my childhood unless I denied Your fatherhood? Have I ever sincerely thought that I am no longer a child subject to a father? If so, Lord, I have lost my true humanity. I am not truly a man unless I am yet truly a child. And when I refuse to offer You the reverence, the awe, the love, the simplicity of a child of God, then may the sight of innocent children, Lord, restore my understanding of true piety.

I will remember that You rebuked Your apostles for holding back the children from You, and You said, "Let the little ones come to me, for of these is the kingdom of heaven made." When I fail to recognize my neighbor as the child of God that he is, or when I myself fail to be interiorly a child of God, I make of myself the inhuman monster of which Shakespeare speaks and concludes, "How sharper than a serpent's tooth it is to have a thankless child."

Of children, Dickens wrote, "I love these little people; and it is not a slight thing when they, who are so fresh from God, love us."

"Call not that man wretched," wrote Southey, "who, whatever ills he suffers, has a child to love."

"Children are God's apostles," wrote James Russell Lowell, "sent forth, day by day, to preach of love, and hope and peace."

Psalm 9

THE WORLD IS SILENT

Lord, why dost thou stand far off? / In days of affliction, why dost thou make no sign? / The hearts of the oppressed burn within them, / so triumphant is the schemer that has entrapped them; / so proud of his wicked end achieved, / still robbing men, blaspheming and despising the Lord.

HERE IS A PSALM for our world, Lord, groaning with the distress of political victims, victims of so much godless bargaining. When, Lord, in all past centuries could Christians have understood any better the psalmist's cry for justice, his pity for the suffering innocent, his horror at the crimes of the powerful? He does not neglect to pray for his brothers and sisters who must pay the price of injustice.

"So triumphant is the schemer," who has lured the poor into his trap by loud promises. "Still robbing men" of justice and happiness, for modern public life—politics, business, entertainment—has often robbed men of the love of God. "God there is none to punish me, the sinner thinks in his pride, and makes that thought his rule." He will praise God as long as God makes no demand of his conscience.

How great must be the victims' temptation to despair! There is no punishment for the unjust. The world is silent; the most horrible crimes are accepted. Where are the men of honor who should cry out against such evils?

"He banishes thy laws from his mind," thus the offender tries to silence the outcries of justice. "Endless time, he thinks, cannot shake his untroubled existence. His mouth overflows with curses, and calumny, and deceit; his tongue is a storehouse of dissension and mischief. Ambushed he lies . . . his eyes are continually on his prey; like a lion in its lair, he watches from his hiding-place, to surprise his defenceless foe. . . . Why not? he thinks to himself, God has forgotten about it; God still turns his face away, and sees nothing."

Who dares say the psalms are out of date, an ancient gem to admire? Are they less true, are they less perceptive, are they less needful today, these cries of the Holy Spirit, this thunder of Divine Justice and Prophecy? Have we not long enough cast the spell of monotonous organ chants and sleepy repetition over these flaming revelations, these awesome judgments and solemn warnings?

When Jeremias warned men to be appalled at how the just are murdered and no man stops to consider it, he was echoing the psalms, which spoke to all ages: No man can spurn God and avoid calamities. The innocent, indeed, must atone for the crimes of the wicked, for the innocent alone are worthy. "Blessed are you when men shall revile you and persecute you and speak all manner of evil against you falsely because of me," said Christ, "be glad and rejoice, for your reward is great in heaven." You can see the mysterious working of God's justice in the sacrifice of the prophets, in the supreme offering of His divine Son on Calvary; you can see the beginning and the fulfillment of the glory to come. And in the wretched despair of the unrepentant sinner, you can see the horror a man accepts when he rejects God. God will repay everyone according to his works; He could not do otherwise.

"God sees the truth, but waits." Tolstoy made this realistic observation of life, and chose it as the title of one of his stories. In that drama of life, we come to appreciate God's work in the soul of an innocent man who suffers unjustly twenty years of enslavement. The interior beauty of the man's character is made visible for a revealing moment, and we catch a glimpse of the mysterious beauty and fitness of God's patience.

Have mercy on those You have chosen for this honor, Lord, and enlighten them; strengthen them, lest they die of despair at the very door-step of heaven.

Psalm 10

THE DAWN

The Lord is just, and just are the deeds he loves; / none but upright souls shall enjoy his presence.

IN THEORY, I believe and I understand, Lord, that this is the purpose of my life: to love justice and to see You, face to face, to enjoy Your presence.

In practice, I am too willing to forget it. How often am I one of those Christians who, You said, are choked by the cares and riches and pleasures of this world and bear no fruit. It never strikes me that nearly all my efforts and worries are for nothing and turn into nothing. I know that these air-bubbles burst as soon as I think I have caught them. Yet I persist in pursuing pet projects rather than perfection.

The psalmist presents a truth so simple in form that I am not impressed when I read it. Yet it is the essential fact of my existence, and without it, my life means nothing: "upright souls shall enjoy his presence."

Without this end, what would the best of human lives be? The most poetic and romantic heroes would have to cry out at the end of life: "To what purpose?" Jacomo, the hero of a novel by Helen C. White, lay dying of a raging fever, and looking back over his years, he said, "It seems a strangely little thing, this life, when it is done. . . . One thinks to do so much and he does so little, and that little is so strangely compounded of blindness and good intent and much effort and much thwarting, and the end is a watch in the night."

So poor and dark is our existence on earth, and we make so much of it! A short hour in the night, and we make no provision for the eternal dawn.

Lord Jesus, my life is covered with a cloud, and it is like the silent tomb on Holy Saturday. It is nothing without the hope, the anticipation, the certainty of seeing You rise before me on Easter morning.

"Flesh and blood," said St. Paul, "can obtain no part in the kingdom of God. . . . For this corruptible body must put on incorruption, and this mortal body must put on immortality." And when it does, "then the prophecy shall be fulfilled, 'Death is swallowed up in victory! Death, where is thy victory? Death, where is thy sting?' Now the sting of death is sin . . . but thanks be to God who has given us the victory through our Lord Jesus Christ" (I Cor. 15:33).

Lord, have I not fallen asleep if I seek only the empty night of this life, and have no desire of seeing You at dawn? Have I no share in the hope and confidence of the heroic seven sons (written about in the second book of Machabees) who with their mother despised this life to see You in the next?

The second son, as he was dying of the tortures, had this to say to the evil king, Antiochus, with his last breath: "Thou, indeed, most wicked man, dost destroy us out of this present life; but the King of the world will raise us up . . . in the resurrection of eternal life." The third son, as he stood in chains, and saw the executioners prepare to cut off his hands, said, "These hands I have from heaven, but for the laws of God I now despise them; because I hope to receive them again from him."

The youngest son of all, as the moment of his torture and martyrdom arrived, saw in his brothers the meaning and accomplishment of God's mysterious way with man: "My brethren," he said, "having now undergone a short time of pain, are under the new law of eternal life."

Lord, my whole life on earth is directed to the day of my entry into Your glorious presence. How much of my attention does it not merit! All my decisions ought to be in terms of that meeting with You, and in as much as my actions are not so, I am not perfect, I am not truly human, I am not Christian.

Psalm 11

TRUE METAL, LIKE SILVER

Lord, come to my rescue; piety is dead; / in a base world, true hearts have grown rare.

THIS IS no cynical sneer or bitter joke. It is the distress of a holy man who pleads with God to save his brethren. The psalmist may not have foreseen how perfect a prayer he wrote for our age, except that he knew well the universal human temptations. He knew how men are prone to lie to their neighbors whenever convenient, how nations in solemn conclave find it a most convenient temptation, how many there are who speak with "false hearts and treacherous lips."

It is all very well to accuse my neighbor, to accuse those more powerful than I, to accuse nations. But I am responsible for my own integrity first of all. Can I justly say, *"they* lie, *they* flatter, *they* are insincere, *they* deceive"? I should remember, Lord, the parable You told to "those who trusted in themselves and despised others," the parable of the Pharisee and the Publican.

Perhaps I have so trained myself, so accustomed myself to my excuses that even *I* am convinced. Very probably no one else is. It would be a most profitable meditation, Lord, to examine myself regularly on my sincerity. I might discover many of my hidden defects by testing my spirit, my "empty forms of speech" against the "promises of the Lord," the "true metal, like silver."

The psalmist says, "Everywhere false hearts and treacherous lips . . . Lord, rid the earth of them!"

Ought I not fear the promise that is made to the psalmist in this divinely inspired poem? "Now, says the Lord, I will bestir myself, on behalf of the helpless who are so ill used, of the poor who cry out so bitterly; I will win them the redress they long for." Have I never been unjust to those who are weaker than I, to those whom I (unjustly enough) consider inferior to myself? Have I never oppressed others by my gossip, my unjust criticism, my sarcasm, my overbearing attitude, my delight in humiliating them, in "putting them in their place"? If so, Lord, I am also one of the oppressors You have condemned in this psalm. I am one of those against whom You will rise, because of the injustice I commit. I myself rise to the defence of the "underdog" whenever my "sentiments" are in sympathy with him. But You are always just; You always rise to defend the oppressed.

The psalmist concludes: "The promises of the Lord are true metal, like silver that is tested in the crucible, the stains of earth gone, seven times refined." How do my words and promises stand, compared to these?

"A man who is not betrayed into faults of the tongue," writes St. James, "must be a man perfect at every point, who knows how to curb his whole body. . . . the tongue is a tiny part of our body, and yet what power it can boast! How small a spark it takes to set fire to a vast forest! And that is what the tongue is, a fire" (James 3:2–6).

If the mouth speaks from the abundance of the heart, as You Yourself said, Jesus, grant us all a true change of heart!

Psalm 12

LEST I FALL ASLEEP

O Lord my God . . . give light to these eyes, before they close in death; | do not let my enemies claim the mastery, | my persecutors triumph over my fall!

LORD, by the very nature You created in me, I have an enemy that may conquer me and cause me to fall asleep in death. For when You created this world, Lord, You created two principles: matter and spirit. The matter was body, destined for death. The spirit was soul, destined for life. While the plants and animals die and decompose, the perfect spirits, the angels, live on in eternal life.

But to us, Lord, You gave a human nature, which bears in itself the fierce struggle between matter and spirit. Thus in this life I have within myself a never-ending battle. On this earth, my spirit is held captive by the body. Yet it may free itself through force of will, and if it succeed, it will live forever, the unconquered master of the body, the undying flame of the spirit. This is the victory or the defeat for which all men are destined.

When Adam sinned, his will lost the supreme mastery, and death—the body—the material world conquered man. But Christ won the victory, and restored true life. As You rose glorious from the grave, Lord Jesus, the spirit was given power again to conquer. "Christ has risen from the dead," St. Paul wrote, "the first fruits of those who have fallen asleep. For since by a man came death, by a man also comes resurrection of the dead. For as in Adam all die, so in Christ all will be made to live" (I Cor. 15:20–22).

Lord, if I ask, as the psalmist does, that You give light to my eyes, lest I fall asleep in death, I am answered by St. Paul, that "as sin has reigned unto death, now grace may reign by justice unto eternal life in Jesus Christ" (Romans 5:21). So then I have reason to trust in Your resurrection. For by Your grace, my will can be strengthened, and the enemy shall never rejoice that I have fallen. Nevertheless my will is free, and that means free to fall from the grace of Christ if I am careless. Thus St. Paul warns me, "Do not yield your members to sin as weapons of iniquity, but present yourselves to God as those who have come to life from the dead, and your members as weapons of justice for God; for sin shall not have dominion over you, since you are not under the law, but under grace" (Romans 6:13).

How pitiable is a man without this hope, without Christ to restore him to grace when he has fallen, when he sees his conquered spirit as already dead. Such is the tragedy of Macbeth, when he cries,

> . . . All our yesterdays have lighted fools
> The way to dusty death. Out, out, brief candle!
> Life's but a walking shadow, a poor player
> That struts and frets his hour upon the stage
> And then is heard no more: it is a tale
> Told by an idiot, full of sound and fury,
> Signifying nothing.
>
> (*Macbeth,* V, 5)

There is nothing but this despair for a man as he discovers that he has allowed deceitful illusions to betray him, to make him far less than a man. Such was the fall we suffered through Adam; there is no rising, but in Christ. In Him, life again signifies everything!

Psalm 13

NO ONE IS GOOD

The Lord looks down from heaven at the race of men, / to find one soul that reflects, and makes God its aim; / but no, all have missed the mark and rebelled against him; / an innocent man is nowhere to be found.

IT IS SHOCKING to hear God in his inspired word speaking like this. "An innocent man is nowhere to be found." Can this be true? There must be someone on earth who is good. Yet God says, "No, there is not one."

Lord, You Yourself took offence one day when a man came up to You and asked, "Good Master, what must I do to gain eternal life?" You answered, "Why do you call me good? None is good but God alone" (Matt. 19:17).

"For there is no distinction," said St. Paul. "All have sinned and have need of the glory of God" (Romans 3:23). Human nature had lost its true goodness. And clearer yet You made this truth, Lord, when You said, "I am the vine, you are the branches. He who abides in me, and I in him, he bears much fruit; for without me you can do nothing. If anyone does not abide in me, he shall be cast outside as the branch and wither; and they shall gather them up and cast them into the fire, and they shall burn" (John 15:5-7).

I know where I stand without You, then, Lord. "An innocent man is nowhere to be found." Without You, I am nothing. Unless I know this, I know nothing of creation or the power that preserves the universe. I have no good but what God has put in me. What a fool am I to consider myself anything, or better than anyone else.

What does it matter that I am honored by men, more fortunate, more talented, more "successful" than my neighbor, if God sees that there is no good in me because Christ does not abide in me? "What does it profit a man, if he gains the whole world. . . ?"

How poor I am indeed, Lord, if I do not see the force of this psalm and this truth. I ought to see clearly that You, my Creator, are far more than a doorkeeper who opened the gates of this world to me. It is You and You alone, who are my life, who preserve my life, whose power keeps me in existence every minute. There is in me no good of itself, Lord. It is Your good, operating in me. "What have you, that you have not received; and if you have received it, why do you glory in it, as though you had not received it?" (I Cor. 4:7).

Every instant I am receiving of You, my Lord; and should You ever cease to give, I would cease to live, cease to exist. It is only ignorance that makes me glory vainly in myself, as though I deserved glory. If You, Jesus, could say truthfully, "If I glorify myself, my glory is nothing; it is my Father who glorifies me" (John 8:54), how much more reason have I to say, "I have no good but what You have in me. You are all my good."

Psalm 14

A WORD FOR CRITICS

Who is it, Lord, that will make his home in thy tabernacle, / rest on the mountain where thy sanctuary is? / One that guides his steps without fault, and gives to all their due; / one whose heart is all honest purpose, who utters no treacherous word, / never defrauds a friend, or slanders a neighbor.

How OFTEN, LORD, You emphasized the evil inherent in gossip. What sin did You condemn more than the sin of slander? You were ever gentle with sinners.

Zacheus the thief won Your affection in the sycamore tree, and You told him, "This day salvation has come to your house."

The adulterous woman was surprised to hear You pardon her: "Neither will I condemn thee; go and sin no more."

Mary Magdalene could tell of Your kindness to sinners: "Much has been forgiven her, because she has loved much."

Matthew the publican knew of Your forgiveness, for You went so far as to make him Your apostle.

Over and over You pardoned sinners. But always You warned them, "Go and sin no more."

Only the slanderers, those who sought to find fault with You, could not accept Your forgiveness. They had hardened themselves against true contrition, since their whole attention was given to finding evil; they looked for matter to condemn. "Now the Pharisees were watching how they might catch him in his speech." You spoke openly to the crowds, warning them of the malice of looking for sin in one's neighbor. "Beware of the leaven of the Pharisees, which is hypocrisy," You said. "There is nothing concealed that will not be disclosed, and nothing hidden that will not be made known. For what I tell you in darkness, speak it in the light; and what you hear whispered, preach it on the housetops" (Matt. 10:26, 27).

In the parable of the Pharisee and the Publican, Lord, You made it clear enough what You think of those who accuse others and justify themselves. And again You called to the crowds in the very presence of the Pharisees: "Hear and understand. What goes into the mouth does not defile a man; but that which comes out of the mouth, that defiles a man" (Matt. 15:11).

Surely it is a cheap and ignoble mind that can attempt to think itself better by searching for evil in others. By seeking to find fault in my neighbor, and by rejoicing that I have found it, I myself have lost the most precious of all treasures: that virtue which You, Lord, proclaimed most beautiful and most valuable: charity.

Is it any wonder, then, that in Your inspired poetry You spoke most of all of that love, and condemned most of all the evil tongue of envy and fault-finding? Is it any wonder that in answer to the question, "who may live on thy holy mountain?" You said, "One that guides his steps without fault, and gives to all their due; one whose heart is all honest purpose, who utters no treacherous word, never defrauds a friend, or slanders a neighbor."

Psalm 15

THE TREASURE

Thou wilt show me the way of life, / make me full of gladness in thy presence; / at thy right hand are delights that will endure forever.

A RICH YOUNG MAN came to see You one day, Jesus, and he asked You what he should do to gain eternal life. You answered, "Go sell all you have, and give it to the poor, and come, follow me, and you shall have treasure in heaven."

You often spoke of heaven as of a treasure—but a special kind of treasure. Heaven cannot be hoarded by misers; heaven cannot be wrested away from me by robbery, or shady dealing, betrayal, or trickery of any kind. I cannot lose it by some outrageous accident. Happiness does not consist in having what others cannot have. Otherwise, why are so many of the richest people also the unhappiest? And why are so many of the poorest people also the happiest? Why do they think themselves far more fortunate than the wealthy? Why can a child with no possessions at all be the greatest possessor of happiness?

A man is not always aware of his unhappiness. He sees only vaguely that he is missing something enjoyed by "enthusiasts." His life is dull, his work is drudgery, but he has grown to expect that. If he is fortunate, his eyes may yet be opened some day, and he will see where true happiness lies.

Do I understand, Lord, how fortunate I am to know that the real treasure of life is heaven, that heaven is the only complete and satisfying treasure? In heaven I will find everything that is good; all that I know to be beautiful, delightful, pleasing, all that I know to be worth loving. No matter what my tastes happen to be, no matter how much my idea of heaven differs from that of my neighbors, You indeed have the power to fill my every desire.

Heaven is far from the proverbial golden city with a silver fence. Heaven is God. Heaven is all perfection and joy, and that is You, Lord of all heavens. Thus You say in the Apocalypse, "Behold I make all things new . . . and there shall be a new heaven and a new earth" (Apoc. 21:1). You will have all things fit to receive the risen bodies of the saints. Yet they should never be satisfied, could they not have You Yourself. They will never see enough of God, nor even of each other, in the glory You shed over heaven.

Could this splendor ever wear out? Impossible, for Your beauty is eternal. A modern songster knew enough to sing that "love is a many-splendored thing," but Your love is infinitely splendored. No man shall ever see all Your beauties; no man shall ever tire of them.

In the Mass of the Dead we beg that You may give the souls of our brethren *requiem aeternam,* eternal rest. But this is not in any sense the rest of eternal sleep. Happiness is not a state of unconscious oblivion. Eternal rest means eternal satisfaction, endless enjoyment, freedom from all the pain of anxiety. On this earth we are unhappy because we do not have all we desire; we are plagued by the search for more and more. Were all our longings fulfilled, we should have rest. This is the "eternal rest" for which we pray.

We shall surely be thousands of times more human, more active, more powerful and glorious than we ever were in our best moments on earth. For here we are ever chained down by our bodies, which drain the soul's strength. We are bogged down by what St. Francis so truthfully called, "Brother Ass," echoing Psalm 31 in which the soul says to the body, "Be not like the horse and the mule, without understanding, whose temper is curbed by bit and bridle." In heaven the body need no longer be dragged about as a bad-tempered mule. Flesh and spirit shall at last see eye to eye, and the flesh shall profit immeasurably.

Lord Jesus, You once said, "I have come that they may have life, and have it more abundantly." The glorious life of heaven is the happiness You have created me for. What a fool I would be, if I should neglect the one thing necessary. What a horrible thing it would be for me to lose this joy, this final accomplishment, toward which my whole being is directed. What a great thing it would be, if I heeded the psalmist, and said to myself, "Blessed be the Lord, who schools me; late into the night my inmost thoughts chasten me. Always I can keep the Lord within sight; always he is at my right hand, to make me stand firm. . . . What do they but lay up fresh stores of sorrows, that betake themselves to alien gods? Not with these will I pour out the blood of sacrifice. . . . No, it is the Lord I claim for my prize, the Lord who fills my cup; thou, and no other, wilt assure my inheritance to me."

How little we understand, how little we think of the things of heaven! Even supposing I am the healthiest of men, and will live to be ninety-five, what are those few years on earth compared with the time I am to spend in heaven?

That is why you send us trials, hardships, failures, Lord. Because we are always forgetting what we were created for. Because we think of heaven as something abstract for pure spirits. We don't say it, but we act as though heaven is not suited to our very earthy human nature. We forget that it *is* a heaven for human beings. If a young boy should ask me, "Will there be baseball in heaven?" wouldn't I have to answer, "Listen, boy, if you get to heaven and look around, and you see all the marvels and beauties of God and His angels, and Mary, and the glorious saints—if then you'll still want baseball, it'll be there for you."

Why, then, does my own concrete interest in heaven seem to falter?

Psalm 16

TEST ME AS BY FIRE

Lord, to my just complaint give ear; | do not spurn my cry for aid. | Listen to this prayer of mine; | they are no treacherous lips that make it. | At thy judgment seat I claim award; unerring thy scrutiny. | Wilt thou read my heart, | drawing near in the darkness to test me as if by fire, | thou wilt find no treachery in me. | Never have these lips been led astray by man's evil example; | still to thy law's pattern thy warnings kept me true; | still in thy paths my steps were firmly planted, my feet did not stumble.

IT WOULD BE WELL for me to attempt to say this prayer daily, Lord. I could not be sincere in it without turning quickly to another psalm, Psalm 50: "Have mercy on me, Lord, and wipe away my guilt." Are my lips not treacherous? Are they not disloyal to You, and that after all my solemn promises? Are they not treacherous to my neighbor—my friends, my brethren? When I am out "entertaining the boys" or "sympathizing" with the pals in my clique, can I then pray with David, "Lord, read my heart; thou wilt find no treachery in me"?

Lord, we all fail many times a day, but nowhere as much as in charity. Yet You called charity the bond of perfection, the Christian commandment. On the most solemn occasion of Your life, on the very night You gave Yourself up for my sake, You said, "This is my commandment, that you love one another as I have loved you. Greater love than this no one has, that one lay down his life for his friends" (John 15:12, 13). Lord, how often have I turned that great commandment around, and have laid down the reputations of my friends for my own selfish ends! By so doing, I could never again say with the psalmist, "Lord, to my just complaint give ear." For how can I now have a just complaint against anyone—I, who have betrayed my friends, I who have indeed found treachery enough on my lips?

But You know very well, Lord, that this truth will not come to life in me, and that I will go on fomenting hateful thoughts against my neighbor whenever he displeases me; I will go on making critical remarks, all most religiously justified. My small jealousies and mean envies will be the soil out of which my "virtuous" concern over the failings of others will mushroom, and the fungi will spread to my "friends" who listen to me, and we will all rejoice in the penetrating, critical minds that a benign Providence has granted us, and we will soon "thank God" in the secret corners of our hearts "that we are not like the rest of men." It is so much easier to condemn evil than to do good.

Let me at least remember the publican You praised, who knew he was indeed "like the rest of men," and whose most critical remark was, "God, be merciful to me, a sinner." And as I beg You to pardon my wrongs, I will remember Your warning that we are pardoned in accordance with the forgiveness and pity we have for our neighbor. "Forgive us . . . as we forgive those. . . ."

Psalm *17*

DO I LOVE?

Shall I not love thee, Lord, my only defender? | The Lord is my rock-fastness, my stronghold, my rescuer; | to God, my hiding-place, I flee for safety; | he is my shield, my weapon of deliverance, my refuge. . . . | All about me surged the waves of death, | deep flowed the perilous tide, to daunt me; | the grave had caught me in its toils, deadly snares had trapped my feet. | One cry to the Lord, in

*my affliction, / one word of summons to my God, / and he, from
his sanctuary, listened to my voice. / . . . Have I not kept true to
the Lord's paths? / Have I not been ever loyal to my God? / No law
of his, but I have kept it before my eyes; / no task he laid upon me
have I refused.*

LORD, THESE ARE THE WORDS of a man who truly loves You. "If you
love me, keep my commandments," You said. The first three commandments pertain directly to You. And see how well I keep
them!

"First, thou shalt not have strange gods before me." Why, never
in my life have I burned incense to a golden calf. I wouldn't dream
of bowing before idols. Second, I don't blaspheme. Whenever I
use Your name in vain, I do it without thinking. And otherwise,
the name of the Lord is so far from my daily conversations that
it would never enter my head to take it in vain. "Third, keep holy
the Sabbath day." Now, Lord, You know as well as I that I never
miss Mass on Sunday.

How does one love You with negatives? Is it that one loves You
by not hating You, by not flinging filth into Your sanctuary? The
psalmist's love is not a litany of negatives. Though I have never
feared the first commandment, Lord, it seems that Your saints did.
They didn't fear worshipping graven images, though many of
them gave their lives for refusing to do so. *They* feared worshipping
more deadly images: vanity, honor, a big name, expensive clothes,
fine cars, handsome looks, money, easy living. These were the false
gods they were afraid of. They knew where the false gods always
hide, and they dragged them out, exposed them, fought them, and
conquered them.

As for taking Your name in vain, the saints never did *anything*
in vain! They used Your name often, and always with the greatest
love and utmost attention. Yes, they used Your name often; they
called on You so much, they praised You so fervently, that they
never stopped using Your name. What irony that while sinful
people use Your name so much, they think of You so little, my

God! People of faith use Your name often, but never without thinking.

And about keeping holy the Lord's day: it is hard to see why the Lord's day can only be kept holy in a church building, and nowhere else. It is harder yet to see how one can keep holy the Lord's day by doing nothing, or by entertainments too worldly for any Christian. No doubt the serious obligation of attendance at Mass is an observance of the third commandment. Yet it is hard to see that a purely negative fear of hell should be given the name *love*. Love at the least requires attention. It is hard to see how I love God if I make no move to know Him, whom I profess to love. How much attention do I really give Him on Sunday?

It is hard to see how I love God if I am absorbed by my own false gods, to which I selfishly cling in so many circumstances.

It is hard to see how I love God by not taking His name in vain, if my thoughts are far from God.

It is hard to see how I love God by keeping the Lord's day holy, when I am not interested in using the day to know God better.

"The first and greatest commandment" of which You spoke, absorbs these three. "Love God above all things, with your whole heart and soul, and all your mind and strength."

"Not death itself is so strong as love," says the Canticle, "not the grave itself cruel as love unrequited; the torch that lights it is a blaze of fire. Yes, love is a fire no waters avail to quench, no floods to drown; for love, a man will give up all that he has in the world, and think nothing of his loss" (Cant. 8:6). If this is what the Holy Spirit means by love, what shall I say of the first three commandments, which tell me I must love God above all things? Shall I yet think them pure negatives?

Psalm 18

THE DAY'S SECRETS

Each day echoes its secret to the next, / each night passes on to the next its revelation of knowledge; / no word, no accent of theirs that does not make itself heard, / till their utterance fills every land, / till their message reaches the ends of the world.

THAT IS TO SAY, LORD, each day I should be wiser than the last. Night after night I should be able to reflect on what You have taught me this day.

What will I have learned, Lord? How You are truly present in every creature, in every event of the day, and how I have again failed to see You there?

Or shall I have learned again that You made my plans fail because they were not Your plans, and indeed were unholy plans, made to glorify myself at the expense of my soul?

Will I have learned how much and how often and how seriously I fail You? Will I have learned that to fail You really means to fail myself? Will I have learned that my restlessness, my unhappiness, my despondency come from trying to make myself and my pathetic pleasures the goal of all my efforts? Will I have learned that unless all my heart and mind and strength go out to You and find their joy in You, I shall have no peace and no justice, and all my efforts shall come to nothing?

Are not these the secrets that each day whispers to the next? Are not these the lessons that each night should pass on to its successor?

It may be true that I have learned these lessons often, Lord. But I am also much too sure that the lessons had no root, and soon

withered. And thus to my own dismay and shame, I must learn the
same words over and over: there is no hope but in God; there is
no love but in God; there is no joy but in God. All else will betray
me. "All things betray thee, who betrayest Me. . . . Naught
shelters thee, who wilt not shelter Me. . . . Lo! naught contents
thee, who content'st not Me." Such was the painful lesson taught to
Francis Thompson over many troubled years.

This is the great tragedy of our lives, Lord: we do not learn
from our mistakes. We are experts in teaching others their mistakes and showing them the way; we profit so little from our own
failures. And yet what we ought to learn You have made so clear:
"How plain are the duties which the Lord enjoins," the psalm
says, "how clear is the commandment the Lord gives, the enlightenment of man's eyes!" But the psalmist knows the answer to
man's withered experience: "And yet, who knows his own frail-
ties? If I have sinned unwittingly, do thou absolve me. Keep me
ever thy own servant, far from pride; so long as this does not lord
it over me, I will yet be without fault, I will yet be innocent of the
great sin." If I will but learn from my failings not to take pride in
myself as being anything, I am yet to be hoped for, I shall have absorbed the grace of this psalm, I shall have learned the secret echoed
from day to day: "God is all, you are nothing—except what you
are in him. Seek all your good in him; if you have learned this, you
have become wise in spite of your ignorance, and you shall succeed
in the very recognition of your failure."

This verse of the psalm is the stuff of which a life-long meditation can be made: "Keep me . . . far from pride; so long as this
does not lord it over me, I will yet be without fault, I will yet be
innocent of the great sin." What more consoling and yet what
more frightening assurance was ever written by the Holy Spirit?
"You sin thoughtlessly, my son, and I forgive you, 'drawing you to
my heart compassionately,' but there is one sin you must not be
thoughtless about, and that is pride. For that is the great sin. And
that is the secret, the great lesson each day must echo to the next.

If you have learned that, you have captured my heart, for God gives
his grace to the humble, and can do nothing else but resist the
proud."

Psalm 19

DIVINE GENEROSITY

*The Lord listen to thee in thy time of need. . . . / May he
send thee aid from his holy place . . . / May he grant thee what thy
heart desires, crown thy hopes with fulfillment. . . . / Shall I
doubt that the Lord protects the king he has anointed? / . . . /
Is not his right hand strong to save?*

LORD JESUS, if I have any doubt regarding Your power to help
me in my real needs, or Your generosity in doing so, I can recall
three simple scenes in Your life. The first I might call "a morning on
the beach." It was after Your resurrection, and since You were no
longer with Your apostles, the funds had run low. So low, in fact,
that Peter had to go back to the fishing trade. "I'm going fishing,"
he announced, not without reason. And the other apostles went
along. All night they caught nothing. Then in the morning You
stood on the shore waiting for them, although they did not at
once know You. To tease them, You called out, "Children, have
you anything to eat?" I can imagine with what dejection Peter answered, "No." Then You put him to the test, to see if he trusted
You. "Cast the net on the other side," You ordered. Most probably
a better man than I would have answered, "Who says so!" Expert fisherman though he was, Peter obeyed Your suggestion. When
a man at last learns to lose that "self-confidence" so respected by the
world, he is ready to find true confidence. And what was his reward for not doubting that Your "hands are strong"? St. John tells

us that the net nearly broke from the weight of the catch, and when the apostles came to shore, they counted 153 fish! What a powerful symbol of Your generosity! (John 21).

Another scene: When You saw the plight of the young couple at the wedding of Cana, You proved, too, how generous You are to those in need. Your mother made the request for them: "They have no wine." We can see in the large size of the six stone jars how generous Your response was!

Shall You be less generous to me, when Your Mother pleads for the graces I need?

A third scene: When You fed the five thousand on the seashore, after all had been filled, twelve baskets of leftovers were gathered. You did all these things, Lord, to show me that You are unlimited in generosity. You Yourself explained these lavish gifts when You said to the Jews, "If you yourselves, evil as you are, know how to give good things to your children, is not your Father much more ready to give, from heaven, his Holy Spirit to those who ask him?" (Luke 11:13).

It was on this occasion, Lord, that You taught us how to pray. You promised to give us what we needed. Why, then, can I hardly live a day without anxieties and worries over the future? "For your Father knows what you have need of. But seek you first the kingdom of God and his justice, and all the rest will be given you besides." What evils, what sorrows, what agony this advice would have saved the world, if it had been heeded!

Some day, Lord, I will see how well You provided for me, when I thought You had abandoned me, and with the psalmist, "I will rejoice at thy deliverance," and see that You have always "granted my prayer abundant fulfillment."

Let others talk of their earthly goods; my refuge is in the generosity of my God.

Psalm 20

THE MEANING OF LIFE

Well may the king rejoice, Lord, in thy protection, / well may he triumph in thy saving power! / Never a wish in his heart hast thou disappointed, / never a prayer on his lips denied.

WHAT A CONTRAST with the first lines of Psalm 21! How differently You speak there, Jesus! "My God, my God, why hast thou forsaken me? Loudly I call, but my prayer cannot reach thee. Thou dost not answer, my God, when I cry out to thee day and night, thou dost not heed."

The contrast continues and deepens. For in Psalm 20 David says, "Great is the renown thy protection has won for him; glory and high honor thou hast made his. An everlasting monument of thy goodness, comforted by the smile of thy favor, he stands firm, trusting in the Lord." This, says the prophet, will be the glorious lot of the king whom God will send.

Then I wonder, Lord, would I have recognized this thrice-favored king as he stood before a Roman governor and said, "Thou sayest it. I am a king. For this was I born, for this I came into the world: to bear witness to the truth." This great king, as he announced his divine mission, had for his "happy auguries . . . [to] meet him on his way" hundreds of welts and bruises from the bitter scourges that "met him on his way", and for the "crown of pure gold" that "thou dost set on his head" a mangled helmet of thorns. This king, the one expected by all nations, is "a worm, not a man; a by-word to all, the laughing stock of the rabble."

It is most fitting, Lord, that these two Psalms should stand together. The prophecy of glory; the assurance that You have never denied his prayer. And then the Psalm of his great suffering. Is this then the glory for which he prayed? Lord Jesus, are these horrors the triumph for which You lived? Are these "the wishes of Your heart" in which You "were not disappointed"? Was this the prayer on Your lips that was not denied?

It was, Lord. All Your life You spoke of that Cross and agony as Your great desire. And thus You showed us how small our minds are, how far above us Your wisdom. You are infinitely wise in the foolishness of the Cross; You are infinitely great in Your humility; You are infinitely beautiful in Your frightful wounds; Your resurrection is glorious in Your death; You have found the highest divine favor in Your desolation; You have won the world's greatest triumph and victory in Your defeat!

Psalm 21

THE NEW CROSS

. . . A by-word to all, the laughing-stock of the rabble. / All those who catch sight of me fall to mocking; / mouthing out insults, while they toss their heads in scorn, / He committed himself to the Lord, / why does not the Lord come to his rescue, and set his favorite free?

THE BEAMS of Your Cross, Lord Jesus, are as wide as the world. The world has tried to forget the Cross for two thousand years, but it has not succeeded. Everywhere we see clearly the story of the Cross.

When the Cross is loved, it brings light and peace. When the Cross is rejected, it brings unrest and the retreat into darkness which we see around us. Because men rejected the Cross, the world stands in the shadow of a terrible new symbol, the cross of tyranny and slavery. There is the Cross of Christ and the cross of anti-God. The world is crushed under the cross of bitterness, for it would not accept the Cross of Love.

Have You abandoned us, Lord of the true Cross? No, You are a lover of justice and mercy. But is it not through that very justice and mercy that the new slavery should spread itself throughout the world, that men may learn what it is to abandon the true Cross? An age that tried to live without You has come to its harvest.

The past century brought such great inventions that everywhere men were saying, "Now we can save the world without God. Now man can rule himself. No more wars, no more suffering, no more poverty, no more ignorance, no more need for religion." Man gave a most ironic twist to that great comforting prophecy of the Apocalypse, "No more tears, for the former things have passed away." Man forgot, Lord, that this comforting prophecy was said only of heaven, and that "God himself will be with them . . . and God will wipe away every tear from their eyes" (Apoc. 21:4).

"We have built our own paradise." So spoke the atheists of 1900, the new scientists whose progress did away with God. What was God to do, then, but let them see what happens without him? You could not really let men find out, Lord, for the world would at once cease to exist without You. But You might, indeed, let man find out what a paradise it is to live without truth, without charity, without humility, without mercy—what it is to serve man instead of God. And man set himself a new record for hatred, brutality, and murder.

We need not bring our whining to You, Lord. You desire nothing but the spiritual good and salvation of every man. But for those who refuse to let You make them holy, You will do nothing. For You have determined that man shall be free. "Daily," writes St. Augustine, "he stretches forth his hand to an unbelieving and seditious people."

At last You are forced to abandon them, for they will have it so, and You have not a mind to dishonor their freedom as they dishonor You.

And when men have abandoned You, Lord, they have no further choice but to be troubled in conscience perpetually, or else to fight themselves by denying that You even exist. Once having denied that You are God, they must go out and find a new god, a small god. For there is no man on earth who does not worship a god. If he has lost the true God, he must sacrifice to a false god: the god of materialism, the god of injustice, cruelty, hatred and greed: the treacherous god of deceit, murder, self-destruction. That god is Satan.

Such is the new, terrible cross of our world. Men wanted darkness, and would not have light. Men wanted hatred, and would not have love.

Have You, then, abandoned the world, Lord? No, rather You have returned to us. Did You abandon Your Divine Son when You brought the evils of pain and desolation on him, so that he cried out, "My God, my God, why hast thou forsaken me? Loudly I call, but my prayer cannot reach thee"?

You did not abandon him, Lord. You only gave him the means to save the world. So now, Lord, You bring us the cross of slavery and hatred, that we might be more than ever Your sons, bearing forth the Cross of Love to set the world free.

Psalm 21, b

ABANDONED IN HIS VICTORY

My enemies ring me round, packed close as a herd of oxen, / strong as bulls from Basan; / so might a lion threaten me with its jaws, / roaring for its prey.... Prowling about me like a pack of dogs, / their wicked conspiracy hedges me in; / they have torn holes in my hands and feet; / I can count my bones one by one; / and they stand there watching me, / gazing at me in triumph. / They divide my spoils among them, / cast lots for my garments.

Lord, it is as though David had stood at the foot of Your Cross with Mary, and there wrote his meditation on what You suffered. Is it any wonder that, after reading a Psalm like this, St. Augustine said that he heard "the voice of Christ in all the Psalms, either praising or weeping or rejoicing in hope, or longing . . ."? All his deepest human emotions are expressed in this most beautiful psalm.

The Biblical Institute of Rome entitles this Psalm "The Suffering Redeemer," and says, "It begins with a terrible cry of affliction. Notice that the first words of the Hebrew were the very words of Jesus on the Cross: 'My God, my God, why hast thou forsaken me?' From this you can easily conclude that He prayed the whole psalm. Or, at least, it is positively certain that He wished to apply the whole psalm to Himself." It may be added that the Jews knew the psalms by their first verses, which served as titles, and when You uttered that cry, Lord, You reminded them of that great prophecy, and the details of Your sufferings which it revealed. This amazing Psalm has the power, the emotion, the accuracy of detail, the beauty, the sorrow, the pity of the prophecies of Isaias, for in this Psalm we see You as abandoned, yet full of trust, as "a poor worm, not a man; a by-word to all, the laughing-stock of the rabble," as mocked and insulted, the prophecy using the very words Your persecutors used, "He committed himself to the Lord, why does not the Lord come to his rescue, and set his favorite free?"

Yet in Your sorrow and agony, You sing already of Your triumph:

"Then I will proclaim thy renown to my brethren. . . . The poor shall eat now, and have their fill, those who look for the Lord will cry out in praise of him, Refreshed be your hearts eternally! The furthest dwellers on earth will bethink themselves of the Lord, and come back to him; all the races of the heathen will worship before him . . . Him shall they worship, him only, that are laid to rest in the earth, even from their dust they shall adore."

Thus the abandonment of the Cross became its triumph. St. Gregory Nazianzen put it this way: "Christ, being the head of the new family, the Church, had to take on himself the infirmities

of the sins of his members, so as to remove them and destroy them."
So Isaias: "He has borne our infirmities and carried our sorrows."

Meditating further on the abandonment of Jesus, St. Gregory
Nazianzen says, "For the sake of our salvation he was willing to
be called *maledictus,* cursed." St. Paul testifies that "Christ redeemed us from the curse of the Law, becoming a curse for us;
for it is written, 'Cursed is everyone who hangs on a tree'" (Gal.
3:13). Abandoned because he took on our sins, "Christ never knew
sin, and God made him into sin for us, so that in him we might be
turned into the holiness of God" (II Cor. 5:21). St. Gregory concludes, "Jesus had to take on our disobedience and our rebellion,
and thus his terrible abandonment on the Cross as told in Psalm 21,
in which he represents us in himself."

And thus the old standards of success and defeat collapsed, and
the old religious convictions about God's blessing and curse
crumbled, and the wisdom of the world became foolishness, and
the defeat of Christ became Divine success, and the abandonment
of the Son of God became the glory of victory, and he who became cursed for us is blessed infinitely forever. And whereas St.
Paul could say that it was once written with sincerity, "Cursed is
everyone who hangs on a tree," today every true Christian must
say with Léon Bloy's Clotilde, "You do not enter Paradise tomorrow, or the day after, or in ten years; you enter it *today,* when you
are poor and crucified." (*The Woman Who was Poor*)

Psalm 21, c

THE DAILY CROSS

*I, too, shall live on in his presence, / and beget children to serve
him; / these to a later age shall speak of the Lord's name; / these*

to a race that must yet be born shall tell the story of his faithful-
ness, / Hear what the Lord did.

LORD JESUS, when I meditate on Psalm 21, the story of Your
Cross, I may make one great mistake about Your sacrifice and Your
redemption. So great was Your final gift of Yourself, Your life,
and Your sacred blood, that it seems to blind me. I say to myself:
it is all very well to look to Jesus on the Cross in all my struggles,
but I cannot imitate You, my Lord. You suffered for three hours,
and then it was over. The third day came a glorious resurrection,
and suffering was for You no more.

But my weakness, my sinfulness, my worries, my labors, my dis-
appointments, my temptations seem never to end. When at last I
seem prepared to imitate Your resurrection, the cross begins all
over again. My cross is as long as my life.

And that is my mistake, Lord. I forget that Your Cross, too,
lasted not for three hours, not for three days, but for Your whole
life. You were happy, indeed, not because Your life was easy, but
because You accepted the Cross willingly.

Born in the cold damp of a stable-cave, You had to flee from a
cruel dictator before You were two years old. You suffered all that
Your parents suffered in the strange land of Egypt, for You knew.

You experienced what it means to be poor and unwanted, without
friends, without help. You returned with Your parents to Galilee,
without a cent, with the poorest of homes to live in. You learned at
a very young age what hard labor means. How often do I stop to
think that the greater part of Your life was not spent in working
miracles, but in quiet, honest, tedious labor? And then I say I
cannot imitate You?

You must have been among the hardest-working men of Your
town; carpentry was an all-day job. No time for taking life easy.
At any hour You were called to help a farmer fix his plow, his
yoke, his tools. Yours was heavy work with very little pay. Your
townspeople considered Your station the humblest, and were indignant to see You appear in public as a leader.

When You began preaching and teaching, You were not deceived about glory or human honors. You experienced constant criticism, opposition, the hatred of religious people who should have welcomed You the most. The criticism You had to bear, Jesus, is so great that I could meditate for months on it. And I say Your Cross is beyond the scope of my life?

And what of Your other burdens? I know from the Evangelists that You suffered fatigue, sleepless nights, that You often spent the night in prayer after exhausting Yourself healing the sick and instructing the people. You experienced every ingratitude, every human injury, unjust treatment. It is hard, if not impossible, Lord, to think of any human cross that You did not carry before me. If I could remember how You lived, Jesus, perhaps my burdens would become much lighter, and my life would become much holier.

"A race that must yet be born shall tell the story of his faithfulness, Hear what the Lord did." If I remember what You have done, I will begin to realize my responsibilities, my opportunities for doing good; how I by my works can imitate You in the honest labor of Your youth, in the wisdom of Your words, in the charity of Your attitude, in the zeal of Your prayer.

I have learned many a year's wisdom in this meditation, Lord, if I only have convinced myself that I really and truly can imitate You in many things—in the most ordinary things of each day. For though You were God, and infinitely above me, You lived more humbly than I do. You lived in a poorer home, in greater want, with more strenuous labors, among people not as kind, not as generous as those around me. Is it not strange, Jesus, that I am so often unwilling to bear the least inconvenience, though I claim to follow Christ? How often must I yet hear what the Lord has done?

Psalm 22

HAPPINESS

The Lord is my shepherd; how can I lack anything? / He gives me a resting-place. . . , / leads me out to the cool water's brink, refreshed and content.

LORD JESUS, Your full-embracing love awaits me everywhere. If anything is written in Your Divine Book, this surely is. How many times did You not say, "Come to me all you who are burdened with work and weary, and I will give you refreshment. Take up my burden and learn from me, for I am meek and humble of heart, and you will find peace for your souls." I have heard this promise of Yours so often, Lord, that I no longer grasp its beauty or power. Yet in the hard, gray realities of day to day living, I should learn this truth easily. If I truly keep my eyes open to myself, I will soon know there is little rest on earth but in You.

Why am I bored by life's burdens, but that I have not found their true meaning? Why do I ever worry or fear, but that I forget You guide my life with a fatherly hand? Why do I become despondent and dejected, but that I fail to respect Your great wisdom and my littleness? Why do I complain and criticize, but that I am depending on things outside myself for happiness? Why do I become selfish and demanding, but that I expect happiness to come to me, when in truth I know that I myself must make it?

In all these troubles, I should have come to You. I should have known that joy must be within me, and I must be in You.

If I have lived true enough to my human nature to know that I want perfect love, perfect knowledge, the fullness of beauty and generosity, then, Lord, I should already have learned the great reality of life.

If I seek all goodness in friends and associates, they will fail to fill half the measure. If I seek all good in honors and fame, I will see them die as quickly as they sprang up; I will see they are not ever without dishonor and rejection. If I seek good in mere pleasure, it will betray me soonest of all my foolish hopes; I will hate the very baubles that I consumed so greedily. For pleasure is the first human hope to explode. If I seek joy in my own abilities, in my own pride and and self-admiration, I will soon find there a dried wasteland. For he who is left with himself alone is soon emptied.

In the end, I will hate myself, who sought to find happiness in things so fleeting and meaningless. And my hands will be empty.

Will You then turn to me, Lord, and bring me life and refreshment? You have promised no less. You have promised that I shall find the meaning and the enjoyment of knowledge, love, understanding, beauty, contentment—all in You, who have placed them in me. You who have made all joy, are Yourself all joy and wealth, the reason and fulfillment of all goodness.

Psalm 23

WHO DARES CLIMB?

Who dares climb the mountain of the Lord, / and appear in his sanctuary? / The guiltless in act, the pure in heart; / one who never set his heart on lying tales, / or swore treacherously to his neighbor. / His to receive a blessing from the Lord, / mercy from God, his sure defender. . . . / Swing back, doors, higher yet; / reach higher, immemorial gates, to let the King enter in triumph!

LORD JESUS, somewhere in my mind there is a faint assurance that someday I may see the gates of heaven roll back to receive me. And remembering that heaven is full of saints, I may take notice of what stuff saints are made of. I marvel at how much purer their intentions were than mine. And sometimes I even tell myself how I wish I could do great things in God; and then a small temptation comes along, and I know again that I can't even do small things in God. I console myself by thinking, "God can't expect that much of me. There are so many other people like me—proud, selfish, critical, stubborn, envious, gossipy, unfair, unkind. Yet all these people must be expecting to get to heaven as I do. God can't be so demanding. He knows I have a good reason for every one of my worldly and unsaintly actions. He knows, at any rate, that I have a good excuse. Go to heaven? Why, of course I'll go to heaven. I'll manage to avoid mortal sin somehow."

Yet I'm bothered by the kind of people I'm afraid I'll find in heaven. Won't I feel a bit embarrassed among them? Here are a great number of pious Hebrews, for instance, from the days of the vicious king Antiochus. They fled to the desert, they died all kinds of cruel deaths rather than disobey the smallest of God's laws. Won't I feel a bit uncomfortable beside them?

And here are the seven Machabee sons and their heroic mother. They suffered merciless butchery rather than eat one piece of forbidden meat. Won't I feel a bit dwarfed beside them? (II Macc. 7)

And here are countless men who suffered for the purity of their service to God, from Abel who died for sacrificing his best lamb to God, and Joseph who was thrown into prison for preserving his chastity, all the way to John the Baptist who died for condemning the crimes of a king, after having himself done heroic penance in the wilderness. Won't I feel a bit eclipsed by them?

Perhaps I had better move on to my contemporaries for consolation. The Roman martyrs have so little comfort to offer.

But here is more embarrassment for me than ever. Millions of men and women, boys, girls, all ages, from all countries, and all of them far too good for me. Which of them enjoyed my comfortable life? Which of them was so honored and befriended? Which of them ever dreamed of my material standard of living? They will surely make me uneasy, because they all fought against the gods of this world, and found the true God. What I have, they would have despised—money, honors, pleasures, vain ambitions—and they would have spent themselves for one thing, even in this *modern* world: the glory of God. And that is what today's saints are doing.

I look about me in this strange heaven, bewildered at the great, strong, courageous heroes of God. I shudder at the things they have done. And I cry, "Indeed, Lord! Who dares climb the mountain of the Lord, and appear in his sanctuary? Is it in *this* heaven, among *these* people that I expect a reserved place? If it is, then I must pay the price, some day, somewhere, some way, I must pay the price. One truth is evident: I have not yet done so."

Another truth is evident: You want me to do so. You have called everyone. You want me to pay my own price, for such is the nature of the freedom You have given me. You want me to begin now. I am indeed a beginner, Lord. And how did these great ones begin?

If I were to ask them, I would learn it was the small things that counted. It was the daily things I neglect, that built them into what they are. It was the small humiliations I will not accept, the small charities I will not perform; it was the ordinary recollection I will not practice, it was their persistent way of finding You everywhere that I do not heed. These things I could do, but will not. They were faithful in small things and acquired the strength for greater ones. Do I want great things, and pay no heed to the small? I am starting at the wrong end, Lord, and I shall fall, and I shall find myself necessarily obliged to begin on what is small and ordinary, insignificant, petty—too much, perhaps, like the twenty years or more You spent in Joseph's carpenter shop. I must return often to that small workshop, and watch the Saint of Saints patiently, faithfully doing the humble, ordinary works of the poor man.

Psalm 24

PERSEVERANCE

In his own laws he will train the humble, / in his own paths the humble he will guide. . . . / Quit my heart of its burden, deliver me from my distress. . . . / Take my soul into thy keeping; / come to my rescue, do not let me be disappointed of my trust in thee.

THESE ARE NOT rare sentiments in Your inspired poetry, Lord. They are found in nearly every psalm. One thinks immediately of the psalmist's perseverance, of his trust in You that long as he may need to wait, You will not in the end fail his desire.

This is a confidence and a long-suffering shared by all the saints. Which saint did not need to practice that divine patience of Job who said, "I know that my Redeemer lives and that I shall rise from the dust when the last day comes. Once more my skin shall clothe me, and in my flesh I shall have sight of God" (Job 19:25). Was not this great hope the strength of David himself when he cried, "Though a hundred trials beset the innocent, the Lord will bring him safely through them all. Under the Lord's keeping, every bone of his is safe; not one of them shall suffer harm" (Psalm 33:20).

Saint Monica was unfailing in this confidence. While her son, Augustine, stuck fast in heresy and sin, she—as her son testifies— "was weeping for me unto You, much more than mothers weep for the bodily death of their children. For she looked upon me as dead, by the faith and spirit which she had from You, and You were pleased to hear her." Indeed, Monica had yet nine years to wait. But she had never doubted that mercy would come. What was her joy, when at last she saw her prayer accomplished, and she could say to Augustine, "Son, for my part, there is nothing now in this life that gives me any delight. What I have to do here any longer or why I am here I do not know; all my hopes of this world are now at an end. One thing there was for which I did desire to stay a little longer in this life, which was that I might see you a Catholic before I died. And my God has granted me this more abundantly, in that I see you now despising all worldly goods and devoted to his service. What have I now to do here?" (*Confessions,* Bk. 9)

"No stranger the Lord is, no secret his covenant, to his true worshippers." "And what should we fear?" wrote St. Teresa. "Our Lord is so generous that He does not leave unrewarded even an upward glance with a remembrance of him." Yet with our greatest desires, holy as they may be, we must learn patience and persever-ance, knowing with St. James that "endurance must do its work thoroughly if you are to be men full-grown in every part, nothing lacking in you" (James 1:4).

"In his own laws he will train the humble." "We are confident even over our afflictions, knowing well that affliction gives rise to endurance, and endurance gives proof of our faith, and a proved faith gives grounds for hope" (Romans 5:3).

If one has never been tried, one does not have deep faith. If one has never suffered in patience, one does not have trust.

Psalm 24, b

FEAR OF THE CRITICS

Let a man but fear the Lord, / what path to choose he doubts no longer. . . . / On the Lord I fix my eyes continually, / trusting him to save my feet from the snare. / Pity me, Lord, as thou seest me friendless and forlorn.

Lord, am I afraid of criticism? Am I afraid to do what I know is right because of what "important" people will say? It will embarrass me to reflect on how much criticism You took, and that from the religious leaders of Your country!

For what did the Pharisees criticize You? Nearly everything. For having friends that were "not in good standing." Friends that did not move in the upper circles: Matthew, the tax collector, a dishonorable man. Zacheus, the publican, a swindler and thief. (They were glad to ignore the fact he had made a four-fold restitution; they would not have had the humility to do half as much.) Your forgiveness of Dismas, the repentant thief, must have shocked their fine religious feelings.

It mattered little to them that You had come to save not the just but sinners—that is, men who know they are sinners.

They criticized You for letting a sinful woman anoint Your feet. One of Your own apostles complained that the money should rather have been given to the poor. They criticized You for being an eater and a wine bibber, for accepting invitations to dine with sinners, for forgiving an adulteress, for breaking the law by healing on the Sabbath, for picking corn on the Sabbath. In the end they accused You of causing sedition and revolution, of blaspheming and declaring that You were the Son of God!

When Your disciples informed You that the Pharisees took offence at Your words because they were words of power and justice, You gave Your answer to the Pharisees of all times: "Every plant that my heavenly Father has not planted will be rooted up. Let them alone; blind guides they are of blind men. But if a blind man guide a blind man, both fall into a pit" (Matt. 15:14). It is better that only one fall into the pit, and that the other be not guided by blindness.

Lord, make me understand how foolish it is to live by human judgments. If others accuse me with reason, let me be humble enough to admit the truth. But if ever I make human praise the end and standard of what I do, I'm a traitor to You and to myself.

St. Gregory's warning is all too necessary: "The desire for praise may overtake you, and what is done for outward effect, will fail of its inward reward. . . . You ought to use the greatest caution, even in doing good things. For it may be that in carrying out a good work, you are seeking only the favor and good graces of men" (Homily 12 on the Gospels). Even in the highest acts of virtue, he warns, one may be seeking only the favors of the critics; for there are many who "keep themselves from the desire of outward things and are drawn by hope to interior things . . . and scorn to receive human praise in return for their labor. . . . But there are many also who afflict their bodies with abstinence, and yet in that very abstinence seek to be approved by men." And these must be the most miserable of humans, for they seek a reward so thin and uncertain, that even the lovers of pleasure are better paid.

"I used to try very hard to be admired, to be liked. That is the world," said the wise old Abbé Chevance to Chantal in Bernanos' novel, *Joy*. It is the way of the world, and if one does not outgrow it with childhood, it is the road to frustration and despair.

We must all face only one critic: the Divine Judge.

Psalm 25

THE BEGINNER

Lord, be thou my judge; | have I not guided my steps clear of wrong? | Have I trusted in the Lord, only to stumble on my path? | Test me, Lord, put me to the proof; | assay my inmost desires and thoughts. . . . | I have not consorted with false men, or joined in plotting evil. . . . | With the pure in heart I will wash my hands clean, | and take my place among them at thy altar, | there making thy praises known. . . .

THESE ARE THE THOUGHTS of a sincere beginner, one who has at last recognized the true purpose of his life. He is not yet perfect, he has not gone far, but he has turned himself toward truth.

Lord, if I am a beginner in the great spiritual battle of life, I must act wisely. I must preserve the good You have begun in me, and I must have sound advice. There are many experts I may consult. One of the best is St. Teresa, whom Pius XI called equal in brilliance and good sense to the great Doctors of the Church.

To beginners she said, "Most of all, be cheerful everywhere and in everything." Gloom and pessimism are the atmosphere of Satan. God created us for joy, and we must walk his way with a cheerful, willing heart. St. Teresa is most insistent that we use good sense and discretion in all matters spiritual; for great blunders can easily be made. "Do not do penances and prayers that your health will not allow," she says, "but also learn to worry less about your health." How much has been paid annually to psychiatrists for the healthy advice this great saint gave out free. "There are many things," she says, " by which you can reach great heights of sanctity without the slightest harm to your health. Despise honor and vainglory, for example; did anyone ever shorten his life by wanting to be less self-centered?" It is far more certain that many a life has been strengthened, prolonged, made happy by unselfishness. "Despise possessions, too," she writes, "for these are the things that shrivel the soul, and build a barrier between it and God" (*Autobiography*).

There is also the matter of "standing on our rights." It is generally a sign of pride. "If we must question rights, let it be this: 'What right have I to the honors and favors I receive?' But God preserve us from ever saying, 'What right had he to do this to me?' "

Lastly, St. Teresa insists that we determine on a time and place for prayer. Here again she speaks like the most experienced of doctors. "Go out into the fields," she says, "where you may experience the peace of solitude and silence, and may speak to God." "The Lord invites everyone, for he said, 'Come to me *all,* and I will give you to drink.' " For the beginner, prayer is refreshment like water: it cools the restless spirit; it washes away our filth; it quenches our thirst. "Whoever drinks of this water will never thirst for the things of this life, but his thirst for the things of the other world will grow in him, and become much greater than any our natural thirst can make us conceive. . . . Blessed be he who invites us to drink!" (*Way of Perfection,* Ch. XXI).

If, following this great Saint's method, I resort to prayer and humility, "with the pure I will wash my hands clean" and You will "never count this soul for lost" but "on sure ground my feet are set."

Psalm 26

FATHER

"True to my heart's promise, / I have eyes only for thee; / I long, Lord, for thy presence. / Do not hide thy face. . . . / Father and mother may neglect me, / but the Lord takes me into his care."

How OFTEN have You not told us, Lord, that we have a knowing and loving Father? You went as far as to say, "Be not anxious, saying, 'What shall we eat?' or 'What shall we drink?' or 'What shall we put on?' for your Father knows that you need all these things. But seek first the kingdom of God and his justice, and all these things shall be given you besides."

You reminded us, "I am the good shepherd, and I know mine and mine know me, even as the Father knows me and I know the Father."

I may remember learning in my earliest school days that God is the "supreme being" and the "pure spirit" and the "almighty creator." But I have never yet got it clear—in a practical way—that You are my Father, Lord, truly my Father in the most real and beautiful sense of that word. You know me completely, everything that I am and that I need, far better than I know myself. You insisted, Lord, that "one" is my "Father, who is in heaven." You came to assure us that our Father loves us, even as You love us (John 17:23). The Son came to reveal his Father: "You know neither me nor my Father," You told the Jews. "If you knew me, you would then know my Father also. . . . He who sent me is true, and the things that I heard from him, these I speak in the world."

Here, Lord Jesus, in the love Your Father and You have for me, I will find life. "For the Father loves the Son, and shows him all that he himself does. And greater works than these he will show him, that you may wonder. For as the Father raises the dead and gives them life, even so the Son also gives life to whom he will." Into this life and love, You have received me: "As the Father has loved me, I also have loved you. Abide in my love" (John 15:9).

I am Your adopted son; all of us are. If anything is written, this surely is. "See how God has shown his love towards us," St. John writes, "that we should be counted his sons, should *be* his sons. If the world does not recognize us, that is because it never recognized him. Beloved, we are sons of God even now, and what we shall be hereafter, has not been made known as yet. But we know that when he comes we shall be like him; we shall see him, then, as he is" (I John 3). What could be more beautiful than this assurance, from one who lived most intimately on earth with You, Lord? You have fulfilled what the psalmist divined; Your care for us is greater than any on earth; Your care for me is complete and intimate and personal.

Psalm 27

RESCUE

Blessed be the Lord's name, my plea is heard; | the Lord is my strength and shield. | Trusting in him, I found redress; | there is triumph in my heart, | on my lips the song of praise.

THIS IS A TRUE PORTRAIT of my life; a constant falling into the pit, and Your repeated rescue, Lord. If I have learned anything in my life, it is that I need redemption, not once, but continually. You have not only made us Your sons, Lord; You are forever re-adopting us. You are forever restoring us to Your family. You began with baptism. "Unless a man be born again," You once said to Nicodemus. And he, not understanding the great failure of man on earth, asked, "How can a man be born again when he is old?" With what beauty You then suggested to him the mystery of redemption! "Believe me," You said, "unless a man be born again of water and the Holy Spirit, he cannot enter into the kingdom of God. That which is born of the flesh is flesh; and that which is born of the Spirit is spirit." You made clear to him, too, that redemption was Your doing. "As Moses lifted up the serpent in the desert" to save the Israelites from plague, "even so must the Son of Man be lifted up, that those who believe in him may not perish, but may have eternal life" (John 3:14).

The psalmist knows well that his life is a recurring failure and an ever-growing need for liberation. "To thee, my Lord, my refuge, I cry aloud, do not leave my cry unanswered; speak to me, or I am no better than a dead man, sinking to the grave." He rejoices that You bring him Your saving power. "Blessed be the Lord's name, my plea is heard; the Lord is my strength and shield."

The great tragedy of man's failure, and the great glory of God's power are often in the thought of St. Paul. He feels these two forces of life at work in his own body. "I know that in me, that is, in my flesh, no good dwells, because to wish is within my power, but I do not find the strength to accomplish what is good. For I do not do the good that I wish, but the evil that I do not wish, that I perform. . . . For I am delighted with the law of God according to the inner man, but I see another law in my members, warring against the law of my mind and making me prisoner to the law of sin that is in my members. Unhappy man that I am! Who will deliver me from the body of this death? The grace of God through Jesus Christ our Lord. . . . The spiritual principle of life has set me free, in Jesus Christ, from the principle of sin and of death. There was something the law could not do, because flesh and blood could not lend it the power; but this God has done by sending us his own Son" (Romans 7:18–25; 8:2, 3).

Psalm 28

THE VOICE OF GOD

The voice of the Lord is heard over the waters. . . . / the Lord's voice in its power, the Lord's voice in its majesty. . . . / The Lord's voice, that breaks the cedars; . . . the Lord's voice kindles flashing fire; The Lord's voice makes the wilderness rock; . . . / The Lord's voice sets the oak-trees a-swaying, strips the deep forest bare. / Meanwhile, in his sanctuary, there is no sound but tells of his glory. . . . / And this Lord will give strength to his people; / the Lord will give his people his own blessing of peace.

THERE IS NO SOUND on earth but announces the power, the justice, the glory of its divine Lord. No sound but tells man of his own

liberation. And yet how long the Lord's people must wait! How
infinitely patient he is, the God of all strength.

"O that thou wouldst rend the heavens and come down," Isaias
pleaded. "The mountains would melt away at thy presence. They
would melt as at the burning of flames, the waters would boil with
fire; that thy name might be made known to thy enemies, that the
nations might tremble at thy presence" (Isaias 64).

How strong must be Your mercy, Lord, that You can withhold
Your judgment and the wrath of Your justice from the appalling
criminals of this world! It is as though punishment has been withheld from sinners ever since the Lamb of God, meek and silent, appeared in the midst of the world's greatest crime, and was its
victim.

In the very cave where You were born, Jesus, young lambs took
shelter. Their presence must have reminded You of the sacrifice
You came to make. Isaias prophesied that You would be led as a
sheep to the slaughter, and that You would be silent as a lamb when
he is shorn.

As a lamb You would plead for us with Your Father; as a lamb
You would not resist injustice. Yet in Your inspired writings You
assured us that there was a latter age of the gentle lamb. You are
merciful now; You wait in silence that You may forgive, but You
will not be so forever. In the end, the time of mercy is over, and
the Lamb of mercy shall be revealed as the terrible lamb of the
Apocalypse, when "the voice of the Lord shall break the cedars and
be heard over the waters" as he comes to accuse those who refused
his mercy.

Of him St. John says: "The kings of the earth, and the princes,
and the rich, and the strong, and everyone, bond and free, shall
hide themselves in caves and in the rocks of the mountains. And
they shall say to the mountains and to the rocks, 'Fall upon us, and
hide us from the face of him who sits upon the throne, and from the
wrath of the Lamb; for the great day of their wrath has come, and
and who is able to stand?'" It is a fearful and awesome sight. The
innocent Lamb of Christmas, the bloody Lamb of Good Friday, the

Paschal Lamb shall appear to accuse those who have rejected his Sacrifice, those who have made light of his mercy, those who have not imitated his humility. Holy Mother Church must have thought of this terrible judgment, when she wrote that cry for pity in the *Gloria* of the Mass: "Thou who takest away the sins of the world, have mercy on us! Who takest away the sins of the world, receive our prayer! Thou who sittest at the right hand of the Father, have mercy on us!"

The voice of God is the voice of life. "Believe me, the hour is coming and now is here, when the dead shall hear the voice of the Son of God, and those who hear shall live" (John 5:25).

The voice of God is the voice of truth. "As he was still speaking, behold a bright cloud overshadowed them, and a voice out of the cloud said, 'This is my beloved Son, in whom I am well pleased; hear him'" (Matt. 17:5).

The voice of God is the voice of judgment. "For the Lord himself with cry of command, with voice of archangel, and with trumpet of God will descend from heaven; and the dead in Christ will rise up first" (I Thess. 4:16).

The voice of God is the voice of eternal youth. "And I turned to see the voice that was speaking with me. And having turned I saw . . . One like to a son of man . . . and his eyes were like a flame of fire; his feet were like fine brass, as in a glowing furnace, and his voice like the voice of many waters. . . . And his countenance was like the sun shining in its power. And when I saw him, I fell at his feet as one dead. And he laid his right hand upon me, saying, 'Do not be afraid; I am the First and the Last, and he who lives; I was dead, and behold, I am living forever'" (Apoc. 1:12-17).

And the voice of life is "the voice of the Lord heard over the waters" when life was first given to the creatures of the earth, those that move about and have their being in him.

And the voice of truth is "the Lord's voice in its power, the Lord's voice in its majesty," the voice of him in the burning bush. Moses asked the voice, "If the children of Israel should say to me, 'What is his name? What shall I say to them?'" And the voice of God answered Moses, "*I am who am*. Thus shalt thou say to the children of Israel, *He who is* hath sent me to you." He is all reality, he is all truth, he exists by himself and in himself and from himself forever.

And the voice of judgment is "the Lord's voice" which "kindles flashing fire; the Lord's voice makes the wilderness rock." When at the end of time the Divine Judge descends, and "the mountains melt at his presence," and "the waters boil with fire," the wilderness, the devastated, scorched earth shall rock, and the dead shall rise at the sound of his voice, and justice shall reign at last.

And the voice of eternal youth is "the Lord's voice" that "sets the oak-trees a-swaying, strips the deep forest bare." And the voice of eternal youth says, "Behold, I make all things new!" And John says, "I saw a new heaven and a new earth. For the first heaven and the first earth passed away, and the sea is no more. And I saw the holy city, New Jerusalem, coming down out of heaven from God, made ready as a bride adorned for her husband. And I heard a loud voice from the throne saying, 'Behold the dwelling of God with men'" (Apoc. 21:1).

Psalm 29

THE MYSTERY OF SORROW

For a moment lasts his anger, / for a life-time his love; / sorrow is but the guest of a night, / and joy comes in the morning.

WE WERE NOT CREATED for sorrow, but for joy. Yet, "Did it not behoove Christ to suffer, and so enter into his glory?"

"But if we are sons, we are heirs also: heirs indeed of God and joint heirs with Christ, provided, however, we suffer with him that we may also be glorified with him. For I reckon that the sufferings of the present time are not worthy to be compared with the glory to come that will be revealed in us.

"For the eager longing of creation awaits the revelation of the sons of God. For creation was made subject to vanity—not by its own will but by reason of him who made it subject—in hope, because creation itself also will be delivered from its slavery to corruption into the freedom of the glory of the sons of God. . . . We ourselves groan within ourselves, waiting for the adoption as sons, the redemption of our body" (which now suffers, but which is destined for an unspeakably glorious dawn). "For in hope were we saved. But hope that is seen is not hope. For how can a man hope for what he sees? But if we hope for what we do not see, we wait for it with patience" (Romans 8:19–25).

Without this hope, sorrow has no meaning. Without the glory toward which it works, sorrow is the greatest of crimes. For God did not create us for sorrow, nor for suffering. And had he not instructed us as to its profound mystery, we should have rejected it as the greatest evil. But now Christ has revealed it to us as a fountain of hidden delights, as the mother and the daughter of saintly love, as the twin sister of Christian joy in this world. So now the Christian rejoices in his sufferings, and sorrowing with Christ enters his joy even in this world.

Yet joy shall ever remain the favorite daughter. Sorrow is not our last end, but the perfect bliss of living with God. Suffering can only lead us, and safely lead us, to the door of heaven. At that moment, pain and tears must suffer their own death. "For a moment lasts his anger" that sin might be wiped away, after which "for a lifetime his love." "Sorrow is but the guest of a night," in which even the saint in closest union with God cannot see clearly, for the night cannot truly be seen. But the dark is given, that the light may be hoped for, and being hoped for, may be attained. And if sorrow, the guest of the night, be accepted with love and entertained, "joy comes in the morning," and as the eternal sun rises, the soul will see all things in the brilliance of the dawn.

Lord, my life's pattern is colored by many sorrows, small in themselves, but often huge to me. Even the fears and worries that magnify my trials are part of sorrow's burden. Yet the burden can be carried with joy. For there is no longer disgust or despair in suffering; the greater part has now been shouldered by the Man of Sorrows, who carried every trial.

Since Your divine wisdom led You to suffering, Lord Jesus, I am assured of its deep value. You never chose anything in vain—neither poverty, nor pain, nor tears, nor rejection. You chose them because they are the very foundation and structure of love. You knew that the way of love in this world and its completion in the next are worthy of much trouble and tears. Life itself teaches us so, and everyone who has truly lived and truly loved, understands with Shakespeare that "the course of true love never did run smooth." Love in this life is toil and sacrifice, but eternity is long enough to repay it.

Psalm 30

INTO HIS HANDS

Thou dost strengthen and defend me; / thou, for thy own honor, dost guide and escort me; / by thee protected, I shall escape from the snare that lies hidden in my path. / Into thy hands I commend my spirit; / thou, God ever faithful, wilt claim me for thyself.

Lord Jesus, I will reflect today on what You told the Jews one day during a festival at Jerusalem. You said, "The Father loves the Son, and discloses to him all that he himself does." Whenever You spoke about Your life in heaven, You spoke especially of the complete love and sharing and unity found in Your family, the Holy Trinity. You told us, and St. John recorded it, that there are no secrets in Your family. "The Father reveals all things to the Son," You said, "and he has greater doings yet to disclose to him, for your astonishment; just as the Father bids the dead rise up and gives them life, so the Son gives life to whomsoever he will. So it is with judgment; the Father, instead of passing judgment on any man himself, has left all judgment to the Son, so that all may reverence the Son just as they reverence the Father; to deny reverence to the Son is to deny reverence to the Father who has sent him." These are Your own words, my Lord. And such is Your complete power over life and death, sharing it as You do with Your Father, that judgment over all the world is in Your hands, as it is in his.

You insisted on the power, the overwhelming beauty of this revelation. A few minutes later You repeated this striking truth, the perfect harmony in which the Father and Son exercise this divine potency: "As the Father has within him the gift of life, so he has granted to the Son that he, too, should have within him the gift of life. . . . Do not be surprised at that. The time is coming, when all those who are in their graves will hear his voice and will come out of them; those whose actions have been good, rising to new life, and those whose doings have been evil, rising to meet their sentence. I cannot do anything of my own impulse; I decide as I am bidden, and my decision is never unjust, because I am consulting the will of him who sent me, not my own" (John 5:20).

As the Son wills with the Father, so should I will with both. I know well enough, Lord, that is what You wanted to tell me. What power is mine if my will is united to Yours! What happiness will be mine, if in all my decisions I say, as You did, "My decision is never unjust, because I am consulting the will of him who sent me, not my own." This is what will bring peace, harmony, fullness to my life.

Psalm 31

THE CHUCK-HOLES

Blessed are they who have their faults forgiven, | their transgressions buried deep; | blessed is the man who is not guilty in the Lord's reckoning, | the heart that hides no treason.

THE PSALMIST warns his fellows of a coming judgment, of the arrival of the great king, "whose winnowing fan is in his hand, and he will thoroughly clean out his threshing floor," and he will rid the earth of pestilence. Blessed are they, then, who can stand inspection with clean hearts as the great Judge passes by.

The psalmist speaks as a prophet, and one can not help thinking of a fiery young man who lived in a rocky wasteland, browned by exposure to sun and weather, a man lean and strong and muscular, wearing a rough camel-skin. "He went over all the country round Jordan, announcing a baptism of repentance for the forgiveness of sins, as it is written in the book of the prophet Isaias: There is a voice of one crying in the wilderness: Prepare the way of the Lord, straighten out his paths. Every valley shall be filled, and every mountain and hill shall be brought low, and the crooked shall be made straight, and the rough paths made into smooth roads, and all mankind shall see the saving power of God" (Luke 3:3-6).

Roads were cleared and widened for the arrival of a great king. Indeed, the great king arrived. But were men prepared for that king? Hardly. St. Gregory the Great observes that his own country could not have been less prepared for its reckoning. Materially, while the Roman empire had one ruler, the small Palestine had *four*. Spiritually, they had no part with him. "He was in the world, and the world was made through him, and the world knew him not. He came unto his own, and his own received him not."

Blessed is he whose heart is prepared to receive his God. Every low place, every chuck-hole must be filled up, to make straight the way of God into his soul. That which is missing must be supplied. "Blessed are they who have their faults forgiven, their transgressions buried deep."

Transgressions are buried deep by good works, Lord. Sins are washouts in my soul, but good works shall fill them up. Let every valley of my soul be filled; let all neglect be covered by the good works I ought to be doing, and have not done. Let the crooked be made straight when I perform the duties of my position in life. Let the rough places be made smooth when I am forgiving, and when I have put on a heart of charity. Lord, when You come to me in the Sacrament of Yourself, You will be stumbling over missing floorboards in my soul, but You will see the house under repair. And I know that You will have to do most of the work, filling the holes, and cleaning out the dirt and filth. But if I may be so irreverent, I remember that You were a carpenter, and that all these centuries You have come to men, and have swept out and remodeled houses in the most appalling condition. I will at least cooperate by "bringing the mountains low," the huge pile of refuse which is my pride and vainglory. I can at least be filled with humility, thus levelling the mounds of rubbish in my soul.

Psalm 32

THE CHARITY OF GOD

The Lord's word is true, he is faithful in all his dealings; / faithfulness he loves, and the just award; / the whole earth overflows with the Lord's goodness. / It was the Lord's word that made the heavens, / the breath of his lips that peopled them.

"I HAVE LOVED THEE with an everlasting charity, and now in mercy I have drawn thee to myself (Jeremias 31:3). "Torrents of water cannot quench charity, floods cannot drown it; if a man should give all the substance of his household for love, he shall despise it as nothing" (Canticle 8:7). There is no sound in the world, there is no word in the universe closer to God than *charity*. It is a word terrible and strong, a word more dazzling than lightning, a word with more meaning than all the books ever written, a word forever falling from the lips of God. "Charity is a fire no water can quench." Charity is that goodness of the Lord which, as the psalmist tell us, overflows over all the earth.

We hear how fearfully Jesus speaks of the "cooling of charity" in the days when men will forget what he stands for (Matt. 24:2). We read that tremendous chapter of St. Paul, in which charity is pictured as a person unable to die, suffering everything, believing everything. We are warned that without charity all is vain; that it would mean nothing to be a martyr, to burn at the stake, without charity. We are assured that it is nothing to speak all languages, to be a prophet, to know all mysteries, to possess all wisdom, unless one has charity; that charity is patient, kind, in no way envious or malicious, having no vanity, no ambition, not even seeking what belongs to her, a stranger equally to anger and pride, an enemy of every evil thought—in a word, that charity is love as found only in God, and in fact, charity is God himself (I Cor. 13). "God is Charity; and he who abides in Charity abides in God, and God lives in him" (I John 4:16).

Lord God, is there any room in Your Heaven for me? Heaven is God, and God is charity. No man can enter heaven unless he has become perfect in charity. How often I have deceived myself, calling myself charitable by some small, silly action done with an insincere heart. Charity is divine love, and it embraces all virtues. The slower my growth in charity, the farther I am from heaven. "Above all else have charity, which is the bond of perfection." Thus St. Paul. When I have charity, I love as God loves. Charity has nothing to do with a smile for everybody and approval of everything, good or evil. Many have corrupted charity, thinking themselves charitable when they act from the "virtue" of good politics. The psalmist describes charity in these words: "The Lord's word is true, he is faithful in all his dealings; faithfulness he loves; the whole earth overflows with the Lord's goodness." The Lord's goodness is not politics. The Lord's goodness is that concern which will lead men truthfully to their last end.

Psalm 33

WHAT IS CHARITY?

Know then, my children, what the fear of the Lord is; | come and listen to my teaching. | Long life, and prosperous days, who would have these for the asking? | My counsel is, keep thy tongue clear of harm, | and thy lips free from every treacherous word. | Naught of evil cherish thou, but rather do good; | let peace be all thy quest and aim.

ONE WOULD NATURALLY EXPECT that on the last night of his life, Christ would have made sure once more that the most important of all his teachings would leave a strong impression on the minds of his followers. He did just that. And it was the counsel given in Psalm 33. Love was the all-important thing. What Jesus and St. John meant by love, St. Paul meant by charity. In the Christian sense, these words are interchangeable: *love* and *charity*. Let us combine them by calling this virtue *Christian love*. What is Christian love?

There are many kinds of love in this world, from the cheapest to the most precious. The cheapest is puppy love, and that is a good name for it. It is merely a liking of the senses. I like that fellow because he looks nice. I might as well say I like a horse because he looks nice. This form of liking because of outward appearance is basically an animal love. It is not love in the sense that Christ spoke of it. It is simply a liking, a sense feeling, a natural feeling not wrong in itself, but not worthy of any reward or of the name *Christian love.*

Now let me investigate some higher forms of love. The love of a father and mother for their children is certainly more than a mere liking. The love of real friends is more than a liking, too. It is a sharing of common interests. It is mutual respect and understanding. Is this the kind of love, then, that Christ meant by charity? No, it is not. He said our charity was to be universal. It was to go out to all men. And these loves, though they are beautiful and good, are very specialized, and are limited to a small group, our own family and close friends.

Lord Jesus, I now understand something about the love You have commanded me to practice. It is not a matter of liking, or feeling attracted toward others. Christian love has nothing to do with liking or disliking at all. Christian love must exist along with the strongest dislikes. Otherwise, how could You have expected us to love our enemies? You did not say, "Approve of your enemies. Agree with your enemies." You did not do that Yourself. But You did say, "Love your enemies. Do good to them that hate you. Pray for them that persecute and calumniate you." Therefore it is not a matter of how gentle and kind I *feel* that makes me charitable. It is the *good* that I do through sheer force of my will. Thus the psalmist, knowing what the goodness of God is, says, "My counsel is, keep thy tongue clear of harm, and thy lips free from every treacherous word. Naught of evil cherish thou, but rather do good." There is no talk of loving, intimate friendship, but of doing good, and of curbing the evil tongue. Thus St. James, who devotes his whole epistle to the practice of charity, observes that "if anyone does not offend in word, he is a perfect man, able also to lead round by a bridle the whole body. . . . And the tongue is a fire, the very world of

iniquity. . . . For every kind of beast and bird . . . has been tamed
by mankind; but the tongue no man can tame—a restless evil, full
of deadly poison. With it we bless God the Father; and with it we
curse men, who have been made after the likeness of God. Out of
the same mouth proceed blessing and cursing. These things, my
brethren, ought not be so" (James 3:2–10).

Charity, Christian love, is indeed no mere sentiment which oc-
casionally warms the lonely heart. It is the whole man, in his complete attitude, and the tongue is its guiding rudder. That tongue, so
prone to curse and condemn its brethren, that tongue ought to be
praying and pleading with God to forgive and convert, to inspire
and to give grace, "for we are all in need of the glory of God."

Psalm 34

MORE THAN A HUMAN LOVE

*Mine to triumph in the Lord, to boast of the aid he brings me; /
this be the cry of my whole being, / There is none like thee, Lord; /
who else rescues the afflicted from the hand of tyranny, / the poor,
the destitute, from his oppressors? See how perjured witnesses have
come forward, / to browbeat me over charges of which I know
nothing; / how they have repaid my kindness with cruelty, and
left me friendless! / Time was, when these were sick; what did I
then? / Sackcloth was my wear; / rigorously I kept fast, prayed
from my heart's depths. / I went my way sadly, as one that mourns
for brother or friend, / bowed with grief, as one that bewails a
mother's loss. / And now it was my turn to reel under fortune's
blows; / what did they? Gleeful they met, and plotted to attack
me unawares; / tore at me without ceasing, / baited and mocked
me, gnashing their teeth in hatred.*

THIS IS DAVID, the man of charity, figure of Jesus, the God of charity. Jesus, You complained as he did, of the reward Your charity met. "Many good works I have done among you; for which of them do you stone me?" Ah, how true it is that our charity must be more than a human love, seeking more than human return. Else we are due for bitter disappointment. Above all, Lord Jesus, I must understand that of its nature charity is not returned in this life, for it is a godly love. "If you were of the world, the world would love its own, but because I have taken you out of the world, the world cannot tolerate you" (John 15:18).

But I have already considered, Lord, that charity has nothing to do with liking or disliking people. Why, then, should I expect that it has anything to do with liking or disliking human return or human ingratitude?

Can I see charity in David's complaint? Well, Lord, Your warnings to the Pharisees were not always sweet and mellow. You were hard where You required it. You were concerned about what was good for them, their eternal salvation, and that is the essence of charity. Charity is not kindness, but goodness. Charity is not the sugar but the salt of life. You desired to save their sinful souls, and that is why You used strong measures and dire threats. You tried to convince them of the seriousness, the horrible danger of their hypocrisy.

Charity is a divine love. I must not confuse it with a merely human love. Human love exists between men. Christian love is more: it is from me to God and through God to my neighbor. And that is why I can love even those I do not like. I do not love them for myself. I love them through God and for God and because of God, and because I want God to be in me, and work through me, and I want to be in God.

Lord Jesus, I know that You have never created a human being that You did not love. I know that Your love creates, and You create no soul You do not want to save. You offer heaven to every man, and as long as he is alive, You give him grace to gain that infinite treasure. I must share this charity of Yours. As long as my fellowmen—any friend, any acquaintance, competitor, enemy, or offender —as long as they live on this earth, I must desire their good, and their good is that they live unto You. I must pray that they will reach their eternal happiness. I must do what is possible to me to help them. I can at least help them with prayers. "Father, forgive them, for they know not what they do." Daily You stretch out Your hands to those who will not accept Your love, and to those who openly and actively hate You. This is true charity. Every Christian can pray like that; if he does not, he is not Christian.

Lord, I may have just complaints. Never mind, the day of justice will come. This life is the day of charity. And what treasures will be mine, what joy on the day of justice, if I come laden with fruits I have gathered in the day of charity. For this is the true love that endures beyond this passing world. This is the love by which all men shall know I am Your disciple.

To apply this great truth: I can imagine the person I would be most liable to dislike. I can visualize the most vicious people in town. Their vices are so appalling I cannot feel secure in their company. Yet I must love them with Christian love. I must desire that they will be converted and will make themselves worthy of heaven. If I can help toward this end, I will do so. I will remember that the Son of God came to save sinners, not the just. I will hate the sin, but never the sinner; I will seek to destroy the evil, but I will seek to save the soul of the evil man.

Psalm 35

MERCY—DIVINE AND HUMAN

Lord, thy mercy is high as heaven; | thy faithfulness reaches to the clouds; | thy justice stands firm as the everlasting hills, | the wisdom of thy decrees is deep as the abyss. | Lord, thou dost give

*protection to man and beast, / so rich is thy divine mercy; / under
the shelter of those wings the frail children of earth will find confidence. / With thy rich store thou wilt nourish them, / bid them
drink deep at thy fountain of contentment. / In thee is the source of
all life; / thy brightness will break on our eyes like dawn. / Still let
thy mercy dwell with those who acknowledge thee.*

THE PSALMIST'S DESCRIPTION of Your mercies, Lord, has overwhelming power and beauty, and all the tenderness and perception
of one who has studied the earth thoughtfully, and has found something of the inner love of its Maker. Mercy without limit—what
better description of the Creator?

The theme of divine mercy is like a song in Shakespeare, who
pictures mercy as so high above the supreme power of kings as to
be truly divine. There is no power on earth that can make a man
merciful, he says, if he does not learn it of God. Fear may compel
a man to exercise mercy, but if he has power, only godliness will do
so. God, who has none to fear, is richest in mercy, and thus it is
in him totally unselfish, totally free, totally beautiful.

> The quality of mercy is not strain'd
> It droppeth as the gentle rain from heaven
> Upon the place beneath; it is twice blest;
> It blesseth him that gives, and him that takes:
> 'Tis mightiest in the mightiest: it becomes
> The throned monarch better than his crown;
> His sceptre shows the force of temporal power,
> The attribute to awe and majesty,
> Wherein doth sit the dread and fear of kings;
> But mercy is above this sceptred sway;
> It is enthroned in the hearts of kings,
> It is an attribute to God himself;
> And earthly power doth then show likest God's
> When mercy seasons justice. Therefore, Jew,
> Though justice be thy plea, consider this—

> That in the course of justice, none of us
> Should see salvation: we do pray for mercy;
> And that same prayer doth teach us all to render
> The deeds of mercy.
>
> *(The Merchant of Venice,* Act IV)

In man, mercy is greater than power. In God, it is all one. Yet if it is humanly possible to speak of a greater in God, it must seem that his mercy is more striking than his power, or even that his mercy *is* his greatest power. His power should never have created me, were it not for his infinite mercy. Most assuredly, his power should have crushed me, but his mercy saved me. Had anyone rebelled against me with half the ingratitude I have toward God, I would long ago have used my power against the culprit. Lord, it surely seems that Your mercy holds back Your power. But I have none of the wisdom with which You rule man and beast. I only know that "thy mercy is high as heaven" while yet "thy justice stands firm as the everlasting hills," though my mind is too small to combine these qualities.

I deserve so little, You so much; I have so little mercy, You so much. Why is it, Lord? How true that mercy is "mightiest in the mightiest." How often have I prayed sincerely "forgive those who make me suffer"?

I wish to have Your happiness, I desire Your strength, I try to share Your justice, I hope to share Your glory—yet I want so little of Your mercy. I have mercy where there is no need for it, but I will not exercise it where I ought.

Truly, Lord, Your mercy is high as heaven, and mine is small and corrupt. What saint did not overflow with genuine mercy? What saint did not heed Your warning, "If you forgive others, your heavenly Father will forgive You, but if you do not forgive men, neither will your Father forgive you your offenses" (Matt. 6:14).

Give me the light and the wisdom to exercise mercy when I ought. Give me the understanding to see that often when I think myself rich in mercy, I have nothing to forgive, for how much can

I in truth say others owe me? Is it not true, Lord, that often when I have a heart of mercy, I ought also have a mind of justice, for those who supposedly offend me do me no wrong, but only graciously give me what I deserve? Let me not be so proud or so blind as to think my mercy is great when I accept from others what I justly deserve. But if it should perchance happen that I receive less than I might reasonably deserve (how rarely this happens!) then I will recall that "the quality of mercy is not strain'd. . . . It blesseth him that gives and him that takes: 'tis mightiest in the mightiest."

Psalm 36

CHRISTIAN PATIENCE

Be content to trust in the Lord and do good; / live on thy land, and take thy ease, all thy longing fixed in the Lord; / so he will give thee what thy heart desires. / Commit thy life to the Lord, and trust in him; / he will prosper thee, making thy honesty clear as the day, / the justice of thy cause bright as the sun at noon. / Dumb and patient, to the Lord's mercy look thou, / never fretting over the man that has his own way, and thrives by villainy. / End thy complaints, forgo displeasure, / do not fret thyself into an evil mood; / the evil-minded will be dispossessed, / and patient souls, that wait for the Lord, succeed them. / Forbear yet a little, and the sinner will be seen no more; / thou wilt search in vain to find him, / while patient souls are the land's heirs, enjoying great peace.

HERE IS THE PATTERN for saintly patience. Why am I always in a hurry that justice be done, before God's time, the time of wisdom? Such was never the attitude of God's saints. They were never in a hurry to punish offenders. Sinners would soon enough be their own

executioners. The true servants of God were only concerned that
the offenders should offend no more.

St. Cyprian, early Roman martyr, is one of the many examples of
the divine patience. As he awaited his trial, he wrote a letter in
prison to the imperial prosecutor of Rome, who, he knew, would
condemn him to death. This is what he wrote to that cruel magis-
trate: "Why bow your captive body before helpless images and
moulded earth? Why rush into the downfall of the devil, his fall
the cause of yours, and he your companion? Believe and live. You
have been our persecutors on earth! we hope you will be companions
of our joy in eternity." At his beheading, Cyprian told his friends
to give twenty-five gold pieces to the executioner, and bandaging his
own eyes, knelt to receive the sword's blow.

Another example (and sound reasoning regarding the existence of
evil) we have from St. Augustine. In his treatise on Psalm 54, he
says, "Never think that the wicked are in this world for nothing,
or that God does no good with them. Every wicked man lives either
to amend his life or to exercise the good men. Would to God, then,
that they who persecute us would be converted and be persecuted
with us. But let us not hate them, though they continue to persecute
us, for we do not know whether they will persevere to the end in
their wickedness. And many times, when you imagine that you are
hating your enemy, it is your brother you hate, without knowing
it. . . ."

What might have happened to St. Paul, had the Christians hated
him instead of praying for him, and bearing patiently his persecution? What might have happened to St. Augustine, had his mother
despaired of him, had not St. Ambrose shown his Christian patience? St. Augustine knew of what he spoke. Of St. Ambrose he
says, "All unknowing I was brought by God to him, that knowing
I should be brought by him to God. That man of God received me
like a father and as bishop welcomed my coming. From the very
first I loved him not only as a teacher of the truth, which I had
utterly despaired of finding in Your Church, but also for his kindness towards me. I attended carefully when he preached to the

people, not with the right intention, but only to judge whether his eloquence was equal to his fame. . . . His words I listened to with the greatest care; his matter I held quite unworthy of attention" (*Confessions*, Book V). Of so unworthy a man, God made one of his greatest saints. For his conversion was prayed for in Christian patience.

And what might have happened to Mary Magdalene, had You not waited for her to repent? How many great saints were once enemies of God, evil-doers? How often a Christian who thinks himself just and despises others is in truth a sinner, one blinded, whom God must forgive much!

Lord Jesus, only You could tell us how many millions of miraculous conversions have been won by Your friends whose Christian charity and patience have brought down grace.

Psalm 37

TO MAKE A MOLEHILL OUT
OF A MOUNTAIN

Thy reproof, Lord, not thy vengeance; / thy chastisement, not thy condemnation! / Thy arrows pierce me, thy hand presses me hard. . . . / My own wrong-doing towers high above me, / hangs on me like a heavy burden; / my wounds fester and rankle, with my own folly to blame. / Beaten down, bowed to the earth, I go mourning all day long, / my whole frame afire, my whole body diseased.

A DIFFERENT MAN would I be, Lord, if I understood my vices as David did his, if I could see my weakness as he could see his. My one strength is my pride; it is altogether too strong. Humble me, Lord, as

You humbled David. I must be humbled by You, for I have not the strength to drive out my own pride. You must do it for me. And if You do, I can become a saint, a true Christian.

Many Christians, sincere as they try to be, are afraid that if they offer themselves to God, and ask him to make them saintly, terrible things will happen to them. They think immediately of the Roman martyrs, or worse yet, of the twentieth century martyrs who have made overwhelming sacrifices in our own time.

It is not as terrible as that, for that is not the beginning of sanctity, nor even the ordinary end of it. What will happen, if I ask God to make me holy, and desire to please him? Small things, simple enough in themselves. Others will not consider my opinion worth much. The important jobs, the positions in which one can wield power, will not be given me. I will not be consulted, even on matters that concern me. No one will ask my advice. Affairs won't be managed my way. I will ask a superior or friend for the same thing another asks. The other will receive it, I will not. I will be corrected for my faults; others with greater faults will go unnoticed. I will not be praised when others are. I will not have friends, while others will seem to have many. I will be passed up when that new job I so hoped for comes along. In short, I will have to lose my pride, in order that I may gain something far more precious.

Is anyone willing to bear this small burden? It is small enough in itself and we must carry it often enough, God knows. But one may carry his cross, or one may drag it and curse it. Will anyone take up this small basket of splinters with joy? Will anyone be glad for humiliation, as the psalmist who said, "Gladden us for the days wherein thou hast afflicted us, for the years wherein we have seen misfortune"? It will make him a saint.

The truth is, if I should honestly undertake to accept all these humiliations joyfully, I should soon be greatly honored. For good people are not blind to virtue. But it is a two-edged sword: once I have sincerely found joy in lowliness, I will then be distressed and unhappy when praised or honored. For I shall have learned to love by being little, and I shall never want to depart from this happiness.

"Learn of me, for I am meek and humble of heart, and you shall find rest for your souls." There can be no doubt that the way of humiliation is the true way. The Son of God could not have chosen a false way.

Those in whom Christ's grace is working, love to be despised and forgotten. They would dread being honored, and they flee from their former pride as from a monster. No saint was ever a hypocrite. Were saints insincere in disliking the honors paid them? They would never have been canonized, were this the fact. The truth will out. One who does not love humiliations knows nothing of Christ or of sanctity. "He humbled himself, becoming obedient unto death, even the death of the cross." Ever since, this has been the blueprint for holiness.

Psalm 38

CHOOSE THE BETTER PART

Lord, warn me of my end, and how few my days are; / teach me to know my own insufficiency. / See how thou hast measured my years with a brief span, / how my life is nothing in thy reckoning! / Nay, what is any man living but a breath that passes? / Truly man walks the world like a shadow; / with what vain anxiety he hoards up riches, / when he cannot tell who will have the counting of them! / What hope then is mine, Lord? / In thee alone I trust.

NO ONE HAS YET DISCOVERED a better philosophy of life than this. And I suspect no one ever will, Lord. With what perception David describes these poor lives of ours! "Labor not for the treasure that is consumed by moth and rust," You said. You knew whereof You spoke, if anyone ever did. I know in my inmost understanding the truth of Your divine injunction: "Do not labor for the food that perishes, but for that which endures to life everlasting, which the Son of Man will give you" (John 6:26). "And that which fell among the thorns, these are they who have heard, and as they go their way are choked by the cares and riches and pleasures of life, and their fruit does not ripen" (Luke 8:14). How many nervous breakdowns, how many heart attacks could have been avoided, Lord, if Christians took to heart this great truth of life?

You gave a clear example of this needless care and worry Yourself one day, to a friend You respected. Martha seems to have been a social lion, probably at the head of every club she belonged to, a go-getter and hustler, although indeed a good woman. She was always the first to invite You to her house when You came near Jerusalem, and for that You were certainly not ungrateful.

Accepting one of her many invitations, You came one evening to her house. She was preparing a great supper, and Lazarus, perhaps, took Your disciples out to look at the cattle and the crops; but You stayed on the porch. You were the teacher, they were the listeners; You had taken on yourself the burden of the day's work, and now You were tired.

Martha was downstairs putting wood on the fire and stirring the soup. Mary came to speak with You and ask You questions. She was interested in Your teachings, in the work You came to do, in the message You brought to men. She was not only a gracious hostess; she was an ardent disciple.

"Martha was worried about much serving." Her interests were swallowed up in the vision of a fine dinner, with well-satisfied guests; she would care for Your material needs. She did not appreciate Mary's attitude. She thought Mary was just idle, slothfully curled up at Your feet. She was indignant, thinking that Mary was doing nothing toward the many preparations. At last she lost patience.

"Lord," she said to You, "is it no concern of Yours that my sister has left me alone to do all the serving? Please! Tell her to come and help me!"

And You answered her, and all of her kind: "Martha, Martha, you are troubled about many things. Only one thing is necessary. Mary has chosen the better part, and it shall not be taken away from her."

You did not mean to condemn the work of a sincere woman. You admired Martha. But You reminded her that she must not forget what is most important. It is not the love of work that makes saints; it is the love of God. She was so busy with external work that she had forgotten the internal spirit of that work.

We live in a time of feverish work and impoverished spirit. The story is an important parable for us, Lord. We like to count successes and "good works" by statistics. Big numbers and astounding turn-outs impress us.

Yet the simplest gesture of a child with a heart full of love is an act more godly than millions given by thousands of the rich with no heart. It's not what we do or what we have that counts. It's what we are and what we love. If You are the way, the truth, and the life, Lord Jesus, there can be no doubt of these values. "God is able to raise up children to Abraham out of these stones." The better part is love. What is man's strength to save souls by a whirl of activity? No one can be "hustled" into heaven. But "to those who love God, all things must work together unto good." To those who are too busy to love God, too full of good works to be of good heart, little may remain but a desolate wasteland. The storm of confusion has passed, and no one will remember. "Lord, warn me of my end. . . , teach me to know my insufficiency. What is any man . . . but a breath that passes," and with what vain anxiety does he work, unless You work in him.

Psalm 39

INTEGRITY

*See then, I said, I am coming to fulfil what is written of me, /
where the book lies unrolled; / to do thy will, O my God, is all my
desire, / to carry out that law of thine which is written in my
heart. / And I told the story of thy just dealings before a great
throng; / be witness, Lord, that I do not seal my lips. / Thy just
dealings are no secret hidden away in my heart.*

ST. PAUL, writing to the Hebrews, pictures Jesus saying these
words as he comes into the world (Heb. 10:5). *"To do thy will, O
my God. . . ."* It is in this will that we are sanctified, the Apostle
says, through the offering of the body of Jesus Christ once for all.
"And I told the story of thy just dealings before a great throng. . . ."

Lord Jesus, when I meditate on the last days of Your earthly life,
I try to conceive what You must have felt. You were innocent, more
innocent than an army of saints; Your trial was among the most
unjust ever seen on this earth; Your enemies were totally blind and
ignorant, according to Your own word. You could have saved
Yourself. Anyone with the slightest knowledge of Your life and
Your trial knows You could have saved Yourself. The Pharisees
didn't ask much, really. They only asked that You keep silent. . . .
"Be witness, Lord, that I do not seal my lips."

They only wanted You to say nothing about them and their
hidden vices. You could have appeased their anger—simply by not
carrying out Your mission. . . . "To carry out that law of thine
which is written in my heart."

If only You had compromised—compromised truth and justice—
You could have gone free. For Your own safety, You could have

let them be. . . . "Thy just dealings are no secret hidden away in my heart."

For a few peaceful years, You could have given in. You could easily have escaped death and suffering, and yet restored us to grace by Your very incarnation. To such a temptation You did not yield. . . . "I am coming to fulfil what is written of me."

There is some doubt about us, Your followers. Each of us has some great temptation in life. It may not be a temptation to save our one and only human life. But it is some great trial, something that demands a choice between a safe, easy, comfortable life, and on the other hand, the struggle of accomplishing our purpose in life.

You have a right, Lord, to expect me to overcome that great temptation. You accomplished Your purpose; I must accomplish mine. The inclination to give up, to drop out, is a serious one. If the temptation is conquered and a full-willed decision is made, the battle is half won, the way is clear, the mind is at rest. If there be hesitation or postponement, and no choice is made between Christ and Satan, there may be a false peace, there may be pleasure, ease, comfort of a sort—but in the appalling blindness there is never real happiness. And some day the realization will strike deeper than a sword.

I am made for one thing, Lord, to become like You. "To do thy will, O my God, is all my desire." And I will never know true life until I accomplish just that. Lord, let no false peace ever deceive me. You know where my weakness is, and I can know it, too. Let me never have peace, until I have conquered my great weakness.

Psalm 40

THE LORD SUSTAINS HIM

*Blessed is the man who takes thought for the poor and the desti-
tute; / the Lord will keep him safe in time of trouble. / The Lord
will watch over him, / and give him long life and happiness on
earth, / and baulk his enemies of their will. / The Lord will sustain
him when he lies bed-ridden, / turn all to health in his sickness.*

PERHAPS NO ONE knew the truth of this psalm better than the
saintly pontiff, Pope Pius XII. There is a triple reason for seeing
this saintly head of the Church in Psalm 40.

For who in the twentieth century has taken more thought for the
poor and the destitute? Who has *had* more poor and destitute people
to care for? How many millions of refugees, war orphans, homeless
families, and crippled veterans has the saintly pontiff helped by his
alms and his fervent prayer! He was our century's outstanding man
of prayer and father of the poor. Blessed is he, indeed, for he did not
forget the cry of the poor.

There is no need to press a meaning out of the second sentence
in the psalm for Pope Pius. The Church, true interpreter of the
Divine Word, has already done so. In the official liturgical prayer,
Holy Mother Church says: "Let us pray for our Sovereign Pontiff,"
and all the people answer, in the Litany of the Saints and other
prayers: "The Lord watch over him, and give him long life and
happiness on earth, and deliver him not into the hands of his
enemies."

Who will doubt that Pope Pius was worthy of this prayer? Who
did not find this prayer truly and completely fulfilled in him? Lord,
You indeed watched over him; You gave him long life; and in

spite of all his sufferings, You gave him happiness on earth. There
was hardly a man on earth happier, for there was hardly a man with
greater love. Yet it would have been harder still to find a man who
had suffered more, who shared more the sufferings of all mankind.
Of him the scripture might well be used, "All who have seen him
have called him blessed. . . ." "Forever let his name be used in blessing, a name to endure while the sun gives light; in him all the
tribes of the earth shall be enriched, all the nations shall extol him"
(Psalm 71). To Pius XII, as to Christ, whose Vicar he was, this
honor came in spite of his enemies.

As for the third sentence, it is known all over the world how
"the Lord sustained him when he lay bed-ridden, turned all to
health in his sickness." In December, 1955, by an "indiscretion that
was certainly neither desired nor approved" by the Holy Father, it
was revealed by his intimates how the Lord had indeed come to him
in his illness, and turned his sickness back to health. On the morning of December 2, during a grave illness, Pius XII was praying the
Anima Christi at the words, "in the hour of my death call me." At
this moment, Christ came in a vision, and stayed near him, and he
understood that he was to get well, though he had said to Christ,
"Call me, and bid me come to thee."

In itself it was a small matter, but a visible assurance given the
suffering pontiff. All his life he gave himself to others, that he
might bring them into the same loving embrace of Christ. One can
hardly imagine a man more worthy of the title, "Holy Father."
How many on earth have been holier? How many have been more
fatherly? Behold here another Christ, a "Father of the poor."

Blessed is he, for he "took thought of the poor and destitute,"
their sufferings were his, and his sufferings were theirs.

Psalm 41

WHO IS GOD?

O God, my whole soul longs for thee, as a deer for running water; | my whole soul thirsts for God, the living God; | shall I never again make my pilgrimage into God's presence?

I KNOW that God has created me, that he continues to keep me alive, that through his power I grow, both physically and spiritually, that he created me to see and enjoy him in heaven. But what is God like? I would like to know God more intimately. I would like a personal knowledge, that I might love him more eagerly.

Lord Jesus, there was a young man, a disciple of Yours, who expressed this desire. His name was Philip. At his last supper with You, he made this bold and curious remark: "Lord, let us see the Father; that is all we ask." That is all we ask! As though it were not enough; as though it were a small matter, a very simple affair! "Let us see God on earth," he asks, not blinking an eye! He might as well have said, "Lord, split open the heavens, and let the terrible day of final judgment come now. That is all we ask." God himself in the Sacred Scripture had said, "No man has ever seen God on this side of the grave." So great is the power and majesty of God, that no living man has the strength to look at him. This didn't seem to bother Philip. He wanted to see God face to face, no more, no less.

Lord Jesus, You could have laughed at him; You could have rebuked him. But You were charitable. You did not refuse him. You accepted Philip's challenge; as impatient as the psalmist, he had asked, "When shall I see the face of God?" You shocked him with the open statement that he and the other disciples had been looking God in the face for three years now, and yet they seemed not to know it. Surely that was not Your fault! Gently You told him, "What, Philip! Here I am, who have been all this while in your company; have you not learned to recognize me yet? Whoever has seen me has seen the Father. What do you mean by saying, 'Let us see the Father'? Do you not believe that I am in the Father, and the Father is in me?" (John 14:8–10). What a clear and simple answer! What an answer for those who try to imagine You as less than Divine! The Son is in the Father, and the Father is in the Son, for they are one and the same God; and he who sees Christ sees God. In fact, he who sees Christ sees God the Father. So simply You stated this amazing mystery. Thus You assured me that God is visible in human form, as a man who truly lived, as a man whose actions I can observe, whose words I can hear, whose love I can see with my human eyes. That is why You became a man, Lord Jesus. So that we could never say again, "Who is God? I do not know God; if only I could see him!" The Father is known through Jesus Christ, whom he sent us for that purpose.

Psalm 42

UP TO THE ALTAR

O God, sustain my cause; / give me redress against a race that knows no piety; / save me from a treacherous foe and cruel. / Thou, O God, art all my strength. . . . / The light of thy presence, the fulfilment of thy promise, / let these be my escort, bringing 'me safe to thy holy mountain, / to the tabernacle where thou dwellest. / There I will go up to the altar of God, / the giver of triumphant happiness.

WHAT MORE MEANINGFUL PRAYER could a Christian make as he begins to assist at the Sacrifice of the New Law, the Holy Mass?

The Church did not choose this psalm to begin the Mass without reason. It is not Christ or his Church who have misunderstood its force. It is that I am not truly Christian, and do not share the depth, the love, the divine desire of the Mass.

Christ has given all: "God will sustain his cause," because he has done nothing for himself but has surrendered everything; only the complete abandonment of charity can "give me redress against a race that knows no piety." Only my own sacrifice can "save me from a treacherous foe," the cancer of disillusioned self-love, the emptiness of a merely human love. I cannot dare to come here without Christian love. I have no part in this world-wide sacrifice unless I have some touch of divine, unselfish surrender. I must leave my house of filth and become true to myself, my nature and my powers, to enter here.

But what have I? It is all too evident. I find in myself no true good, no honest selflessness, nor even the strength to do genuine good. "I have nothing," was the profound remark of the Abbé Chevance in Bernanos' novel, *Joy*. "It took me thirty years to discover that I have absolutely nothing. What weighs on a man's heart is his dream. . . ."

I have nothing but the overflow of Your goodness: "Thou, O God, art all my strength." I have nothing to give me confidence, no merit of mine can bring me worthily to a place so hallowed, to an action so divine. But Your goodness supplies: "The light of thy presence, the fulfilment of thy promise, let these be my escort, bringing me safely to thy holy mountain, to the tabernacle where thou dwellest. There I will go up to the altar of God, the giver of triumphant happiness."

Psalm 43

BOWED IN THE DUST

Thou dost put us to flight before our enemies; | our ill-wishers plunder us as they will. | Thou hast made us like sheep sold for food, | scattered here and there among the heathen. . . . | Thou hast turned us into a laughing-stock for our neighbors, | mocked and derided by all who dwell around.

THIS IS THE WAY You have treated Your people throughout history, Lord. Every age has the same story to tell. The nation that knows You best is the one that must suffer most.

Not only Your chosen race and Your bride, the Church, have been hated and crucified; individually Your most intimate friends are without consolation. "Ever my disgrace confronts me," says the psalmist, "as I hear nothing but reproach and reviling, see none but enemies, none but persecutors."

Is it punishment for sin, Lord? Is it that Your favorites offend You the most? At times it has been so, but more often the innocent suffer. Therefore the psalmist's justifying plea, "All this has come upon us, and it was not that we had forgotten thee. We have not been untrue to thy covenant, or withdrawn our hearts from thee." The early Christians, the Roman martyrs, the very Apostles themselves had not forgotten You or offended You. Never had men on earth loved You more. Nor indeed had Your Son forgotten You.

To us the mystery is dark and obscure. "All the while thou wouldst bring us low," says the Psalm. "Anguish on every side, darkness hanging over us."

Where might our answer be? We have indeed sinned and deserved punishment, but not more than the rest of men. Those who have completely abandoned God and give themselves to avarice and lust and envy—have they merited more reward than the martyrs? It cannot be that God is deceived about them: "He can read the secrets of men's hearts." His own saints have not failed to take up this burden. "No, it is for thy sake that we face death at every moment, reckoned no better than sheep marked down for slaughter."

Nor is it that Your holy ones are insensible to pain, or have some peculiar, unnatural desire for suffering. For the psalmist complains of his abandonment, yet in his complaint suggests an opening into the mystery of God's doing: "Bestir thyself, Lord, why dost thou sleep on? Awake, do not banish us from thy presence forever. How canst thou turn thy face away, without a thought for our need and our affliction? Our pride is bowed in the dust; prostrate, we cannot lift ourselves from the ground. Arise, Lord, and help us; in thy mercy, claim us for thy own."

As his complaint concludes, the psalmist shows that he has learned what You wished to teach him by his humiliations: there is no crime like the crime of pride. His trials have saved him from the world's most godless vice, the vice of superiority. All evils entered the world through that crime. Lucifer forgot that all his good was of God. Lucifer forgot that, in comparison to God's wisdom, his own knowledge was ignorance and nothingness. Lucifer forgot that the creature can never be the creator. In short, Lucifer forgot that only God is God. Pride poisons the very heart of human goodness, because it cuts off human good from its source. It breaks the essential link of the universe; it cuts off the creature from the Eternal Creator. It kills human life at its fountainhead.

There is in nature itself a recoiling from pride in creatures. Even the animals rise up against those who strive for the full mastery. But men, to whom it is given to understand their nature, are most resentful of pride in their fellowmen. No man will disagree with that well-known criticism of the street-corner philosopher: "I won't have a guy talking like he knows better than God himself."

Almost any kind of sinner can be tolerated and loved sympathet-
ically by his fellows. But in every case humility is the reason. The
drinker who struggles against himself is loved like a wounded
lamb, the petty thief is pitied, the slothful man may be admired
for his kindness, the angry man may be respected for his loyalty to
principles, the impatient man will be loved as energetic, the
amorous are tolerated for the sake of their weakness. But let any of
these sins be joined with a noticeable pride, and men draw away as
from a hardened criminal. For pride cuts off forgiveness and
sympathy. A sinner can be tolerated if he is ashamed, and loved
if he is repentant; but others draw away in fear if he is unbending.

Though in its deepest sense humility may be the world's most
forgotten and most misunderstood virtue, its opposite, the vice of
pride, will always be by its nature the most abhorred. It is instinctively recognized that the good man, the lovable man, the trust-
worthy man, the man one must seek out for a true friend is the
humble man. For humility preserves and pride destroys.

From the day of Adam and Eve to that of Cain, from Cain to the
tower of Babel, pride was the crime detestable before God.

From the crime of Joseph's brothers to the Pharaoh of Moses' day,
You punished the proud, You favored the humble, though indeed
not before they had "passed through fire and water, and You led
them at last to a place of rest."

You rejected Saul the proud excuse-maker; You accepted David,
the humble, ashamed sinner.

All history is a story of the miseries caused by men's pride, and of
the beautiful humility learned by the sorrowing victims of injustice.
The pride of Rome tried to crush the humility of the Christians,
but at length the humble prevailed, and the blood of the martyrs is
the glory of the Church of God.

And after all these lessons, pride is yet man's strongest enemy,
his most dangerous temptation. The holiest are plagued by its secret
inroads.

That is why we must suffer at Your hands, Lord—lest we begin to think of ourselves as great and powerful, as all-knowing and all-justified, lest we become as those who have no god but themselves, and are cut off from the living God.

Psalm 44

GODLY LOVE

Listen, my daughter, and consider my words attentively; | thou art to forget, henceforward, thy own nation, | and the house of thy father; | thy beauty, now, is all for the king's delight; | he is thy Lord, and worship belongs to him.

WITH WHAT NOBILITY the psalmist speaks! A father leading his daughter to God, showing her how to return to God the gifts she had from him. There is no nobler work in the world than that of teaching and inspiring the young to love God.

How often I should pray, "Lord, God of all beauty, reveal Your glory to those innocent children You have entrusted to me. You are their creator; let all their beauty be for Your delight!" Fathers, mothers, guardians, teachers—God has honored us with the most beautiful vocation on earth. God himself is father to his children, yet he allows us to share his fatherly love, to create his love in them, as it were.

Lord, we are all directors of souls, whether we perceive it or not. We have a powerful influence on the young, often when we are least aware of it. How often have we warped their pliable natures! "All things are seen," says St. Augustine, "and seen by those the culprit least suspects." It is the tragedy of human curiosity that it sees so quickly what is wrong, and understands so slowly what is good and beautiful. And the young are swift to see.

Oh, with what trembling and with what loving respect ought we to approach the soul of a child! With what fear we ought to honor their innocent hearts, for God is there! "Take care what you do to these little ones, for I tell you, their angels gaze forever at the face of my Father in heaven." Thus You assured us, Jesus, that these innocent ones are temples where You ought to be adored and reverenced. How perfectly this truth was understood by Clotilde, the saintly heroine of Léon Bloy's, *The Woman Who was Poor:* "Whenever she encounters a child, she kneels down before it, as did the great Bérulle, and, with its pure little hand, traces upon her forehead the Sign of the Cross." Such is the supernatural treasure of a child's soul. We who understand, Lord, must guide them heavenward. If we refuse that honor, they will fall victims to him who goes about seeking innocents to devour.

There is nothing more truly human than that instinctive sense of respect and reverence I ought to have as I face a human soul, and loving it, try to give it something of my good—or rather, of God's infinite good.

Yet our weakness may overcome us, and we love these lovable ones selfishly. We fail to love them unto God, and thus we really fail to love. We rather take pleasure in them, than love them with divine charity, which alone is love.

Our sole interest, Lord, should be that of the psalmist who asks of you (in psalm 89) that Your works might be manifest to Your servants, and Your glory to their children.

God knows how many doting parents have ruined their children by a false, indulgent, earthly mercy. God's mercy is unto salvation. Too often man's mercy is unto damnation. "If you allow your brethren to perish for want of correction . . . you are not less guilty than they. If your brother had a bodily injury which he wished to hide because he dreaded a surgical operation, would it not be cruel of you to keep it a secret, and an act of charity to reveal it? How much more, then, ought you to uncover his spiritual decay, lest a more terrible rottenness devour his soul!" This from the Rule of St. Augustine, who spoke from experience. His own father had neglected to love him unto God, and approved what would lead to

his son's ruin. Augustine contrasts this attitude of his father with
that of his mother. When he was sixteen years old "owing to the
narrowness of the family fortunes I did not go to school but lived
idly at home with my parents. The briars of unclean lusts grew over
my head, and there was no hand to root them out. Nay, when my
father saw me in the public baths now growing towards manhood
and indued with a restless youthfulness, as if from hence he looked
forward to grandchildren, he related it to my mother with joy. He
rejoiced with the drunkenness with which this world has forgotten
its Creator and loves the creature instead of You, inebriated by the
invisible wine of a will perverted and inclined to baseness. But in
my mother's breast You had already begun Your temple, the foundation of Your holy dwelling; for my father was as yet only a
catechumen, and that but recently. She, therefore, upon hearing it,
was seized with fear and trembling; she was concerned for me, because I was not baptized, that I might stray into those crooked ways
in which worldlings walk, who turn not their face but their back to
You."

Recalling how earnestly his mother had admonished him to keep
himself pure, St. Augustine writes, "They were Your admonitions,
and I knew it not; and I supposed You to be silent while she spoke;
but by her You spoke to me, and in her You were despised by me,
by me her son, the son of Your handmaid, Your servant" (*Confessions,* Book II, iii).

Here were two loves—the father's worldly love, and the mother's
Christian love. History records examples enough—and sad enough—
of the ruins of worldly love. But here, because it was genuine, because it was persevering, St. Monica's love won out, saved the soul
of her son, made of him the great Saint he is today, and indeed
turned her careless husband away from the foolishness of this world.
It is Godly love that perseveres; it is Godly love that conquers; it is
only Godly love that saves.

Psalm 44, b

VIRGIN ALL FAIR

She comes, the princess, all fair to see, | her robe of golden cloth, a robe of rich embroidery, to meet the King. | The maidens of her court follow her into thy presence, | all rejoicing, all triumphant, as they enter the king's palace! . . . While time lasts, mine it is to keep thy name in remembrance; | age after age, nations will do thee honor.

How MUCH THIS LAST PROMISE sounds like another prophecy the same Holy Spirit placed on the lips of the fair princess who said, "Behold, henceforth all generations shall call me blessed." And thus the chorus of holy virgins, "the maidens of her court follow her into thy presence, all triumphant."

The children of Mammon are scandalized. Too much honor for the humble princess. Too much reverence for you, Mary, for never having sinned, and never having sin. Too much love for you, Mary, for being the greatest woman God ever created, for being the only perfect woman.

The children of Mammon have a home, too, and a mother whom they might revere. They might reverence her company, we trust, and praise her virtues. Is God's family, then, different? Should the mother be forgotten, ignored, unnoticed?

The children of Mammon—and we, the faltering children of light, the stumbling, unworthy children of light—need to see You, Lord, and be seen by the piercing look of Your mercy. Yet it is too much for us. Who will assist us, Lord? Whom will You send? Who is the smoked glass, through whom we may view Your infinite brilliance? Who is the morning star, the gate of heaven, the comforter of the afflicted? Who is the help of Christians that will spare not her soul, seeing the anguish and tribulation of her people? Who is the new Israel, strong before God? Who is she, whose name He has so magnified that never again shall her praises depart from the lips of men? Who is it, if not she who said, "He has regarded the lowliness of his handmaid; for behold, henceforth all generations shall call me blessed, because he who is mighty has done great things for me, and holy is his name."

Mother most powerful, it is you who brought us Christ. It is you who know Christ, if anyone does. There is no woman on earth or in heaven holier.

Is it any wonder, then, that the Church sorrows with your sorrow, saying, "Whither is thy beloved gone, O thou most beautiful of women? Whither is thy beloved turned aside, and we will seek him with thee? Pray for us, Queen of Martyrs, who didst stand by the cross of Jesus." Is it any wonder that she rejoices with you, singing, "Virgin most prudent, where goest thou, glorious as the ruby dawn? Daughter of Sion, all beautiful and gracious art thou, fair as the moon, chosen as the sun."

Psalm 45

HE DARED TO BE DIFFERENT

God is our refuge and stronghold; | sovereign aid he has brought us in the hour of peril. . . . | Come near, and see God's acts, | his marvellous acts done on earth; | how he puts an end to wars all over the world, | the bow shivered, the lances shattered, the shields burnt to ashes! | Wait quietly, and you shall have proof that I am God, | claiming empire among the nations, | claiming empire over the world.

WHAT A striking prophecy! God Himself is coming to claim empire among the nations, over the world! The prophecy is fulfilled when God-made-man, the great king, comes to save the world!

To save the world! "What an operation," the ambitious go-getter would have assured us. "Why, he'll have to start organizing, gather lots of money, rally huge armies, hire a raft of officials and secretaries, contact all the important people; orchestras, megaphones, slogans, rousing speeches and big promises—all to stir up the public sentiment." After all, what had every king before Christ done to "win the world"? Wealth, military might, bloody wars of conquest, absolute power—these were essentials!

But Christ the King dared to be different. Your answer, Lord, was Christmas. You dared to defy the "Apostles" of this world, for You said, and lived it: "Blessed are the poor in spirit, for theirs is the kingdom of heaven." Not, blessed are the power-hungry conquerors, but "blessed are the meek, for *they* shall possess the land." Not, blessed are they who succeed by promising and deceiving and betraying and enslaving peoples, but "blessed are they who suffer persecution for justice' sake, for theirs is the kingdom of heaven."

How much of the modern world lives on pure externals! In order to do great work you've got to impress the crowd; you've got to sway the mob with fine words and a display of flashy "successes." But the King who had "the favor of the most High with him" turned the world's standards upside down. He showed the world how wrong it was about what makes a great king.

Surely You could have chosen power, position, wealth, tremendous influence, Lord. You could have impressed the millions with Your might; You could have turned the very sun and stars out of their courses, so that a cry of fear and amazement would have swept over all the earth. But You lived a simple life of prayer and work: love and sacrifice in a hidden life. This is the amazing fact of Christmas: Christ the King shocking the world, awaking the world at last to true greatness.

Chesterton observed that the cave in which Jesus Christ was born was probably underground, dug out of the side of a hill. And so in

Your very first appearance, Lord, rather than descending from heaven in glittering rays and blazing clouds, You came up out of the ground, like a little beggar, who had no place to go. You appeared, King of kings, not in a flaming vision, but as an unknown infant. The very humility of Your coming and of Your whole life on earth assures us, once for all, that the lowliest of us who imitate You might be kings of whom the psalmist could say, "Glory and high honor thou hast made his. . . . The favor of the most High is with him" (Psalm 20:6, 8).

Psalm 46

THE SEARCH FOR CHRIST

God is King of all the earth; sound the hymn of praise! / God reigns over the heathen, God sits enthroned in holiness. / The rulers of the nations throw in their lot with us, that worship Abraham's God; / a God so high, he has all earth's princes for his vassals.

HE IS KING of all the earth; he wishes to reveal himself to all. All earth's princes are his vassals; he will draw them all to himself. Such is the psalmist's prophecy.

Such is the event, too. From the day of Your birth, Lord, You set about fulfilling this prophecy. And the first fulfillment we know by the Feast of the Epiphany. You immediately became "a light to the Gentiles." Learned men came from the East, from a great distance to find You, born "King of all the earth." They brought You gifts; three gifts are mentioned. The number of men was most probably greater. Early paintings show the Magi accompanied by a large train of followers. It would have been necessary for the kind of journey they made. In artistic representation, this becomes such a colorful procession, with such a display of fine robes and riches, that it is easy to forget the mystery it illustrates.

You do indeed reign over all the earth, Lord, enthroned in holiness. And all earth's princes are indeed Your vassals. But as Isaias exclaimed, "Truly You are a hidden God!" And when earth's princes come to be Your vassals—and to profit unspeakably by it—they must search You out! We all must search You out, if You are to reign over us.

If I consider what the Wise Men had to do to find You, I know the strength of their loyalty. I know they are not the vassals of a tyrant, but vassals who have chosen the hidden King by loving free will, and, in fact, by an act of heroism.

They saw a star in the heavens. It was no easy sign to understand; they must have studied it, discussed it, doubted, worried, prayed over it. What is important is that they were fully determined to carry out the divine will expressed in that sign.

There was little consolation in setting out to "throw in their lot" with those "that worship Abraham's God." A long distance to travel, and they did not know where they would find Christ. There was no one to tell them; most probably no one encouraged them on the way; no guide, no information, no assurance that they *would* find the "king of all the earth."

Their reward, their everlasting glory and honor for the perseverance with which they sought Christ—this speaks clearly, Lord, of what You expect of us.

Do I search for You everywhere, as they did? Will I do so much to know Your will, and to fulfill it? Do I accept difficulties half as great as theirs, as my duty in Your service?

Psalm 47

THE GREAT KING

The Lord is great, great honour is his due, | here in the city where he, our God, dwells. | Fair rises the peak of his holy mountain, | the pride of the whole world, and the true pole of earth, | mount Sion, the city of the great King.

CHRIST IS "The Great King." And what is a great king? This, Lord, You have revealed to us in a most striking manner, through Your Church.

At first glance it seems strange that in celebrating Your glorious Kingship, the Church has chosen for the gospel of the Mass that scene in which You stand before Pilate as a common criminal.

Why not the glorious scene on Mount Thabor, when You were transfigured and shone as bright as the sun, and were adored by Moses and Elias? Why not the scene of Your glorious Resurrection, when You conquered death forever, and showed Your divine power? Why not the Ascension, when You took Your throne at the right hand of Your Father forever? Or why not at least Palm Sunday, when You entered Jerusalem in triumph?

How revealing that the Church has chosen the picture of the suffering Christ to show us His true Kingship! Indeed, Lord, You could have saved the world with a great show of armies and trumpets and flags. But this would have been all too selfish for You. You left the triumph and the pomp to Your Church. You chose nothing for Yourself, because Your love was completely unselfish; Your love was perfect. You could have chosen every easy way; You chose what was hard, humble, selfless, because of Your great love. Can we understand a love that empties itself of everything man holds dear? Can we understand a love that renounces all pleasure, that renounces a just return for what it gives?

If we can understand, we can perceive something of the infinite power and beauty and tragedy of the scene in the praetorium. Christ the King in a bloody crown of thorns, abused by the Jews, misunderstood by Pilate, abandoned by His own apostles, rejected by His own people, deserted by those men, women, children for whose good He had worked countless miracles. He who thus "emptied himself and took the form of a slave" is surely the most worthy of kings.

It is easy to be king and rule your people, if you are wealthy, honored, and accepted; if you face no difficulties, no prejudice; if all is prosperity.

The true king is he who will sacrifice his life for his people; he who gives his blood to save his friends from perdition is the true king.

"My kingdom is not of this world," You told Pilate. Yet only Your kingdom could save this world. Yours was a far greater kingdom, Yours a far manlier kingship, Yours an empire "of truth and life, of holiness and grace, of justice, love, and peace" (Preface, Feast of Christ the King). You are the king for whom we have longed.

It is almost blasphemous to speak of Your kingly character in terms so human. What right have we to expect human satisfaction from the divine King? Nevertheless, to our weak minds all the greater cause for reverence and love, when we see that everything about the God-man, the King of both heaven and earth, makes him more and more lovable to men. He enlightens our blindness, he supports our weakness, he deepens and broadens our narrow perceptions, he shows us what it means to be human at last, to be true to the glory we once were.

In every way divine and human, Jesus, You are the one King who by all Your actions have truly deserved the complete love of Your subjects.

Psalm 48

HE CAME TO RESCUE

No man can deliver himself from his human lot, / paying a ransom-price to God; / too great is the cost of a man's soul; / never will the means be his to prolong his days eternally and escape death. / True it is, wise men die; but reckless fools perish no less; / their riches will go to others, and the grave will be their everlasting home. . . . / But my life God will rescue from the power of that lower darkness, / a life that finds acceptance with him.

The psalmist saw clearly enough the misery of fallen man without rescue. He saw that man had no means of "paying a ransom-price to God." Yet as he looked into the dismal future of fallen man, it seemed as though the Cross suddenly appeared to him. Though he had just said, "No man can deliver himself," he now exclaimed, "My life God will rescue." Whether or not he understood the manner or means of rescue, the Christian surely understands. He knows by what means that ransom was paid; he knows this might have shocked the ancient Hebrew, so accustomed to saving himself by fire and sword, so accustomed to describing salvation in a materialistic way.

St. Augustine, observing the paradox of God's rescue, wrote: "That Cross which was the derision of his enemies is now displayed on the foreheads of kings. The effect has proved his power; he conquered the world, not by the sword, but by the wood. The wood of the Cross was thought a thing of scorn by his enemies, who stood before it and wagged their heads, shouting, If he is the Son of God, let him come down from the Cross."

We can almost hear the very wood of the Cross begging the

rescuer not to descend. The wood personified by St. Augustine as the
conqueror of the world, the wood scorned by men has been exalted
to the heavens, united with God the rescuer to save men *from the
power of that lower darkness.*

This beautiful personification was taken up by an eighth-century
English poet, who made of it one of the most beautiful masterpieces of Christian literature. The Cross itself speaks:

> "Well I remember, a day in the woodland,
> How I was hewed, hacked from my trunk,
> Fierce fiends snatched and shaped me
> For a spectacle of shame to men;
> On their backs they bore me, bade me stand,
> Made me bear their beaten criminals.
> Standing I saw the Lord of love,
> Maker of man, hasten Himself,
> Come to the hill with courage high,
> Me He ascended, mighty and strong.
>
> "The young Hero stripped Himself, He who was mighty God,
> Strong and stout-hearted, He climbed the towering Cross,
> With spirit manly, for man He would save.
> I trembled as He touched me, cowered as He clasped me;
> Break down I dared not, nor fall with fear.
> "Stand fast," my Lord commanded;
> A rood I was raised; aloft I lifted the Lord,
> King of high heaven; nor bend nor bow. . . .
>
> "Hear and believe, my hero beloved,
> That bitter woes had I to bear;
> Hate and horror have happiness brought,
> Far and wide men pray, as they ought,
> By this saving sign; redemption bought
> By the Lord of heroes, on me was wrought.

"For that am I splendid, high under heaven,
That I may heal my worshippers all.
The cruelest of gibbets I once was judged,
Hateful to men. But He, the Hero,
Opened by me the doors of life."

It was indeed a salvation by strength and violence, by an unparalleled act of heroism. The paradox is in the manner: the world
is saved by him who does violence to himself, not to his neighbor.
We should have known—but we never would have, Lord, had You
not given us the supreme example. When has man, in all his history,
understood the truth and followed it, unless it was impressed upon
him in a most shocking and concrete and bloody manner?

We are redeemed, Lord, because You were unjustly condemned.
You have won the everlasting victory because You were defeated.
We are "rescued from the power of that lower darkness," because
You voluntarily steeped Yourself in unutterable darkness.

Shall we learn by Your example, by the tragedies of history, by the
seeds of spiritual truth You have planted in us? Shall we learn that
when man conquers man it is a false victory, and when man conquers himself it is the one true victory?

Psalm 49

A GREAT FUGUE

*It is the Lord God that speaks; / his message goes out to all the
earth, from the sun's rise to its setting. . . . / The heavens themselves pronounce him just, God who is our judge.*

How MUCH WISDOM, how much happiness we could acquire, Lord,
if we truly recognized that great truth: "It is the Lord God that

speaks." Whatever happens to us, whatever success we meet, whatever failure, whatever difficulties, whatever discouragement, "it is the Lord God that speaks." It is so easy to pray, "Lord, teach me to do Thy will." And when his will is made known, how hard to accept it!

Our lives are like a great fugue. A humorous commentator was once asked, "What is a fugue?" He answered, "It is a musical number in which the voices enter one by one, and the audience leaves, two by two." Thus we can say that God's will in our life is like a great fugue: his wisdom, his divine plan unfolds, one incident after another. To the inexperienced ear, a "fugue" appears to be musical confusion. And so to the inexperienced, worldly, thoughtless Christian, God's wisdom is confusion. But to the expert musician a fugue is to the ear what a gorgeous Persian rug is to the eye; so to the man of faith, God's will and God's wisdom is a work of unspeakable beauty.

As God's words "enter, one by one," how many Christians, like the unappreciative audience, walk out on God, "two by two." Their ideals may have been high, but when God tries to teach them true wisdom, the deep wisdom of the saints, they fail Him. They cannot make the reality live up to the ideal.

The painful sorrows and limited joys that one after another slip in and out of our lives in apparent disarray—what meaning have they? Are they not the threads of His infinitely beautiful pattern, are they not His weaving, a weaving far beyond our sight and hearing?

Lord, teach me the difference between words and actions. Teach me the difference between ideal and reality. It is not enough for me to say I love You, and I love Your will. It is only a dream, if I will not accept the concrete incidents, the concrete persons, the everyday fact by which You are leading me to my final goal.

"The heavens," the beauties of nature "pronounce him just, God who is our judge." Why, then, do we of all creatures, who should know You best, why do we reject Your wisdom?

Lord, let me never fail to hear and appreciate the "great fugue"

You are composing out of my life. It may be a mystery to me now, but if I accept it, because I accept You, I will come to know and love the unlimited beauty of Your work.

Psalm 50

MISERERE

Have mercy on me, O God, as thou art ever rich in mercy; | in the abundance of thy compassion, blot out the record of my misdeeds.

OF ALL THE HEARTFELT CRIES of David, none has been repeated so often, nor any with as much sincerity as this psalm. It has been the companion of all great Christian repentance, the treasure of all Christian centuries.

Popes and kings died with its pleading rhythms still in their ears; canons sent it roaring to heaven from their cathedrals; innocent virgins murmured it softly for their daily venial faults; hermits and penitents mingled it with their sighs in their night vigils; soldiers and crusaders mumbled it on their marches, and many a straying novice, perhaps, whispered it hastily in a dark corner of a chapel, for it is the best known and most beautiful of the penitential psalms.

What psalm is equal in power to the *Miserere?* It is the universal act of contrition, written for us by God in the Sacred Scriptures. It has a high place on the honor roll of Divine Poetry, as important as the *Magnificat* of Mary, the *Benedictus* of Zachary, the *Nunc Dimittis* of Simeon. It is the prayer of penance common to all the Saints, the prayer which no Christian has a right to ignore. The unbroken history of the *Miserere* is a striking testimony to the common weakness of all men. . . . for who cannot pray it in all truth and sincerity?

And yet, it was originally one man's personal confession of his secret sins. What is universal, after all, is the truth that every man is personally responsible for his actions, and must make genuine, personal atonement, must make a personal request to God for pardon.

There is much for meditation in David's story, though it is the old, oft-repeated story of the world and the flesh. David, filled with humility and loyalty to God, is assailed by curiosity. He has seen a beautiful woman bathing, and he must find out who she is. When he is told that she is the wife of Urias, it is high time to distract himself from her. "Watch and pray, lest you enter into temptation."

But David is not watchful this time, because he has been idle. He sends messengers out to bring her in. The holy king has become a slave to curiosity and selfishness and lust. What has happened to him, the beloved man of God, who had refused to kill his persecutor, Saul, even in self-defense? Twice he had Saul in his power, but allowed no one to touch him, because he was the Lord's anointed. From his early youth, David has been God's favorite— but now, he is blinded by the flesh.

One sin brings on many others. He commits adultery, then deceit, then murder—the clean type of murder. He sends Urias into the worst position in battle, without providing for his protection. Urias is sure to be killed, and no one will know. Innocent hypocrisy; a sin cloaked in a royal command. Thus did God's chosen leader fall.

A silence follows; not the silence of peace and love, but the awful silence of murder, of horror. David has nothing more to say to the Lord.

The Lord, on the contrary, is not heartless but merciful. Though David had destroyed Your beloved servant, Your love would still save David. So You sent to the king Your prophet Nathan, with a story for David to hear:

"Your majesty, there was a rich man in one of the towns who had everything he wanted, all kinds of sheep and oxen. And there was a poor man who had only one little lamb, which was his own dear pet. But the rich man stole it and killed it."

The king burned with indignation at hearing the tale, and said to Nathan, "As the Lord is a living God, that man deserves to die! He shall pay fourfold for this cruel deed!"

Nathan answered firmly, "Thou art the man." What must have been David's surprise as this prophet recalled the evil the ungrateful king had committed against God, Who had favored him above all kings.

Ah, the crime of abusing God's favors! "I saved thy life. . . . I gave thee thy master's goods to enjoy. . . . All Israel and Juda are in thy power, and if that were not enough, more should be thine for the asking."

Your favors to me, Lord, are greater in so many ways. The Faith and the age in which I was born—how can I set a price on these privileges? How can I set a price on life itself?

And when Nathan struck David the final blow: "Thou hast killed Urias by the sword of the Ammonites," he understood that God is never deceived. Indeed, how seldom is man deceived about the sins of his neighbor!

God is the enemy of hypocrites because He is Truth itself. "Thou didst this secretly," He tells David, "but I will punish thee in the sight of all Israel, in the sight of the sun."

Here is the key to David's sorrows, expressed in so many of the psalms. Why was he always in trouble? Alas, the misery that one sin can bring on a man, as good a man as he might be!

Yet David's is a truly humble soul: "I have sinned against the Lord." Most of the kings killed the prophets that were sent to them, and completely ignored the warnings they had come with. But here is, after his fall, a repentant servant of God. It was a terrible fall, and God spared no words assuring David of that. Nevertheless, Lord, You were still interested in him; You saw his sorrow and forgave him.

Psalm 50, b

TRUE CONTRITION

Wash me clean, cleaner yet, from my guilt, / purge me of my sin, the guilt which I freely acknowledge, / the sin which is never lost to my sight.

WASH ME CLEAN, cleaner yet, wash me thoroughly, Lord. Not only do I need my sins forgiven; I need to rid myself of the smudges and dents and ruts left behind; the bad habits, the weakness, the worldly tendencies must be purged. Thus I have a constant need for the renewed sacramental absolution, to get at the roots of my sins.

"The sin which is never lost to my sight. . . ." An active conscience is one of Your greatest gifts, Lord, a sign of Your mercy, and worth praying for. If the saintly king David had to be told by a prophet, how much sinfulness have I ignored?

"Thee only my sins have offended. . . ." I sinned against goodness, and all goodness is of God. We are made only to have God, and thus the Jews conceived the deep, poetic concept that He is a "jealous God." They were not to have any strange gods in His sight.

Indeed, I am only what God is *in* me. I am His creature; I have only what is from Him. And thus when I sin, I attempt to destroy myself. It is really myself that suffers; that is why sin is so foolhardy. That is why it can never bring real happiness. I have destroyed something in myself by it.

"I have done what You know is evil, Lord. . . ." As I look back, I know that choosing myself instead of You has only brought evils on me. Indeed, whenever Your law is called in question, Your side is always right. "Thy sentence was deserved, and still when thou givest award thou hast right on thy side," says the psalmist. How many messages God sends us daily; and if we are not seeing them, not hearing them, it is time to sound the alarm. We are losing time that will never be regained.

"Thou art a lover of faithfulness . . . deep in my heart, thy wisdom has instructed me." David saw how useless it was to be a sinner interiorly, and merely to appear good in the eyes of men. Only the reality is of interest to God; only the reality can make us happy. And, ironically, after we are in our graves—if not before—only the reality about us is remembered by men. If we tried to make an impression on men with what we were not and had not, all that remains in the memory of men is the humor of our attempt and failure.

Appearances are cheap and easily recognizable. We are all born performers, carrying a "front" about with us, and we have a certain right to hide our less-lovable selves, but when we come to realize that we are known, after all, at our worst, there is much we can learn from it. We can learn that, in the long run, all things work together for the good of the honest man, the man who is more concerned with secretly pleasing God in his own soul than with making a display of anything. We can learn, too, that nature itself conspires to betray and expose the hypocrite. No one is so much abused by the tongues of his fellowmen as the "false-front" man, and though the criticism may be sinful in itself, there is a poetic justice about it. "Seek first the kingdom of God and His justice," said Jesus, "and all these other things will be given you besides."

Psalm 50, c

RESOLUTION AND REVOLUTION

My God, bring a clean heart to birth within me; | breathe new life, true life, into my being. . . . | Give me back the comfort of thy saving power, | and strengthen me in generous resolve. | So will I teach the wicked to follow thy paths; | sinners shall come back to thy obedience.

CONTRITION is not found in fine words and phrases, but in a change of heart. If I am sorry, I must be genuine about it. I must say, "Because I am sorry, I intend to do this particular good work. . . ."

A boy could hardly be called contrite if he said to his father, "I'm sorry I broke the window, but I won't pay for it." Nor is anyone really sorry for his sin if he will not resolve to repair the harm he has done. It is in the psalmist's "generous resolve" that his sorrow is genuine. He knows that he must do something concrete to crush the selfishness that broke through when he offended God by his grievous sin. "I will teach the wicked to follow thy paths." What more generous reparation for one's own sins than that of helping others to avoid a similar fall, instructing others in godliness, spending one's energy in positive good works?

But how else could he merit God's favor? What good would it do to ask God, "Sprinkle me with a wand of hyssop, and I shall be clean" if he were only to soil again what God had washed clean? David's choice of the "hyssop branch" was most fitting. Sprinkling with the hyssop was a ceremony for pronouncing lepers cured. The high priest dipped a hyssop branch in the blood of a sparrow and sprinkled the former leper; then after many ceremonial washings the man was pronounced cured. Cured; whole and healthy, completely restored—not temporarily washed, only to fall back into the same disease.

If David were to be cured, then, there must be a new, positive way of life, a godly, unselfish way, a way directly opposed to the sin by which he had fallen. The real good of David's resolution was, of course, that he *kept* it. This must undoubtedly be the test of true sorrow. A new life must be born: "Bring a clean heart to birth within me; breathe new life, true life, into my being." David's principal occupation hereafter was to praise God's mercy with heart and soul; to feel it deeply in himself, to teach it to others, to fill his people with it.

His request was answered, "Lord, thou wilt open my lips, and my mouth shall tell of thy praise." The sincerity, the genuine manliness and humility of his psalms show that his resolution was effective.

Sorrow is a real movement of will, not a magic formula. Mere words of contrition cannot change us; there must be a re-education and re-direction of our will. Sorrow is an all-important change of heart: we must see our sin for what it is; we must see what it has meant to us—how it has injured us, damaged our happiness, endangered our way to God; we must honestly *expose* our weakness before God, knowing that only He can cure us; then we must make an effective promise, a resolution that will produce the necessary change, that will "breathe new life, true life" into our inner being.

Psalm 51

ROOTED IN PRAYER

And I? rooted like a fruitful olive-tree in the house of my God,
I will trust forever in his divine mercy; / I will give thee eternal

thanks for all thou hast done, and boast, as men should ever boast,
of thy name.

ONE who is "rooted like a fruitful olive tree" in the house of God
has established himself firmly in the habit of prayer. This, after
all, is our principal duty in life. Not that it is in any way necessary
for God to hear our day-to-day thanks, or our "boasting of his
name."

It is that we need it, Lord. We need the constant expression at
least in our mind, of our love and adoration of You, of our needs
and desires of the spirit, grace that You alone can give.

The very act of this kind of prayer, this habit of raising mind and
heart to God everywhere, will bring an infusion of God into my
soul. It will make strong my desire to see God, to know Him better,
to love Him at last with a genuine self-surrender. The psalmist has
this true spirit of prayer; he trusts forever in the divine mercy, he is
grateful and desires to be so eternally, he is thrilled at the very name
of God. He does not regard prayer as some kind of chore to get
done, as some necessary but disagreeable exercise. Prayer, the inspired poet implies, is the full and spontaneous expression of love.
We might almost say it is the habit of happiness in God.

The habit of prayer, we will find, is the only sure habit of constant happiness. Even though we practice a generous self-sacrifice
toward our neighbor, even though we keep busy with much outward activity, even though we belong to every lively organization
in reach, there will be a certain pain amidst all if there is emptiness
inside us.

We become weary of ourselves and our own limitations, just as
surely as at times we are disappointed even in our best friends. God
has not left it in our imperfect nature to be fully happy apart from
him. We came from his hand, and are to reach our full perfection
only upon returning to him. St. Augustine could say from much experience and thought: "Whichever way the soul of man turns,
unless towards God, it is affixed to pain."

The spirit of man is not static, like a sculpture in stone. It is a living thing, like a camp-fire that must constantly be supplied with fresh wood, lest it gradually die out. The spiritual life is like every other form of life on earth: it needs constant attention and sufficient fuel, if it is to stay alive. Prayer is the life of man's soul; it needs continuous encouragement. It grows on the love and the good will and the thoughtfulness that places a man constantly in the presence of God.

By the habit of prayer we are "rooted like a tree in the house of God," where we find peace, contentment, the silence of love and the fullness of life.

Psalm 52

THE AGONY OF CHARITY

What, can they learn nothing, / all these traffickers in inquity, / who feed themselves fat on this people of mine, / as if it were bread for their eating, / and never invoke God's name? / What wonder if fear unmans them, / where they have no cause of fear?

THERE IS MUCH SORROW for the modern Christian as he views the crimes committed daily all around him, as he prays earnestly for those millions who suffer injustice, persecution, and torture, as he grieves for the young whose open and innocent hearts are fouled by the world's temptations and snares. Indeed, there are all too many who in a criminal way "feed themselves fat" on the innocent, on the weak and foolish, who make out of the young and curious reader "bread for their eating," and who certainly "never invoke God's name" except thoughtlessly in their selfish anger.

The modern Christian who is willing to sacrifice himself for the rescue of these unhappy souls, must experience some of that supreme agony of Yours, Lord, on that terrible night in the garden of olives. Will he not feel, Lord, as You felt when You began the shedding of Your blood in that cold, death-like sweat?

It was an agony of charity, of a broken heart at seeing the sinners that all Your sufferings would not save, Lord, because they would reject You. You could have had no selfish fears of the pains to come, since Your every reason for coming to this world, for choosing the time and place, was selfless, was for us and surely not for Yourself. And now You saw all the Judases, the betrayers, the self-condemned, the lost chances, the lost souls.

Is it any wonder that many of the great mystics, seeing You in Your agony, heard You exclaim, "Ah, much good it does to bleed so copiously, to suffer such intense pain, to receive so many blows, so much spittle, so many lashes, to be so atrociously crucified! Much good it does to be the Son of God and die as a son of man, only to be trampled on for centuries by those who should love Me for it."

In those moments You experienced in Yourself all the mental agonies of the human race; You were carrying all the horrors and evils of mankind on Your shoulders. Then You prayed, "Not my will, but Thy Will be done," and rose up, self-possessed, majestic and strong, and gave up Your life for us.

Psalm 53

DIVINE HUMOR

I joyfully offer thee sacrifice, | and praise thy name, Lord, as praised it must ever be; | who else has delivered me from all peril . . . ?

How DOES ONE EXPLAIN this joy of the saints in the very face of torturous suffering? How can one explain the feelings of St. Paul when he rejoices at all his troubles? Just where is the joke, in all the pains and trials of the saints? How can one "joyfully offer sacrifice"?

We must investigate this "divine humor" of the saints. There is so much for us to learn in it! What is a joke, anyway? Why do we laugh when we see a small, thin man walking down the street with a huge, fat woman as his partner? The humor is in the lack of proportion. They don't appear to belong together. All good jokes grow out of some lack of proportion like this.

And that is the divine humor of the saints. That is the paradox of their good cheer in the face of great trials. To the saints, the biggest joke of all was this: they knew how little they were paying for the kingdom of heaven. They rejoiced over the amazing bargain they had discovered. A few humiliations, a few pains, a few good drops of blood—this was the small price for God's infinitely magnificent heaven. "What exchange shall a man give for his soul?" What can we answer You, Lord, but to laugh at the thought of making any exchange?

Only saints can truly laugh at earthly hardships. For only they see how truly small they are, how out of proportion with the things they are purchasing. They see, as St. Paul did, that "the sufferings of this life are not worth comparing with the glory that is to come."

Their true sense of proportions, and of the divine joke in it all, is what made the saints seem so extreme in their penances and devotions. When we are told, for example, that St. Patrick insisted on praying all 150 psalms every day, and soaked his feet in ice cold water that he might stay awake to do so, we laugh. And it is, indeed, part of the grand joke that made the saints so happy. They had struck the world's greatest treasure, and they knew it; why shouldn't they laugh through all of life?

If we understood this great truth, Lord, if we realized what a tremendous offer You have made us, would we find limits to what we would gladly do for You? Wouldn't we be as eager as the saints, as inspired by the divine humor of it all? Wouldn't we "joyfully offer sacrifice" to You, Lord, knowing well that after the brief opportunities of this time of trial, You will "deliver us from all peril," and show us the glory You reserve for those who can laugh at how little they are asked to pay for it!

Psalm 54

THE RIDDLE OF DEATH

My heart is full of whirling thoughts; / the fear of death stands over me; / trembling and terrified, I see perils closing round me. / Had I but wings, I cry, as a dove has wings, to fly away and find rest!

WHEN MEN SORROW over the death of a loved one, they are ever and again confronted by the most important fact of human life: this life can in no way explain itself. In how many ways have men throughout history bewailed this riddle, this mystery!

Omar Khayyam, in the *Rubaiyat,* observed:

> Strange—is it not?—that of the myriads who
> Before us passed the door of Darkness through,
> Not one returns to tell us of the road
> Which to discover we must travel too.

Like a man facing death with bewilderment and without faith, Thomas Hobbes exclaimed, "Now I am about to take my last voyage, a great leap in the dark."

Poets who have pondered and perceived the beauty of life, its mystery, its power and possible meanings, have suspected, indeed, that we have here on earth no lasting home, but are created for another. "What is life," they ask, "but the prelude to an unknown song?" Yet they fear, as Hamlet did, that unknown song. The fear of death stands over them. Who, asks Hamlet, would

> ". . . grunt and sweat under a weary life,
> But that the dread of something after death,
> The undiscovered country, from whose bourn
> No traveler returns, puzzles the will,
> And makes us rather bear those ills we have
> Than fly to others that we know not of?"
>
> (*Hamlet,* III, 1)

What is more consoling, then, amidst the darkness and confusion, the fears of human life, its sorrows and despairs, than the ever-calm and grave voice of the Church, the ever-living assurance of Christ: "I am the resurrection and the life; he who has come to believe in Me, though he be dead, shall live." Thus the Church sings at the Preface in the Requiem Mass: "The life of those who are faithful to thee, O God, is but changed, not ended; and when their earthly dwelling place decays, an everlasting mansion stands prepared for them in heaven."

In the face of death man can make one of three choices: 1) he can despair, seeing death as the end of all things for him; 2) he can ignore the truth; he can wonder, merely, stand confused before the great mystery of life and death; he can miss the divine order and beauty of life and death; 3) he can open the flood-gates of hope and strength and truth: the gates of grace; he can see life, even in its sorrows, as the sure road to joy; he can see with St. Paul that if we suffer and die with Christ, we will surely rise with him. And if he lives with Christ, every sorrow, every sacrifice becomes a sweet death, in which this natural, earthly life is given up so that the eternal life of glory might enter in.

Psalm 55

KING OF FREEDOM

My trust is in God, man's threats cannot daunt me. | The vows which thou claimest from me, O God, | my sacrifice of praise shall fulfil; | hast thou not saved my life from every peril, my feet from every slip?

THE vows You claim from me, Lord, are not the vows of servitude or slavery. Even though You have "saved my life from every peril," even though all I have I owe to You, even though You have absolute power over me, You will not force me into Your service.

You were called "a king" even by Pilate. But You are only the king of freedom. You refuse to force anyone into Your kingdom; You will not accept anyone who does not freely and cheerfully offer his service. If I am reluctant or hesitant in accepting Your will, I am, after all, not Your loyal subject.

You alone, Lord, of all kings, have absolute power. That is why You can afford to make us free. "You shall know the truth," You told us, "and the truth shall make you free." When the Jews heard this, they became angry and said, "We have never been slaves to any man." But they had been slaves to every empire in every civilization: Egypt, Assyria, Babylonia, Greece, and Rome. They had constantly been enslaved, because they had always refused to do God's will. That is why St. Stephen told them, "Stiff-necked race, you are forever resisting the Holy Spirit, just as your fathers did. . . . you, who received the law dictated by angels, and did not keep it." Those who will not choose the freedom of God must fall into the slavery of men.

History has taught men over and over that there is no freedom but in carrying out the will of God. Communism is teaching us that once again—but we should have learned it long ago.

Christ alone is the King of true justice and the King of true freedom. If it were not for You, Lord, we as individuals would count for nothing. In nations where You are not worshipped and Your will is not done, a human life means nothing, an individual is a mere tool, an economic or political number, and this is not enough to keep him alive. It is only in Your Precious Blood that each of us becomes free.

You did not come to this world to be made a king. King You were from all eternity, before the world was created. But You came to save our lives from the deadly peril of eternal loss. You came that we might learn the truth, and the truth would set us free. "Everyone who is of the truth listens to my voice." And if we listen, You will show *us* how to become kings; masters over ourselves, and true conquerors of the world. "The flesh profits nothing; it is the spirit that gives life."

Psalm 56

THE RESURRECTION

O God, mount high above the heavens, | till thy glory overshadows the whole earth. | See where they have laid a snare for my feet, | to bring me low, dug a pit in my path; | may it be their own undoing.

THANKS TO GOD'S INFINITE MERCY, the snare and pit were the undoing of his enemies, of sin. Judas had laid the snare, had delivered up Jesus; the Jews and the Roman governor had "brought Him low," had beaten Him, insulted and spit upon Him, had tortured

Him and sentenced Him to death; they had "dug a pit," His tomb. It was truly their "undoing," for He arose, glorious, eternally victorious, mounting "high above the heavens, till His glory overshadowed the whole earth."

And this was the message of the risen Christ to his disciples on the road to Emmaus. Was not this divine plan of suffering, agony, death, and resurrection most fitting? Jesus told them, "Too slow of wit, too dull of heart, to believe all these sayings of the prophets! Was it not to be expected that Christ should undergo these sufferings, and enter so into his glory?

"Then, going back to Moses and the whole line of the prophets, he began to interpret the words used of himself by all the prophets" (Luke 24:25–27).

Lord Jesus, what a day of glory was the day of Your resurrection! For this day You came into the world: for Your resurrection, and for that of Your saints. This day is the beginning and the proof of man's resurrection; the glorification of those who become other Christs. For this we were born; for this You created sun, moon, and stars; for this You gave us a mind and a will: to hope and to love and to anticipate that day. Our life would have no meaning, our life would make no sense, but in the fulfillment of the resurrection.

Truly, if we knew the glory, the splendor, the beauty of our resurrection, no one would ever be satisfied with another day on earth. Dante visited heaven and saw the souls supremely happy there; yet they all were talking about the day of their resurrection. They have won the battle, they are happy, they are with God; yet they long for the day when they will be restored to their bodies; for they are human, they are body and soul, and they understand something of Christ's risen beauty.

Glorious and resplendent, You are with us in the Holy Eucharist, our hidden God, "high above the heavens." Yet in the Blessed Sacrament "thy glory overshadows the whole earth." And is it not true, You come to us in the Eucharist in order to prepare our bodies and souls for the resurrection? Is it not Your desire to come to us frequently, as the pledge of our future glory? For You said, "He

who eats my flesh . . . shall have life everlasting in himself, and I
will raise him up on the last day."

Psalm 57

PSALM OF CURSES

*My God, break their cruel fangs. . . . Like spilt water let them
run to waste . . . melt into nothing . . . perish like the untimely birth
that sees never the light of the sun. . . . / The innocent man will
triumph at the sight of their punishment, as he dips his hands in
the blood of the evil-doer; / Sure enough, men will say, innocence
has its reward, sure enough, there is a God who grants redress here
on earth.*

THE OLD TESTAMENT "psalms of curses" seem to have been the
most difficult for Christians to assimilate, heart and soul, into the
Church's prayer. We do not find the "curses" used freely in the
Church's daily liturgy. In fact, we might suspect the note of embarrassment that prompted the Church to relegate the strongest and
longest of the cursing psalms, 108, to the very end of her weekly
psalm-arrangement, the hour of Nones on Saturday.

We ourselves in reading this psalm and looking for meditation in
it, may wince over the downright hearty good will with which the
psalmist hopes the sinner will be destroyed. We may almost choke
at the image of "the innocent man" dipping "his hands in the blood
of the evil-doer." Yet this is part of the inspired prayerbook, and it
has something to teach us.

The psalms are poetry, and as such they may make use of our
emotions in the service of God. If in the psalms we are prompted to
love You, Lord, as our generous Creator and tender Father; if
these songs of praise inspire us toward joy and thanksgiving and

courage in suffering, as well as to sorrow and even depression; why should they not also stir within us a holy fear of evil, a horror at the thought of losing You, who are all our good?

It is true that since You revealed to us that the commandment of love is supreme, Jesus, we have come to a much finer distinction between the sinner and the sin. If to the mind of the ancient Hebrew it was nearly impossible to separate the crime from the man in which it had "taken up its abode," there is still much for us to learn from the curses. We realize as fully as the ancients the dangers and the tragedies born out of sin. We fear no less, let us hope, than the ancients for the innocents—the young, the pure, the child-like. We would give our lives, let us hope, to "keep scandal from these little ones." We would burst into nearly uncontrolled anger, let us hope, on seeing harm done to innocent souls. We would not think it wrong to say that the hatred of evil, like the fear of the Lord, is "the beginning of wisdom."

Can we not see a paradox, then, in the cursing psalms? Not only are these curses like a prophecy, warning the sinners of what God's justice must bring them, if they do not repent. Not only are they a warning to us, who "think ourselves just" and may be falling into evils we have not the humility to recognize. But the curses serve also to remind us how the infinite mercy of God brings good out of evil. "All Scripture was written for our correction," writes St. Paul. And so, we may add, Lord, the curses were also written for our correction.

Though we cannot wish literally that the sinner will "perish like the untimely birth that sees never the light of the sun" we can surely wish that his prosperity may perish, that God may punish him here on earth, if that will save his soul from worse evils. If we ourselves, Lord, need punishment for our correction, if suffering the consequences of our sins has enlightened us and brought us wisdom, can we not desire the same grace for those who persecute us? St. Augustine understood this paradox of salvation through a curse, when he prayed, "Would that those who persecute us now, might come to be persecuted with us." For then they, too, will be saved through the cross.

Here is the mystery, then, and the value of these curses: not only the blessings of God, but the inspired curses will save us, if we have the wisdom to heed them. May, then, the "curse of sin" come upon the sinner now—while he has yet time to learn wisdom from it, and repent.

Psalm 58

AWAKE, ARISE!

Lord of hosts, God of Israel, awake! / . . . To thee I look, the God who strengthens me, the God who watches over me; / my God, and all my hope of mercy. / With that divine aid, may I triumph over my enemies.

IF MANKIND has always looked to God for hope and strength, if we have always turned to God for rescue from our enemies, if we have in all centuries sought God's aid against the fear of evils and of death—we shall not be disappointed. There is one event, one day, one hour that has answered all. It is the central point of all history; it is the climax, the greatest joy on earth, the beginning and end of every Christian life: it is the resurrection of Christ.

"Lord of hosts, God of Israel, awake! . . . Arise, Lord, stand up to save us!" Could the psalmist have guessed how literally, how beautifully this prayer would be answered? Not even the apostles expected that glorious event.

That is why Thomas doubted. That is why he boldly insisted, "Unless I put my finger into the prints of the nails, and unless I put my hand into his side, I will not believe." He *was* really dead, after all, and buried. Now some women come and claim that the tomb is empty; he has arisen. Small wonder that Thomas insists on absolute proof.

What must have been his surprise, Lord, when he got that proof! When You scolded him for not believing! Yet, in a sense, we rejoice that he doubted. It was not only Your resurrection that was at stake; it was the resurrection of all of us. If You could raise Yourself, then You could raise us. If this was true, then everything men had ever hoped for would come true. Now he felt with his own hands and saw with his own eyes that it was really true!

What a frightening joy it must have been! All the martyrs, all the suffering on earth, all the crippled, the blind, the sick, the dying, the imprisoned, the tortured, the abandoned—all suffering men could rejoice now. They could laugh some day at all they had ever suffered. What difference did it make, except that there was an unbelievable glory in it? They would rise from the dead—perfect, joyous, beautiful, strong, healthy, brilliant for all eternity! What did anything else matter now?

All the tragedy in the world had suddenly disappeared. There was really no sadness anymore; only one sadness remained—not to love Christ, so as not rise with Him.

Psalm 59

LOVING PROVIDENCE

. . . thou, O God, has disowned us, and wilt not go into battle with our armies? | It is thou that must deliver us from peril; vain is the help of man. | Only through God can we fight victoriously; Only he can trample our oppressors in the dust.

WE HAVE HERE a glimpse at the mysterious, loving providence of God. Clearly in ancient times the most important lessons of life were learned in suffering, since men could learn them no other way. And, it seems, every century, every generation, every race, nation, and individual must learn these vital truths in the same difficult manner.

When the Israelites' pride was bowed in the dust, when God at last turned away from these arrogant, self-sufficient, covetous children of his, then at last they understood that man can never safely indulge in his successes or his talents or his material comforts apart from God. Nature herself will turn against men who forget her Creator. Men, in fact, turn against each other when they forget their Creator.

We have heard often enough—in theory—that the beginning of all sin, the head and roots and citadel of all sin is pride. It is a sin of excessive strength rather than weakness; it brings no shame with it; it is boastful, self-righteous, and hypocritical, and therefore it traps us so easily. We are pride's victims long before we recognize it, and still longer before we confess it.

That is why it was so necessary for God at times to refuse "going into battle with Israel's enemies." His chosen people, his favorite sons too soon forgot his mercies; he complains of that often enough in the sacred writings. We are perpetually in danger of taking a benefactor's gifts for granted. It is best that we are often and forcefully reminded, by a temporary loss of gifts, of our own insufficiency.

The Israelites often fell into the temptation of trying to make God the instrument of their will, just as we do. This could not lead to anything but disappointment. For God can never be the instrument of human wills; he would then no longer be God. It is we who must be his instruments; it is we who must await his word.

The Israelites, like us moderns, were deceived by pride into thinking that human happiness was achieved by coming to possess what man humanly and selfishly desires for himself. They had to learn—by suffering the consequences—that the very things they most wanted brought them the greatest unhappiness.

As Dorothy Sayers wisely observed, "human happiness is a by-product, thrown off in man's service of God." No one knew this better than Israel's prophets, but Israel's people seldom listened to them. The psalmist, like the prophets, reminds us that only God can "deliver us from peril"—the peril of unhappiness—and "vain is the help of man."

Psalm 60

DAY AFTER DAY

Listen, Lord, to this cry of appeal; / do not let my prayer go unheeded, / though it be from the ends of the earth that I call upon thee. / When my heart misgives me, thou wilt set me high up on a rock, / thou wilt bring me repose; / thou, my only hope, my strong tower against the assault of my enemies. . . . / Lord, thou hast listened to my prayer, / a domain thou hast given me where thy name is held in awe. . . . / Eternally I will sing thy praises, day after day perform my vows.

Of all men that ever lived, there was only one who did not need to pray. There was only one who did not need to adore God, or thank God, or make reparation to God, or ask God for his needs —for this man *was* God: he was Christ, God and man.

Yet, Jesus, when I examine the New Testament, I see how often You prayed! St. Matthew says that after the miracle of the five loaves of bread and the two little fish, with which You fed five thousand men, not counting women and childen, "Jesus obliged his disciples to take their ship and cross over to the other side of the lake, while he would dismiss the people. And when he had finished sending them home, he went up the mountain-side, alone, to pray" (Matt. 14:23).

St. Luke tells us that You "passed the whole night offering prayer to God."

St. Mark tells us that one evening, "after sunset, they brought to Jesus all the sick, the blind, and the lame, and he healed them all. And rising very early, he left the city and went to a desert place, and there he prayed" (Mark 1:35).

By Your example You taught us not only that no one escapes the need of prayer, but You taught us *how* to pray. In the "Our Father" You taught us how to pray unselfishly. "Thy Will be done, . . . Forgive us . . . as we forgive those who trespass against us . . . lead us not into temptation, but deliver us from evil."

You taught us especially that prayer must be persevering. "Eternally I will sing thy praises, day after day perform my vows," said David in the psalm. You told the parable of the man begging bread of his friend at night, illustrating "how we should always pray and never fail," said St. Luke. Again the evangelist assures us that when You went out to Gethsemane to pray on the night before You died, You went out "according to Your custom."

Perseverance, then, is the first rule of prayer. No one can be called a man of prayer if he is not in the *habit* of prayer. Anyone can pray once in a while; it takes no great virtue to pray in distress, and then soon give up. But to pray when no answer seems to come, when there seems no reward to the prayer, when one hates to pray or sees no reason to pray—this is perseverance in prayer; this is honest, sincere prayer.

Psalm 61

ATTENTIVE TO GOD

No rest has my soul but in God's hands. . . . I have no other stronghold, no other deliverer but him. . . . Yet even now, my soul,

leave thyself in God's hands; / all my trust is in him. . . . God is
all my defence and all my boast; /my rock-fastness, my refuge is
in God.

NOTHING CALMS the restless soul better than attentive prayer. If
one is attentive to God, says David the psalmist, confusion flees:
"No rest has my soul but in God's hands. . . . Safe in his protection,
I fear no deadly fall."

A restless rattling of words, a rush "to get through," distractions
over petty cares and concerns—these are the destroyers of true
prayer. When we go to prayer, we must remember, with David,
that "man is a breath that passes; in Adam's sons there is no trust;
high in the scales they rise, weighed all together and lighter than a
breath" (Psalm 60).

We cannot truly pray if we do not give ourselves attentively to
God. This was Your point, Lord, in telling us, "When you pray,
you are not to be like hypocrites, who love to stand praying in syna-
gogues or at street-corners, to be a mark for men's eyes; believe
me, they have their reward already. But when thou art praying, go
into thy inner room and shut the door upon thyself, and so pray to
thy Father in secret; and then thy Father, who sees what is done in
secret, will reward thee" (Matt. 6:5-6).

Thus, from David and from the Divine Teacher who humbly
called himself the "Son of David," we have the second important
rule for prayer; be attentive to God; shut out all distraction. "Go
into thy inner room and shut the door." We must go within and
shut the door on distractions. This is the external preparation for
true prayer. "Leave thyself in God's hands." This is the first step.
"God is all my defence and all my boast." This is the outcome of
true prayer.

But distractions will come; they have come to the greatest of
saints, to the contemplatives who made prayer their full day's
work, who were experts in prayer, who loved nothing more than
prayer. How are distractions overcome? By perseverance, the first

rule of all virtue, the first rule for the formation of all good habits. And every human being in this world who is truly happy, truly at peace, who "is at rest," who has "a stronghold, a rock-fastness, a refuge" in which he can always trust—every such person has the habit of prayer.

Psalm 62

WHO IS THIS SPEAKING?

O God, thou art my God; / how eager my quest for thee, body athirst and soul longing for thee, / like some parched wilderness, where stream is none! / ... To win thy favor is dearer to me than life itself; / my songs of praise can no more be withheld. . . . / My thoughts shall go out to thee at dawn, / as I lie awake remembering thee, and the protection thou hast given me. / Gladly I take shelter under thy wings, / cling close to thee, borne up by thy protecting hand.

There is a knock on the door; I open it. Two policemen are waiting for me, and immediately carry me off into an armored car, manned by two more men in uniform. They drive me to the city hall, where a vast crowd of people is gathered—for what reason? I have no idea. The police hustle me to the balcony of the city hall, and stand me before a well-dressed, dignified royal personage. I have never seen him before, I am unable to say who he is, where he comes from; but he is clearly someone very important. Now they tell me, "You have been appointed to deliver greetings and a message to his highness on this great occasion." Of one thing I am sure: there will be very little conversation, if any, and my message will profit no one, until I find out who this person is, and what my position towards him happens to be.

The psalmist knew well what royal personage he was addressing. "Thou art my God," he says in all simplicity. "To win thy favor is dearer to me than life itself." Even at dawn (a time when most of us are not the clearest thinkers), as he first awakens, he remembers all that God has done for him. He is overjoyed at being favored by this gracious Lord. And surely he knows his own position before this Lord: "Eager my quest for thee, body athirst and soul longing for thee. . . . Gladly I take shelter under thy wings, cling close to thee. . . . My songs of praise can no more be withheld."

Here, indeed, is a profitable conversation. Here is deep understanding, genuine love, recognition of the Great One's generosity, of His care, of His favors. Such is the third rule, and a most important rule, for true prayer. It is the rule of true humility.

Without sincere humility, we cannot pray. You illustrated this, Jesus, in Your parable of the Pharisee and the Publican. The Pharisee knew neither You nor himself. Otherwise he would not have presumed to "tell You all about himself," as though to impress You with his greatness. He did not see where he stood, nor how small he stood before God.

The Publican prayed, as St. Augustine did, that he might know God and know himself. That is why "he went down to his home justified." Lord, I cannot truly pray unless I understand clearly who I am, and try to understand, as far as humans can, who You are.

Psalm 63

ON ONE CONDITION

Let the thoughts of man's heart be deep as they will, / yet God has arrows, too, to smite them with, sudden wounds to deal them; / all their conspiring plays them false. / Scornfully the onlookers

shake their heads, awe-stricken every one; / who but will acclaim
God's power, / who but will ponder his great acts? / Honest men
will rejoice and put their trust in the Lord; / upright hearts will
not boast in vain.

No ONE HAS MEASURED accurately the worries of man. No one can
say in fractions or percentages how much of human suffering consists of futile worrying. But we are all sure that if our worries, our
fears of the future, were scrupulously measured, the figures would
be shockingly high. There is untold suffering in the fear and the
outright non-acceptance of our lot in life.

Is there any remedy? Can we prevent this needless unhappiness?
A magazine columnist stated that the best advice she had ever received was this, from an old priest: "Why should *you* worry? Trust
God; isn't He *infinitely wiser* than you are?" Strange, Lord, how
we never stop to think of the obvious!

The psalmist is remarkably familiar with the obvious. He, the
clear-headed poet, the man of sound thought and experience, knows
that not the most cunning of men can outwit God. God's will
must always be done, whether *we* want it or not. "So take my advice," says St. Teresa, "and make a virtue out of a necessity," by
accepting God's will cheerfully. If we accept it grudgingly, or even if
we rebel, His will must be done. He *is* God, after all. And if He is
God, He must of necessity do many things that we, His feeble
creatures, cannot understand. "For the wisdom of God is foolishness to men, and the weakness of God is stronger than men," St.
Paul reminds us (I Cor. 1:25).

Whatever we desire, whatever we ask God for, whatever we plan
to do for His sake—all this must always be "under one condition." And this is the fourth rule for true prayer: "Thy will be
done." Without this condition, prayer is a kind of foolish coaxing.
We would laugh to hear some eager soul praying, "O Lord, be
faithful to my promises!" Yet any prayer in which we do not
absolutely and expressly accept the Will of God as infinitely

superior to our own, as having absolute right over ours, as being at times contrary to ours—any such prayer is just as foolish as that.

Lord Jesus, at the moment of Your greatest pain, in the hour of Your death-agony, in the garden of Gethsemane, You taught us how to pray. "Not my will, but Thine be done."

Psalm 64

A FEARFUL JOY

To thee all mankind must look for pardon, | weighed down by its sinfulness till thou dost forgive. | Blessed the man on whom thy choice falls, | whom thou takest to dwell with thee in thy own domain! | . . . What power girds thee about! | In thy strength the mountains stand firm; | thou dost calm the raging of the sea, | raging sea-billows, ay, and the turmoil of angry nations. | Thy portents strike terror at the world's end, | fill the lands of sunrise and sunset with rejoicing.

How WELL the psalmist understands at once the joy and the dread that possess a man as he stands before God. Even the best of men, the greatest of saints, who could rejoice that God's choice had fallen on them, who had given their whole lives to him—even these greatest never forgot what they owed him, and how little they had paid.

The great Catholic scholar of Anglo-Saxon England, St. Bede the Venerable, was known and loved widely for his remarkably gentle disposition, his total dedication to Christ, his outstanding humility. All his various talents—teaching, preaching, translating, writing—were completely given to God.

Such a man, we would think, had nothing to fear from God's

judgment. He could say with the psalmist, "Blessed the man on whom thy choice falls, whom thou takest to dwell with thee in thy own domain!"

Yet on his death-bed, this gentle, humble saint exclaimed, "It is a fearful thing to fall into the hands of the living God!"

What had he to to fear? A man of exceptional innocence and total dedication—how could he call it "fearful" to stand before You, the rewarder of good works?

His "trouble" was that in living close to You, Lord, he came to see something of what God is. He came to understand something of Your infinite holiness, Your supreme perfection; he had been given a glimpse of the boundless distance between man and God.

His very joy at Your excellence caused him to fear. "How shall I, puny, and limited as I am, ever be worthy to face my Creator? How shall I ever make a fitting return of love to my Redeemer?"

This is the deep feeling of simultaneous joy and pain experienced by the holy souls in Purgatory. They rejoice at the prospect of appearing before You; but their unworthiness pains them exceedingly. And thus again they rejoice at the opportunity of cleansing themselves, of making themselves a little worthy of You, however painful the task may be.

If only we could understand this deep truth on earth, how much more worthy we would be at the hour of death!

Psalm 65

SONG OF THE UNBELIEVABLE

Let the whole world keep holiday in God's presence, / sing praise to his name, pay homage to his glory! / . . . Come near, and see what God does, / how wonderful he is in his dealings with human kind, | how he turns the sea into land, and lets men cross a river dry-shod; | ours to rejoice in his mercy.

A FITTING PSALM for the great paradox of Christmas! The wonder of God in his dealings with our kind. "How he turns the sea into land," the infinite ocean of distance between his supreme perfection and our earth-bound weakness, between his spiritual brilliance and our human flesh. This boundless "sea" which no man could cross is now suddenly turned into land, which we can travel "dry-shod," with no special equipment but our trust in his mercy.

Rather than "Glory to God in the highest," we can sing, "Glory to God in the lowest." Glory to God, the helpless infant, the child of poverty, laid in the manger of a wind-swept cave, "because there is no room in the inn."

Here is meditation for a life-time: how God stoops down to lift us up. It seems unsuitable, improper: he of infinite majesty should not lower himself like this! He should realize that we are too ignorant, too unappreciative to recognize the miracle and the mystery involved. Or can we, after all, perceive some of the infinite beauty of that divine gesture?

The Church and her Saints have recognized it, have gazed in awe, have knelt in love and reverence before this mystery. In the "Gloria" of the Mass, the Church jubilantly sings her praise of the event: God has done the unbelievable; He has become man. True joy grows out of the unbelievable, the dream come true. If that is true, Christmas is surely the greatest joy. What greater reason for hope, for love, for security, for comfort? What greater reason for poetry and song? Many poets, indeed, have devoted their most beautiful work to this mystery. Chesterton asks, "Who is proud when the heavens are humble, who mounts if the mountains fall?" For now we know, he writes—

> There has fallen on earth for a token
> A god too great for the sky.

He has burst out of all things and broken
The bounds of eternity.

Into time and the terminal land
He has strayed like a thief or a lover,
For the wine of the world brims over,
Its splendour is spilt on the sand.

(*Gloria in Profundis*)

Psalm 66

HIS SAVING POWER

Make known thy will, O God, wide as earth; / make known among all nations thy saving power. / Honor to thee, O God, from the nations, honor from all the nations! / The Gentiles, too, may rejoice and be glad; / a whole world abides thy judgment, / and the Gentiles, too, obey on earth thy sovereignty.

As THOUGH IN GRACIOUS COMPLIANCE with the poet's request, God came, and made known to all nations His saving power. But what a scandal to those who waited for him, yes, and boasted that they waited for *him* and had no trust in man!

It is not fair simply to assert that God's people did not know him, and therefore could not recognize him when he came. The Old Testament is filled with the boast that they, of all nations, knew the true God, and knew him very well; and this was a reasonably justified boast.

It is not fair, either, nor correct to say that His people only knew Him as the Lord of justice, and greatly to be feared. A surprising number of pages are given in the Old Testament to the assurance that God is a loving Father, that he is an ocean of mercy, that his

concern for man is as tender and unselfish as that of a mother for
her only child. We find it in the psalms, in the Song of Songs, in
Isaias, and in many other books. In fact, the most beautiful and
tender passages often surprise us, coming just at the conclusion of
some awesome description of God's power, of the terror and fear
which he ought to inspire in men, of the grave punishments he has
inflicted on the disobedient.

If the writers of the Old Testament seem at times to look at
God from afar, to set him at too great a distance from us, they can
shock us a moment later by making him almost too human, by
thinking of him in terms surprisingly earthly.

When the promised Redeemer came, then, when God visibly came
to save a falling world, what would He be like? What would we
see? Basically, they understood His love, His concern for every man,
His will to save not only Jew, but Gentile; He created all; He loved
all. He was very demanding; He was boundlessly merciful. They
understood all this.

What they hadn't guessed, what they couldn't have guessed, what
we couldn't have guessed, Lord, was the incredible weakness, the
insignificance, the poverty in which You would choose to come. We
couldn't have guessed the fierce opposition You would meet with, the
simplicity in which You would choose to clothe Yourself. The cave
at Bethlehem, the dangerous flight into Egypt, the lowly cottage at
Nazareth, the years of toil as a village carpenter, the three short years
of preaching, during which You had no place to lay Your head.

The Redeemer who had at His command the power to save the
world, who had built and could destroy the world, becomes the poorest of vagabonds. Should He not have been the most beloved of
vagabonds? Yet He was hated by so many! If there is not a world
of things for me to learn here, Lord, I shall never learn a worthwhile thing in my life!

Psalm 67

THE VICTORY OF LIFE

Blessed be the Lord now and ever, | the God who bears our burdens, and wins us the victory. | Our God is a God of deliverance; | the Lord is our Master, that saves men from peril of death.

As GOD created the world to bring forth life, so Christ in redeeming the world restored life. His Resurrection is the feast-day of life itself. It is the answer to the mystery of suffering and death. Christ came to this world to reveal to us the real meaning of life: "Unless the grain of wheat fall into the ground and die, it remains alone. But if it die, it brings forth much fruit. He who loves his life, loses it; and he who hates his life in this world, keeps it unto life everlasting" (John 12:24-26).

How often we ask ourselves, "Why must I suffer sickness, disappointment, loneliness? Why must so many of the innocent suffer injustice, betrayal, destitution, undeserved punishment?"

Christ came to answer this by His own life.

I have heard people of faith and a good Christian life express their bewilderment at the great sufferings of innocent peoples and nations. The twentieth century is surely the century of martyrs; we have had millions of them. But worse, perhaps, is the living martyrdom of more millions of enslaved people; a life of infinite fear, weariness, poverty and pain.

"It would seem that God abandoned these people," said a good lady.

"Yes," answered a young man, "if you forget what happened to His Son on Calvary."

And not only on Calvary; the cold and hunger at Bethlehem, the precarious journey to Egypt, the twenty years of thankless labor as Nazareth's carpenter, rejection by neighbors, Pharisees, Sadducees; the ingratitude of those who owed Him most. His whole life was the beginning of Calvary; it was Calvary in various forms.

But You were the Son of God; You could choose only the best. And You chose to be poor, to be hated, slandered, condemned, despised, imprisoned, accused, laughed at, spat upon, tortured, left to die on a tree. The best? How can such things, by any stretch of the imagination, be called "the best"? There is no good in them; otherwise we would have to say that evil is good and good is evil.

It is a mystery to our earth-bound human ways of thinking. But there is a hint in that word *victory*. Victory—over what? "God gives His people strength and courage," the psalmist tells us. Strength and courage—for what? For traveling the road, the only road to Resurrection.

This should come as no surprise—in one sense, at least. For everything on earth has its price. Everything good must be paid for or worked for. Happiness, most of all, must be earned. It is not easily earned, as experience has taught us all.

Christ had decided to become one of us; thus He, too, subjected Himself to the law of human achievement—the things of greatest value demand the greatest sacrifice; they have a high price, sometimes a heroic price.

Sorrow today is for joy tomorrow; death today is resurrection tomorrow—if one has paid the price. "Blessed be the Lord now and ever, the God who bears our burdens, and wins us the victory." He has paid the price, but we must share it with Him, if we are to share the victory.

Psalm 68

THE GREAT TEMPTATIONS

What more could I do? I humbled myself before them by fasting; | and that, too, was matter for finding fault; | I dressed in sackcloth, and they made a by-word of me. | Idlers in the market-place taunt me; | the drunkards make a song of me over their wine. . . . | Should I make amends to them, I, that never robbed them? | . . . Was it not jealousy for the honor of thy house that consumed me; | was it not uttered against thee, the reproach that I bore?

To WHAT LENGTHS, Lord, could Your self-abasement extend? Could You have humiliated Yourself more than by coming before us fasting, like a sinner atoning for his past? Many saints spent days and nights fasting, in order to conquer the desires of the flesh, in order to atone for having lived in too great ease and pleasure when young, in order to make more certain their perseverance in grace.

You had no need of such things. Clearly Yours was from the beginning a heart of heroic sacrifice and reparation—sacrifice and reparation for us, since You had not the slightest need for it Yourself.

Reparation, however, was not the end of Your humiliations. You suffered Yourself to be *tempted* . . . the greatest mystery of all. As an example to us, You allowed the arch-tempter of all, Satan, the spirit of pride, to tempt You to those three greatest snares: comfort, pride, and power.

If we consider Your temptations artificial or unreal because You were perfect, then we do not understand them. The first was the simple and strong temptation of seeking comfort after forty days of severe fasting. You had denied Yourself food and drink to what is nearly the utmost of human endurance. We ought not be surprised at Your strength, both of soul and of Your human body. Hardened by years of labor, of frugal living, of the heavy exercise demanded by Your occupation, You were in the truest sense a man, not "a reed shaken by the wind," or a king "clothed in soft garments." You were no softer than John the Baptist, whose manliness You praised. Nevertheless, the strongest of men will have an overwhelming hunger, an overpowering ache for comfort after forty days of prayer and no food and cold nights on a mountainside. How easy it would have been to work a miracle to satisfy Your hunger! And could anyone have said it was wrong? But You refused to display Your power, even to Your greatest enemy, Satan.

The second temptation was that of presumption: to glory in Your strength, to boast of being the Son of God by throwing Yourself headlong from the dome of the temple and landing unhurt. Would not all the people cry, "Look, there is a man with the strength of God!" Would not all the people know that this is the Son of God? And how cunning Satan was! He asked You to do this in fulfillment of a prophecy in Psalm 90: "He has given His angels charge over thee, and they shall bear thee up, lest thou dash thy foot against a stone." This was a temptation to human pride, to glory in Your strength, to display the qualities that You alone enjoyed. As true man, this was a real temptation to You.

When You completely refused this, there was a third and greater temptation. It was the temptation of fear, in part: it was the temptation to give up the hard life You had chosen, a life of suffering, poverty, humiliation, men's ingratitude, pain and death—to give this up to become powerful, to show the world *now* that You were the King of glory. This, too, was a real and severe temptation. If it were not, You would not have been human. Alas, the vast majority of men do not resist the temptation of power when it is offered them. Perhaps yet fewer overcome the temptation of fear.

It was also a temptation to conquer the world in the spirit of the world, that is, to accept "the kingdoms of the world, and their

glory," to master the world with weapons that the world understood. You had a choice now, at the beginning of Your public
life: to take the pain and sorrow, or to take the devil's bargain and
live a comfortable, important earthly life, wielding the power that
You truly had. In fact, You could have done this without giving in in
the least to Satan—at least, we must confess that if anyone can at
any time do so, You certainly could have done it. But to teach us
caution against the insidious temptations of the world, even in
innocent matters, You chose the most difficult.

Earthly power and the easy life! How willingly we fall into
these traps, lose our love of Christ, lose our concern for our neighbor, lose our true purpose in life.

These three efforts of the devil represent the greatest earthly
desires of man: his comfort, pride in his exalted position, a desire for
worldly goods and power. Christ overcame them all.

To conquer His own comfort, He chose hard labor and troubles
of every kind. To conquer pride, He chose the simplest life in a
nation that on the whole did not appreciate Him. To conquer all
desire for worldly goods, He chose to live like a vagabond, satisfied
to live on the kindness of His loyal friends, content to have for
Himself not so much as a stone to lay His head on—no property, no
palace, no endowments, no business but His Father's business . . .
to save the world from the world, to save us from ourselves!

Psalm 69

IT ALL DEPENDS . . .

*Deign, O God, to set me free. . . . / Thou seest me helpless and
destitute; / my God, help me. / Thou art my champion and my
deliverer.*

"IT ALL DEPENDS on your point of view," says the corner politician, who feels himself losing an argument. "It all depends on your way of counting," says the embarrassed businessman who fears being undersold. "It all depends on your definition," says the exasperated philosopher, who cannot come to terms with his antagonist. It all depends. . . .

How true their statement, with a truth deeper than any of them suspect. Not only an argument, but life itself and death and life after death depend on your point of view, your way of counting, your definition.

"My God, help me. . . ." A substitute for ingenuity, a selfish plea for superior strength, a coward's whine for mercy—that is one view of the psalmist's cry. "What humiliation, what abasement, what lack of self-confidence in religion and prayer"—that is one point of view. "Believe in yourself, trust in your own abilities, follow your instincts, fear no one, stand up for your rights, have faith in yourself"—there is a popular point of view!

Rather, it *was* a popular view—a generation ago. Somehow in the nuclear age it got lost. Somehow the great materialists' code of courage shrank to an atom; self-confidence went underground at the sight of a mushroom cloud. Men were suddenly faced with an unparalleled fear of one another, and the former philosophers of courage fell on their knees and begged for negotiations. "Bargain, barter, or beg, however fruitless," became their motto. Freedom, the great trumpet of agnostic humanists, was silenced beneath a heap of broken promises, hopeless corruption and mistrust, and a new slavery and savagery.

Shall men ever be free, really free? A question worth asking. Can it be answered? "It all depends on your point of view." The psalmist knew the only answer, thousands of years ago. "Deign, O God, to set me free." He does not "believe in himself," for he is wise by experience. He has suffered, he has enemies who plot against him, who rejoice at his misfortunes, who abuse him with every insult. It will not do to "believe in himself."

What, then? Can a man still be free when his enemies deny him

freedom? Can a man still conquer when he is beaten to the ground?
Is there still a champion to befriend him when all on earth have
forgotten him? In our age, when we hear of the population explo-
sion, the machine and mass production, the proletariat and mass
movements, the government and the almighty party, more than we
hear of the individual soul—what freedom is assured us?

Did the psalmist really cower and cringe? Far from it! He
triumphed in unquenchable courage because he was assured of his
"champion and deliverer." Did he tremble at the loss of his freedom? He rejoiced, he said, that God would set him free.

"It is all in your point of view." The psalmist's is the one point
of view large enough to save all. Self-confidence alone is inadequate;
we constantly find ourselves too small for the problems that face
us. Human freedom alone is too small; we are constantly chained
by our countless limitations, contantly stepping on each other's
freedom. We need a humility which can regain our pride, and a
wholesome fear that can regain our courage.

The nuclear age has much to teach us, Lord: we are lost, unless we turn to something great outside ourselves, in which we find
absolute trust, absolute control and absolute freedom—unthreatened,
unchanging, undying. The psalmist, fortunately, found it long before our time.

Psalm 70

THE SIGN OF CONTRADICTION

Men stare at me now as a strange portent, / so signal the protec-
tion thou hast given me. / And evermore praise was on my lips, /
my constant theme thy glory. . . . / A mark thou seest me for en-
vious eyes and tongues; / they conspire together, and whisper, God

*has abandoned him; / now is the time to overtake and seize him; /
no one can bring him rescue now.*

THE PSALMIST, as a figure of Christ, is like Him a prophetic "sign
of contradiction." For when the Redeemer comes, even His chosen
people, His very own, will "stare at him as a strange portent," and
will literally "conspire together, and whisper, God has abandoned
him; now is the time to overtake and seize him." We consider the
overwhelming power and beauty of Christ's personality, His pure
generosity to the poor, the sick, the sinner; we consider the brilliance
and power of His teaching, the endless stream of miracles, the ir-
reproachable holiness of His life. And we are puzzled.

You asked Your enemies one day on the steps of the temple,
"Which of you can convict me of sin?" Not the worst of Your
enemies could answer You, Lord. None could accuse You. Why,
then, had You become a "sign of contradiction," why had You become a public enemy? How was it possible for those who publicly
professed to be awaiting Your redemption to reject You when redemption came?

We are shocked at their blindness, their ignorance, their apparent
ill will.

If so, we are simply shocked at our own defects. How often we
treat You as a "sign of contradiction," Lord! How often Your
teachings are cast aside! How often we have refused You, con-
spired against You! Simeon's prophecy is fulfilled in us. We always
want the finest, the biggest, the most: the finest house, the biggest
car, the most of praise and importance. You took the least for Yourself: the poorest home, the least of worldly goods, choosing to live
in a town of no importance, living by an occupation that required
hard work but promised no importance, no pleasure, no wealth, no
praise, no admiration.

What Your Father required, that You did, at the cost of Your
security, Your comfort, Your life. But for Yourself You took
nothing. With a singleness of purpose, with a purity and simplicity
that not the greatest of prophets had equalled, You brought a re-

demption men had not expected! Yet, as we look back, and as we look about us, we can truly ask, "What else would have brought redemption? What other redemption did we need?"

You are far too good for us, Son of Man; You did too perfectly what we hope for and are never able to accomplish. You will always be the "sign of contradiction." And for that very reason, You will always be the sign of hope and redemption, the one true sign of final salvation.

Psalm 71

THE FORWARD LOOK

Ageless as sun or moon he shall endure; | kindly as the rain that drops on the meadow grass, | as the showers that water the earth. | Justice in his days shall thrive, and the blessings of peace; | and may those days last till the moon shines no more. | From sea to sea, from the great river to the ends of the earth, | his sway shall reach. . . . | He will give the poor redress when they cry to him, | destitute folk, with none to befriend them; | in their need and helplessness, they shall have his compassion.

THIS GREAT SONG of longing for truth and justice, called "A Psalm of Solomon," expresses man's highest ideals. People of all ages and nations, evil as they can be, have always desired this perfection, this fulfillment of their greatest aspirations. In an earthly sense, little progress has been made toward that goal over the centuries. One could not be proved wrong if he said that the accomplishment of this end is farther away now than ever, that, if anything, the hope has deteriorated.

All these centuries of failure should have taught us one thing, however: we must look for this fulfillment in a spiritual sense. We have here on earth no lasting home, and we are wrong to insist on a heaven on earth.

But the prophecy has been fulfilled; Christ Jesus "shall endure," and we are sure that "justice in his days shall thrive, and the blessings of peace," and the poorest, the most unjustly treated, the most helpless shall indeed "have his compassion." Christ has not failed to bring all our hopes to reality; it is we who fail. We do not view our lives as we should; we think of life merely in terms of a few years on earth. It is like thinking of health only in terms of curing sickness; it is like thinking of an education only in terms of registration day; it is like thinking of an opera only in terms of the first measures of the overture, or like thinking of a baseball game only in terms of the warm-up. This life is really not life; it is the preparation for life. Until we understand that, we have got the universe wrong, we have got human nature wrong, we have not the slightest notion of God's plan.

See and admire a strong and hearty man, ninety-five years of age, if you please, and you are right in saying he has not even reached infancy in the life God has planned for him. So long a life we have ahead of us; so little we plan for it!

Why do we Christians know so little about the resurrection of our bodies, the eternal life for which body and soul are destined? This is the event for which we were created, and to which, according to St. Paul, all creation looks forward. Books ought to be compiled, containing all the beautiful literature of the Church on the resurrection, and all Catholics should read it, and live by it, meditating on it every day! Exaggeration? A simple case of logic.

A little boy once told me in catechism class, "Father, I don't want to go to heaven."

"Why not?"

"I don't know anybody up there," he answered.

Must this tragic ignorance persist? Are we to remain so ignorant of the real, the everlasting life to which God created us?

Psalm 72

AM I IN THE WAY?

What bounty God shows, what divine bounty, / to the upright, to the pure of heart! / Yet I was near losing my foothold, / felt the ground sinking under my steps, / such heart-burning had I at seeing the good fortune of sinners that defy his law. . . . / Why, then, thought I, it is to no purpose that I have kept my heart true, / and washed my hands clean in pureness of living; / still, all the while, I am plagued for it, / and no morning comes but my scourging is renewed. . . . / Yet ever thou art at my side, ever holdest me by my right hand. . . . / What else does heaven hold for me, but thyself? / What charm for me has earth, here at thy side? / What though flesh of mine, heart of mine, should waste away? / Still God will be my heart's stronghold, eternally my inheritance.

THE ONLY REAL SOURCE of unhappiness is our constant foolishness in placing obstacles between ourselves and God. As soon as we desire to possess things for ourselves, instead of desiring to give ourselves to God, anxiety is born and the assurance of happiness flees.

The famous conductor, Arturo Toscanini, had a phenomenal knowledge of the musical score of his orchestra, down to the finest details. One day at a rehearsal, as the orchestra reached the climax of an overture, Toscanini suddenly shouted, "Stop!" And when they stopped, he asked, "What was that noise?"

There was a puzzled silence, until the first violinist solved the riddle. "Sorry, Maestro," he said, "that noise was yourself, humming."

"Oh, yes," answered Toscanini, enlightened. "So it was, so it was."

He had gotten between himself and his orchestra, and the strange sound disturbed him. Strange sounds disturb us, too, when we get between ourselves and God. And when the obstacles appear, whom do we blame? Do we blame the friend who has not done our will because God, after all, has given him a will of his own? Do we blame our companions who within the natural limits of their human knowledge have not anticipated our every whim and taste? Or, worst of all, do we blame You, Lord, for desiring to enlarge our puny souls by spoiling our little plans, so that we can rise out of ourselves to something greater?

Lord, we know that Your plan for the personal life of each of us is a beautiful, harmonious symphony, if we perform it according to Your Will. But as soon as we get in the way of Your wisdom, and want to do things our own way, indeed we'll hear strange noises. Then if, like Toscanini, we stop to ask, "What was that noise? What's wrong here?" will You not answer, Lord, "Sorry, child, that noise was yourself, getting in the way, and spoiling a beautiful harmony. Your pride has caused this confusion. You are making your own unhappiness. Why not try loving others genuinely, without intruding yourself so much? Why not try appreciating the mystery and the beauty of the divine plan, without making a mess by trying to improve upon it?"

How different my life would be, if I could follow this sound advice in practice. Then I would never be "near losing my foothold," as the psalmist says, because of my impatience "at seeing the good fortune of sinners that defy God's law." I might understand in some measure that God's patience, as well as His wisdom, is infinite; that God's mercy, as well as His justice, is infinite. And what if I do become impatient, and try to intrude myself into God's plan? Shall that change His plan? Shall that diminish His wisdom? Shall that bring me any success? "What though flesh of mine, heart of mine, should waste away?" asks the psalmist. "Still God will be my heart's stronghold, eternally my inheritance." There is nothing else worth the asking.

Psalm 73

TROWEL AND SPEAR

See what havoc thy enemies have wrought in the holy place. . . . /
Blow after blow, like woodmen in the forest, they have plied their
axes, / brought it down, with pick and mallet, to the ground. . . . /
O God, shall our enemy taunt us everlastingly, / shall blasphemy
still defy thy name? . . . / Must the dove be the vulture's prey? /
Souls unbefriended, but for thee, wilt thou leave us quite forgotten?

AFTER YEARS of captivity in Babylon, when the Hebrews under
Nehemias attempted to rebuild Jerusalem, they soon found themselves attacked by enemies on all sides. Arab, Ammonite, and
Philistine alike took up arms to throw the project into confusion
and failure. This seemed the final blow to God's people, who were
tired enough of carrying materials over ground choked with rubble,
trying to rebuild walls charred and crumbled. They came complaining to Nehemias, and asked, "What should we do? Fight or build?"
If they ceased building, they went unprotected. If they did not fight,
they would be destroyed.

Nehemias answered, "There is only one way: we must both fight
and build. We must have a trowel in one hand, and a spear in the
other." And thus the wall was at last rebuilt. "The warriors among
us were divided into two companies," he wrote, "one of these remained at work, while behind them, under the clan chiefs of Juda,
the rest stood arrayed for battle. . . . And even while they were at
work . . . it was one hand to work with, and one closing still on a
javelin; nor was there a workman but must build with his sword
girt at his side" (II Esdras 4:16–18).

This, too, is the way of prayer. It has two jobs to do; it must fight and it must build. It must fight off the world and its false standards; it must build the love of God and the true happiness it brings.

"See what havoc thy enemies have wrought in the holy place," says the psalmist. See, Lord, how Your enemies, the false and failing allurements of this life, have left Your holy place in ruins. My soul was once a holy place. You cleansed it and sanctified it and adorned it by baptism, renewed it by confession; You made it sacred by Your presence in Holy Communion. Then the armies of this world rushed in—pride, envy, greed, sloth, pleasure-seeking, selfishness in a vast array of armor and weapons—and "blow after blow, like woodmen in the forest, they have plied their axes, brought it down."

But You have not left me without aid. You have taught me how to pray; You have shown me that it is a strong weapon: "Watch and pray, that you may not enter into temptation." If my prayer is sincere and humble, it is like trowel and spear. It builds up my soul, high enough to catch a glimpse of Your glory; it fights off my enemies, so that at last the fear, the anxiety, the confusion of this world is calmed; and there comes a silence in which I can hear Your voice.

Psalm 74

OF NOBLE BLOOD

When the time is ripe, I will judge strictly; / earth rocks to its fall, and all that dwell on it; / I alone support its fabric. / Rebel no more, I cry to the rebels, / Abate your pride, to the transgressors; / would they match themselves against the most High, / hurl defiance against God? / Look east, look west, it will avail you nothing; / no help comes from the desert, or the high hills; / it is God who rules all, humbling one man and exalting another.

TIME WAS—in the days of kings, queens, dukes, duchesses, counts and countesses—that one had to be "of noble blood" to count for something. One was nothing, unless there was a discernible strain of nobility in his family.

In our own time—a thing in itself fortunate—not much fuss is made about a man's "noble" lineage. This, we say, is very democratic and very correct. Basically this is true, for it leaves room for true greatness; but we must guard against the other extreme: that of forgetting how much nobility God has put in man. We might forget family lineage, but we cannot forget the sacred nobility that man has inherited from God without grave danger to our freedom, and indeed to our salvation.

"Behold what manner of love the Father has bestowed upon us, that we should be called children of God; and such we are," St. John writes (I John 3:1). It is tragic that so much of our modern world, in revolting against the false nobility of family ancestry, wealth, and connections, has revolted against the true nobility and dignity that every man, woman, and child has received directly from God. When men lose sight of their true nobility, they are soon less than men.

St. Paul in his famous epistle on charity assures us that we are nothing unless we have the love of God and of neighbor in us. It is the Church's insistence on this inner nobility of man that makes her truly democratic. The Church, in the spirit of Christ, her head, requires us to love every human being as God loves him, because he is noble, made to the image of God; and because he becomes increasingly noble and valuable and lovable as the love of God and neighbor grows in him. This is true democracy, where the smallest child can be the greatest in nobility; where a little child praying the Our Father with love in his heart is much greater than a dictator who holds the fate of half the world's population in his murderous hand, but whose mind knows no God, and whose heart is empty.

Lord, give light to our darkened minds, so that we can see the true image of man as You have created him. Let us strip the world of its false standards, not to find other—and perhaps worse—standards of materialism, but to see beyond this world into the true, noble, eternal dignity of our human nature. "It is God who rules all, humbling one man and exalting another." The man of false nobility, of earthly domain, shall be humbled; the man who has found his true self, his true and lasting worth, shall be exalted.

Psalm 75

NOTHING TO LIVE FOR?

Loud rings in heaven the doom thou utterest; / earth trembles and is silent when God rouses himself to execute his sentence, / giving redress to those who are scorned on earth. . . . / To the Lord your God let vows be made and paid; bring gifts from every side to God, the terrible; / he it is that cows the hearts of princes, / feared among all the kings of the earth.

EVERY DELIBERATE ACTION of man prepares him for judgment, leads him to judgment. But there is nothing fearful in this, unless the action itself is fearful. Judgment is necessarily bound up with every free choice: there is a judgment before we act, there is judgment that follows it, that measures its wisdom or folly, that measures its value, its importance, its consequences.

Christ, in His whole life and teaching, showed us how to judge wisely. He showed us how hard it was for those who acted only for material aggrandizement to attain happiness. If they acted for material goals, judgment was already pronounced; their happiness would depend only on material fortunes; their happiness was therefore always in danger, and was at best to end with death. A judgment after death for such people could not be other than terrible; they had not prepared for anything beyond death, and so they came before God stripped bare. They had lived for this world, and this world had nothing more to offer them. Could they blame God, then, could they object that God was "a terrible judge" when He told them, "Depart from this place; you are not prepared to enter here; you did not direct yourself to this goal, your final end is elsewhere."

There is only one real tragedy in death: that at the last moment we find ourselves with nowhere to go. To find at the hour of death that everything for which we were striving, everything for which we prepared, everything which cost us so much effort, all at which we became skilled and experienced—all this is to end forever, this is the greatest of tragedies.

That is why You said, Jesus, "How hard it is for those who hope in riches to be saved." If we have put our trust in the things of this world, we shall be bitterly betrayed.

Here is the eternal paradox, which grows out of a justice and a balance that God has put into all created things: if we live only for the goods of this world, we will cherish them anxiously and feverishly, afraid that they will be consumed. And at the end of life we will suddenly become aware of the awful truth that they have consumed *us!* We were so careful to preserve our riches, alas! We have not consumed our riches, but they have eaten out our souls! What a shocking revelation, to find we have made a monstrous error in judgment. "Loud rings in heaven the doom . . . earth trembles and is silent."

How often we had been warned! "To the Lord your God let vows be made and paid," says the prophetic psalm. All else will end in bitter failure. Nothing to live for? Nothing, until we have stripped away the false hopes that make creatures turn traitor on us. It is He who gave us life; it is He who knows what there is to live for! "I am the resurrection and the life."

Psalm 76

AMID THE DARKNESS

To the Lord I look when distress comes upon me; | in his presence I lift up my hands amid the darkness, never wearied; | grief like mine there is no comforting. . . . | I reflect upon days long past, the immemorial years possess my mind; | deep musings occupy my thoughts at midnight, | never will my mind be at rest. | Can it be that God will always leave us forsaken, | will never show us again his old kindness?

AMONG THE SAINTS of the Old and New Testaments we find much evidence of mental suffering, of great distress for which they could find no consolation. This leaves us puzzled, for we know these saints were men and women of most excellent character, of noblest motives, of most heroic unselfishness, of strongest faith. Where, then, could they find cause for such deep grief? Surely there was all joy and consolation in God; they had not sought it elsewhere. And surely they were not victims of self-pity, these men and women of boundless charity. Did they not agree with St. Paul that "for those who love God, all things work together unto their good"?

Yet we cannot dispute the fact of mental anguish in those closest to God. We need only turn to Christ in the garden of Gethsemane, to see in Him the most appalling of mental sufferings.

The cause of their torment of soul is one and the same as the cause of their joy: it is love. If the charity of Christ and of all the saints caused them the greatest happiness, it also brought them the greatest grief.

And if the saints loved their neighbor with a total dedication, they were eager to see this love take its effect. They were filled with a complete and selfless longing to see God's love in the hearts of all.

And what effect did their work have on the majority? Painfully little. This, if we understand the charity of the saints, was their greatest suffering: seeing their good work apparently coming to ruin. The early Christian martyrs suffered more at seeing their weaker brethren fall away, than at their own pains. They grieved more at seeing fellow-Christians dragged into sin by the pagans, than at seeing themselves dragged to death in the arena. Thus the excessive wish of St. Paul that he might be "anathema" to Christ in order to save the Jews.

This, too, is the greatest sorrow of priests, nuns, catechists, lay apostles in the captive nations—to see the apparent ruin of their labors. They have given the best of their life for their friends, to make them holy, to save their souls; then to see the powers of evil overrun their good work, this is hardest of all. They are men of great faith; to see the innocent massacred would be far less pain than the fear that they will lose their innocence under pressure and threat.

Their only answer is to trust in the infinite wisdom and mercy of God. God, they know, has not been defeated, and there is no danger that He ever will be. Nevertheless, as far as they can see, many are lost. And here on earth we must judge by what we see, and the tragic destruction of the good that might have been is no cause for rejoicing. Any true Christian suffers from this, and feels the desolation of the saints, who had labored so much for these souls, had spent their energy, had prayed to God with tears. Good results there had been, yes, heroic souls in whom the faith is firmly grounded. But what of the many others? "The blood of the martyrs is the seed of the Church," a fact quite beyond denial. But the blood of the martyrs is accompanied by numerous defections, lost opportunities, appalling scandals, frightening corruption, and great general harm to the Church and to souls outside the Church. This, too, is a fact quite beyond dispute. If every heroic act of the martyrs brought down blessings, did not every vicious act committed against the Church also increase the world's evil?

It is well to appreciate the great sanctity of many, to see that God does indeed dwell in men by His overflowing grace, and to see that He does bring much good out of evil. We cannot, on the other hand, help seeing that evil. The presence of so many evils, so many dangers to souls, cannot but bring grief and suffering to the soul of a true Christian. For this grief there is, in a sense, "no comforting," except in an ever-greater and more heroic gift of ourselves, in an ever-rising crescendo of prayer, a lifting up of hands "amid the darkness, never wearied." Against such evils human help is vain. The mystery is penetrated only by God; it is only to Him we can turn.

Psalm 77

A LESSON NOT LEARNED

Do not turn a deaf ear to the words I utter; / I speak to you with mysteries for my theme, / read the riddles of long ago.

THE PSALMIST, like all the prophets, had an urgent story to tell, with a lesson that had to be learned. Was he young and optimistic? Did he expect men to listen, to follow the obvious course the lesson taught them? Was he old and cynical? Did he know that men would hear but not listen, or would learn the lesson briefly and would do nothing to act upon it? Or was he wise and mellowed—whether young or old—with a kind of divine patience that told him his story would mostly not be taken to heart, but that he must continue to tell it? Was he wise and mellowed with the endless patience and mercy of God?

In any case, the lesson he taught was this: neither man nor society nor nation can scorn God and escape the consequence. The tragic story of the Hebrew people is a miniature of the tragic failure of the world, the failure of man, from political bungles of the highest level down to the smallest personal blunders of the individual.

"He gave Jacob a rule to live by, framed for Israel a law," the psalmist explains. "They were to put their trust in God, ever remembering his divine dealings with them, ever loyal to his commands; they were not to be like their fathers, a stubborn and defiant breed, a generation of false aims, of a spirit that broke faith with God."

The Hebrews could not plead ignorance, they could not put the blame on a "confusion of policies and purposes." Their goal and the means to it were clear enough: "Follow the law of God and you cannot go wrong."

God had warned them often enough that as soon as they abandoned Him, He would abandon them, as if by mutual agreement. Men were left freedom of action; but action always brings consequence. Action always leads somewhere; if it leads away from God, then we must learn what it is to live without God. To impress His people with the seriousness of their duties, God in Scripture often used the terms "anger" and "vengeance" and "punishment." Not that God could ever in a human sense give way to anger or vengeance. Natural consequence alone was fully strong enough to teach man the folly of disobeying God. Those consequences which the Hebrews called "punishment" were as much the loving providence of God as the consequences they called "reward." Ever patiently and gently, through good and evil, through prosperity and trials, God was teaching them. What the psalmist observed was that the Hebrew race, like all the race of fallen man, were extremely thick-headed students.

We are taken through all the history of God's people, all the wonders He performed for them, when He led them out of Egypt into the plain of Tanis, through the days of the Judges, to the days of Israel's foolish insistence on a king and a kingdom, in imitation of their pagan neighbors. Many wonders He worked for His people to save them, the nation from which the Redeemer would spring.

"Yet, with all this," the psalmist laments, "they continued to

offend him; all his wonderful deeds left them faithless still. . . .
When he threatened them with death, they would search after him,
feel their need of God once more; they would remind themselves
that it was God who had protected them, his almighty power that
had delivered them. But still they were lying lips, they were false
tongues that spoke to him; their hearts were not true to him, no
loyalty bound them to his covenant. Yet, such is his mercy, he would
still pardon their faults, and spare them from destruction."

We have here the best summary of history ever written. What is
the history of man, of nations or of any individual person, if it is
not this described by the psalmist? Is it not the endlessly repeated
story of God's mercy and man's ingratitude, followed by new mercy
and renewed daring and sinfulness on man's part, followed by another shower of God's mercy and yet greater defiance from man—
and so on without respite?

Psalm 78

THE PRICE OF BLOOD

*Shall the heathen ask, What has become of their God? | Shall our
eyes never witness thy vengeance upon the Gentiles, | that open
vengeance thou wilt take for thy servants' blood? | Could but the
groaning of the captive reach thy presence! | Thy arm has not lost
its strength; | from our bonds deliver us, a race doomed to die.*

MY GOD, who can blot out the appalling blood stains of this earth
of ours? The injustices of our generation, the cruelty of Communist
persecutions, the degradation of human dignity, the destruction of
human freedom—who can tell what great sanctity, what overwhelming reparation can purge the earth of its guilt?

For how many centuries has a cheap price been set on human

blood! By how many criminals—criminals of high position and power—has the blood of the innocent been spilled unregarded! Had You not warned Your chosen people that upon them would come "all the just blood that has been shed on the earth, from the blood of Abel the just unto the blood of Zacharias. . . . Amen I say to you, all these things will come upon this generation." And then, Lord, the most fearful condemnation of all: "Brood of vipers, how are you to escape the judgment of hell?" (Matt. 23:36, 33).

What sanctity can undo all this evil and cruelty, these crimes against what is most precious on the earth—innocence, truth, devotion, love of God? At the sight of these horrors, the temptation to despair is great. Yet it is only a temptation. God has in no way been overcome, nor has His grace departed from the earth. In the infinite mysteries of His loving Providence, this innocent blood is priceless.

Was not the Divine Blood sold at a cheap, ignominious price? The crime of all crimes—to set a price on the Blood of God! In this terrible act, had not the earth sold itself to the cruelest of crimes for all centuries to come?

Yet in its most frightful act of murder, the earth was redeemed. In God's incomprehensible mercy, we were washed and purged in the blood of our own guilt! Such is the infinite height and depth of God's forgiveness. The very crimes are atoned for by the innocent blood they shed! In this unspeakable patience and generosity of God and His Saints, the earth is saved from destruction. "Forgive them, for they know not what they do." Had they known, they would have been struck dead by the horror of it. Not that they are without guilt, but that there is a blindness in crime, a blindness in all of us, which makes us forget the awful significance of every act of selfishness, every sin we commit. Only the saints understood; when their eyes were opened, is it any wonder they wept?

Psalm 79

THE PURITY OF JOSEPH

Give audience, thou that art the guide of Israel, / that leadest Joseph with a shepherd's care. / Thou who art enthroned above the Cherubim, / reveal thyself to Ephraim, Benjamin, and Manasses; / exert thy sovereign strength, and come to our aid.

THE HEBREWS, as they called upon God, must have realized what wisdom there was in reminding Him of their ancestor Joseph, and his brother and his sons. For of all their great ancestors, Joseph was probably the most pleasing to God. Joseph was the most manly, the most virtuous, the most lovable of Jacob's sons. He is indeed the worthy patron of that great Joseph, the foster-father of Jesus, the model of chastity and obedience. As soon as we meet him in the Book of Genesis, we are aware that he is a boy of great innocence, simplicity and purity. His honesty and chastity become the more outstanding as we see how he preserved them perfectly all his life, and that despite the bad examples of his brothers, and the temptations into which he was led.

We are told some of the crimes of his brothers, for which their father Jacob cursed them even on his deathbed. We are also told that as a young boy Joseph had reported some of these deeds to his father, that he might correct his sons. For this his brothers hated him and plotted to kill him. Ruben, the one sensible older brother, tried to save Joseph's life, and persuaded the others to throw him into a pit rather than be guilty of his blood. It was Ruben's intention to rescue Joseph after the others had gone. But while Ruben was absent the others dragged Joseph up out of the well and sold him for twenty pieces of silver to slave-traders who took him off to

Egypt. These brothers, not having the honesty of Joseph, lied to their father, telling him that the boy had been killed by a wild beast.

In Egypt the virtues of Joseph continue to flourish. No word of complaint against his murderous brothers, no thought of revenge. Sold as a mere boy of sixteen into a strange country, to people whose language he could not understand, he was yet so attractive in goodness that Putiphar, the captain of the Egyptian army, bought Joseph to have him as his personal servant.

These strangers and pagans soon recognized the virtues of Joseph. We are told in Genesis that the captain "saw clearly enough how God was with Joseph, giving him success in all he turned his hand to. Thus Joseph became his master's favorite servant and had the management of all his affairs and of all the property that was entrusted to him. For Joseph's sake, God blessed the household of this Egyptian."

Meanwhile most of Joseph's brothers continued their sins and crimes in the distant land of Chanaan. And now Joseph's time of temptation came. He had already suffered exile for his innocence, but he would be tested yet more severely. When God prepares a man for great things, He purifies him through fire, like gold tried in the furnace, an image used by psalmists and prophets. What is important about Joseph's trial is not simply that he withstood the temptress, Putiphar's wife—which he might conceivably have done through mere disgust at her brazen approach—but that he knew clearly the reason why, that he showed perfect integrity, incorruptible simplicity of purpose. Genesis leaves us no guesses about Joseph's character:

"Joseph had beauty of form and face, and after a while his mistress cast longing eyes at him, and bade him share her bed. But he would have nothing to do with such wickedness. 'My master,' he said, 'entrusts everything to my care, and keeps no count of his belongings; there is nothing of his but I, by his appointment, have the keeping of it, save thee only, his wedded wife. How canst thou ask me to wrong him so grievously, and offend my God?' Such was the talk between them day after day, she ever more importunate. A day came at last when Joseph must needs be within doors, busy with some task when no one else was by; and she caught him by the hem of his garment, inviting him to her bed. Whereupon he went out, leaving his cloak still in her hand."

The outcome is easy to guess: the spurned woman vowed revenge, and upon the return of her husband, she accused Joseph of every sin he had resisted. Putiphar, "too easily convinced," was enraged at Joseph, and had him thrown into prison. This was now a second monstrous injustice that Joseph suffered, but even so, he was never bitter against God. He was soon a favorite of the jailer, and a close friend of the other prisoners. His charity and patience were never diminished. God had not forgotten him; He simply gave him the opportunity to let men see his virtues. If all Scripture is written for our correction, as St. Paul observes, surely the life of Joseph has much to give us. God gave him the grace of prophesying the future of Egypt, of being released from prison and becoming at last the Pharaoh of Egypt. But he paid the price that all must pay for victory.

Now Joseph was in a position to take revenge on his cruel brothers. But it is clear that no such thought ever entered his mind. As they came to him begging for food—for the whole country of Chanaan was then starving in a famine—Joseph gave them all they desired, and returned their money. In tears he begged them to come back and bring with them Benjamin, his youngest brother.

It is easy enough to read the story of Joseph with interest; it has all the power of a thrilling novel. While it is indeed full of amazing insights into human nature at its worst and at its best, it is also the true history of a man who was in every way pleasing to God. God, in return, had led Joseph "with a shepherd's care." Scripture assures us repeatedly of God's great love for his faithful servant, Joseph. And like all God's friends, Joseph paid the price.

This law of price and reward can be observed in every phase of physical and spiritual life; it can be discovered in any corner of the world. Yet how few of us accept it and act on it! The world is heaped with failures, with people who would not work for happiness, who would not pay the price—and so, of course, they did not win the crown.

How many are there in the divorce courts, in the jails and in the mental institutions, who are there because they could not accept this law of life? How many more are suffering needless discouragement and despair, unhappiness and failures of many kinds, because they do not realize that all good things have their price—or because they are not quite willing to pay the price?

Psalm 80

"THIS WAY OUT"

Give heed, my people, to this warning of mine; | Israel, wouldst thou but listen! | . . . am not I the Lord thy God, I, who rescued thee from Egypt? | Open thy mouth wide, and thou shalt have thy fill. | So I spoke, but my people would not listen; | Israel went on unheeding, | till I was fain to give their hard hearts free play, | let them follow their own devices.

IT SEEMS that man as an inventor of excuses is no new institution. It seems that year after year, century after century, God's own people found excuses for ignoring Him, found excuses for neglecting the things that really count.

Some years ago an unknown wag posted this sign near several exits in the Boston Symphony Hall: "This way out, in case of Brahms."

We can reasonably doubt whether certain music lovers are as afraid of Brahms as certain Christians are of serious thought. And these are "good" Christians, those with some sense of justice and duty. Yet there is an effective sign posted on every exit of their interior soul: "This way out, in case of meditation." The very word frightens them. They rather expect to find meditation as difficult as the hieroglyphics of ancient Sumeria.

Are we afraid to try meditation for fear that our conscience will bother us forever after? Are we afraid we may discover in ourselves something that must be driven out before God can enter? Are we afraid of meditation because that is something we can do only in the darkest corner of a church? Are we afraid that serious thought is a kind of imprisonment?

To avoid serious thought, to postpone those hours of meditation, is like taking a trip without a single map, without so much as a glance at the highway signs. How can one live, you may wonder, without ever asking himself, "Why am I here? Where is my real happiness? How did I get here? Where am I going? Where should I be going? How do I know I am not deceiving myself? How can I find my way? If God created me, what is He like? What does He expect of me? What should I expect of myself? What do I owe to others? Does my happiness depend on them? Does theirs depend on me? How can I avoid failure?"

These are the "curiosities" we probe in meditation. They require hours of serious thought, but they do seem important enough to merit these hours.

Suppose I come out of meditation with that for which it is intended—with a deeper and fuller appreciation of Who God is, the beauty of His creation, the marvels of that creation which is my own immortal spirit, the thrilling promises He has to me and my fellow-men—is this dull, is this punishment, imprisonment? Suppose I come out of meditation prepared to live happier, full of a new freedom, truer to myself, a far greater blessing to those around me—is this something to find "a way out" of? Or if I come out of meditation convinced that there is something in my life I must change, if I wish to avoid ruin, unhappiness, emptiness of purpose? Can I afford to neglect such an opportunity?

Tomorrow a new sign will hang over the exits of my precious soul: "This way in, for serious thought."

Psalm 81

CLEANED IN THE WINTER

Will you never cease perverting justice, | espousing the cause of the wicked? | . . . But no, ignorant and unperceiving, they grope their way in darkness; | see how unstable are the props of earth! | Gods you are, I myself have declared it; | favored children, every one of you, of the most High; | yet the doom of mortals awaits you!

"How UNSTABLE are the props of earth!" Who has not experienced it? Who has not experienced pain in the greatest of earthly joys? Who has not rejoiced to hear an innocent child whisper in his ear? And who has not saddened at once to think of that same innocence marred by ignorance, led astray by evil forces? Or who has not, in experiencing the joy of maturity with its deeper perception of truth and its truer satisfaction in beauty, experienced at once the ebbing of his strength, the disappointment in his own limitations?

How brief is the period of a man's full physical and intellectual power—if indeed he ever enjoys it! Most of our lives are spent "ignorant and unperceiving"; we grope our way in darkness. While the body is strong, the spirit is green, unprepared, blind, shallow. When at last experience and sorrow, when failure and humiliation have awakened the spirit, the body has aged, its energy is faltering.

These things cannot be imagined; they must be felt in our very bones. We are spirit and flesh; we must know the truth in our spirit, but we must also feel it in our flesh.

Lord, we pray to You to spare us from pain and suffering; but when we do so, in a sense we pray against ourselves; we pray to our own harm. There is a depth of truth and appreciation which only

soul-cracking suffering can bring. We see it in the resurrection of a
country devastated by war—if its people have learned the lesson of
war, have felt the curse of evil, of pride and vanity; if they have
learned the lesson of peace, have felt the blessing of charity, sacrifice,
patience, humiliation. In the words of T. S. Eliot's Chorus:

"War among men defiles this world, but death in the Lord renews it,
And the world must be cleaned in the winter, or we shall have only
A sour spring, a parched summer, an empty harvest."

(Murder in the Cathedral)

Man himself must be cleaned in the winter: he must be cleaned
by seasons of darkness, days of deep suffering, or there will be no
resurrection.

This is to say what Christ said on Easter Sunday to two dejected
disciples: "O foolish and slow of heart. . . . Ought not Christ to
have suffered these things, and so enter into His glory?"

Psalm 82

FALSE FAITH

*Let their cheeks blush crimson with shame, Lord, | till they come
to sue for thy favor; | confusion and dismay be theirs for ever, | for
ever let them be abashed and brought to nothing, | till they, too,
know the meaning of the divine name, | acknowledge thee as the
most high God, the Overlord of earth.*

A STRANGE WAY of attracting men to God, you might say. Will
men come to know God's goodness and mercy through misery and
suffering? Will they reach Him through faith and love because He
has left them in the pit of abandonment and despair?

When St. Teresa of Avila complained to God out of her anguish, He answered her, "This is the way I treat all my friends."

Her answer, too, came of the wisdom in experience, "Yes, Lord, and that is why You have so few of them."

Few friends, because even those who try to be his friends have a mistaken notion of faith. They think faith is believing in God's goodness "because He gives me whatever I ask Him for." They say, "I have faith in St. Anthony, because whenever I lose something, I pray to him, and then I always find it."

One might have the same "faith" in a wash-machine, because it never fails to get the clothes clean. One might have the same "faith" in a furnace, because it has never yet broken down.

It has become common to say someone lost his faith because he was embittered by some personal tragedy. "God did not hear his prayers," so now he has shut himself off from God, he thinks. He may go as far as saying that "God is cruel" to him.

A mother lost her only child, a seven-year-old boy, and said, "It's so terrible to think of, I know I'm going to lose my faith." Why? Because God did not follow her scheme of life? We cannot deny that these people have a heavy cross to bear, but we can ask what kind of "faith" can be thus destroyed.

We have no faith if we do not accept God for what He is. We have no faith if we do not accept His wisdom as infinitely superior to our own. And thus every time God shocks us with His wisdom, every time we cannot understand why our most deserving efforts fail, or why the world seems to have turned against us, we should see all the clearer how far His wisdom is above ours.

To applaud, to praise God when He sends you a jolly good time may be gratitude; it is not proof of strong faith. It may be the same genuine faith that makes us see good as coming from God's hand, as well as hardships. But genuine faith is not weakened by trial. It is tested; it is found true, and strengthened; it has learned that when God's wisdom is hardest for man to understand, it may then be most clearly divine.

Psalm 83

NO OTHER HOME

For the courts of the Lord's house, my soul faints with longing. /
The living God! at his name my heart, my whole being thrills with
joy. / Where else shall the sparrow find a home, the swallow a nest
for her brood, / but at thy altar, Lord of hosts, my king and my
God?

No ONE can deny the statement of St. Paul that "we have here on
earth no lasting home." Science has tried to prolong man's life, and
has succeeded to some extent. Nevertheless, one does not daily meet
men who sincerely expect to live forever on this earth. If they did,
they would be most unpopular in these days of overpopulation fears.
But you do not consider a man an outcast for wishing to "live
happily ever after." Eternal happiness is not an unpopular idea. A
man is not enthusiastically applauded for saying, "After this life
there is no other."

Yet he is generally approved if he lives so attached to the things
of this world as to indicate he is not much aware of another life to
come. We are afraid to face the dismal suggestion that "perhaps
there is no other life." We are equally afraid, in practice, of acting
upon St. Paul's meaning—"Our home is heavenly, eternal." We are
afraid, because for such a home we must be prepared, worthy,
cleansed, chastised, purged of all filth. We are afraid, because we
know that the supreme moments of earthly happiness do not come
unprepared. They come at a great price; they have been earned.

We know that preparation for such a home must be painful. It
will necessarily tear us away from our earthly home; it will forbid
us to be satisfied with things temporary; it will allow us no rest in

the resting places of this world. We know that it will cost us more than words to earn this lasting home; it will take painful experience. We need no one to tell us this; we can read it ourselves in the histories of men and nations.

It is a frightening picture: our true purpose in life is great beyond our own comprehension. David uttered the true sentiments of every man when he said to God, "Such wisdom as thine is far beyond my reach, no thought of mine can attain it." He gave words to every man's fear when he added, "Where can I go, then, to take refuge from thy spirit, to hide from thy view?" (Psalm 138:6–7).

But every man that is true to himself knows that he must not shrink away from his lasting home out of fear or ignorance. He must know the way, and he must pay the price. No great thing is ever without its price. People boast about knowing "the facts of life," but they seem never to have heard this, the most important fact of life. There is no victory if nothing is overcome. The world is heaped with failures, men and women who would not work for happiness, who made no plans for eternity, who in consequence (we fear) have not won the crown. History's pages are filled with kings, emperors, poets, generals, artists who could have won everlasting fame and true glory, had they but kept their eyes on their lasting home, had they but heeded less the comforts of this passing home.

When at last their eyes were opened, how many of them echoed the cry of Wolsey, "O Cromwell, Cromwell, had I but served my God half as well as my king, He would not have left me naked to mine enemies." It is a tragic echo to the joyous cry of the psalmist: "Willingly would I give a thousand of my days for one spent in thy courts! Willingly reach but the threshold of my God's house, so I might dwell no more in the abode of sinners" (Psalm 83:11).

Psalm 84

PEACE WITH JUSTICE

What blessings, Lord, thou hast granted to this land of thine, / restoring Jacob's fortunes, pardoning thy people's guilt, / burying away the record of their sins, / all thy anger calmed, thy fierce displeasure forgotten!

HERE is a man with a heart full of gratitude for the blessing Christ comes to give us: He fulfills the prophecy of the great Redeemer (thus "restoring Jacob's fortunes"), He pardons our guilt, washing it away, drowning it in baptism, "burying away the record of our sins."

The psalmist is a realist, however. He fears for men; he fears that we will go on angering God by making all too little use of the redemption. Knowing what dangers lurk in the heart of man, he asks God, "Must thy resentment smoulder on, age after age? Wilt thou never relent, O God, and give fresh life, to rejoice the spirits of thy people? Show us thy mercy, Lord; grant us thy deliverance!"

Then, as though seeing from afar the arrival of God the deliverer, he already knows what God's answer will be. "Let me listen, now, to the voice of the Lord God; it is a message of peace he sends to his people; to his loyal servants, that come back, now, with all their heart to him. For us, his worshippers, deliverance is close at hand; in this land of ours, the divine glory is to find a home. See, where mercy and faithfulness meet in one; how justice and peace are united in one embrace! Faithfulness grows up out of the earth, and from heaven, redress looks down. The Lord, now, will grant us his blessing, to make our land yield its harvest; justice will go on before him, deliverance follow where his feet tread."

"It is a message of peace he sends," but only to those "that come back, now, with all their heart to him." And how gently he invites us! By the marvel of all marvels, God has taken our human form, has become one of us, so as to raise us up, so as to make us more like Himself: "in this land of ours, the divine glory is to find a home."

What would our world not gain by understanding this statement of the psalmist: "Justice and peace are united in one embrace!" You cannot separate them; you cannot have peace without justice, and that is precisely why we have no real peace. Only the justice of God, the justice that "will go on before him," when men are ready to accept His law and His will, only this can bring us any peace. It is because the world has not sought God or His justice, that unhappiness, fear, and misery have spread.

That same justice of God is needed to bring peace to each of us, too, as individuals. If our everyday life is not one of interior peace, it is because we are not seeking the justice of God: His justice in dealing with our neighbor; His justice in always putting God's law first; His justice in that we are His creatures and owe Him our attention and our loving service; that we do not love others truly if we do not love them in God. Too much of our love is not "mercy and faithfulness," or "justice and peace," but a kind of glorified selfishness. True love must give, not grab.

"Seek first the kingdom of God and His justice," You told us, "and all the rest shall be added to you." Those who seek God and His justice are at peace with all men. They are the peace-makers, those You called "the sons of God" in the beatitude.

But if we do not seek God, we will have neither justice nor peace; "the rest" will be taken away from us, too. We will have less and less to live for, until at last our little world collapses. It had no foundation; it was a house built on sand.

Psalm 85

NO ANSWER?

Who is so kind and forgiving, Lord, as thou art, / who so rich in mercy to all who invoke him? / . . . There is none like thee, Lord, among the gods; / none can do as thou doest . . . so great thou art, / so marvellous in thy doings, thou who alone art God.

THE PSALMIST'S PRAISE of God's mercy to all who call on him has been echoed through the centuries, by millions of saints, by millions of the faithful. They recall, Lord, Your promise that anything asked in Your Name would be given: "Ask and you shall receive."

But there is another echo, another sound heard through the centuries: the cry of suffering, injustice, and despair. Cries, soft and loud, weaker and stronger, piteous and vehement, of prayers unanswered, of men complaining that God has abandoned them. The Church herself has prayed for unity, for peace and justice, for freedom that men might serve God according to their consciences. What, then, has happened to the kindness and mercy of the Lord, His goodness to those who invoke Him?

The answer lies in God's infinite wisdom and man's incredible weakness and ignorance. The psalmist in reply to his own question observed that God's wisdom is too sublime for us. We Christians, with the full benefit of Christ's revelations concerning life and eternity, and with the full benefit of Christ's example, can behold some of the mystery unveiled. We can see, at least, how often people think their prayers unanswered because they have asked for the wrong things, have made the wrong things important, have prayed for their own destruction; they are, in Christ's words, "a scandal" to Him, because they "mind not the things of heaven, but of earth."

Three years You spent, Lord, trying to teach Your disciples to look at life in the light of eternity, and then how miserably they failed You!

A story is told of a young man who was one of Rossini's music students. It seems that some time after the death of Beethoven, this eager student came to Rossini with a large pack of papers, his own musical composition. "Sir," he announced, "I have written a funeral march to commemorate the death of Beethoven. I believe it has great promise. Could you inspect it for me?"

Rossini agreed, and the student eagerly awaited word on his new masterpiece. When word was slow in coming, he went to Rossini's house and asked for the maestro's verdict. Rossini seemed reserved at first, so the student begged, "Tell me your honest opinion, sir, every word of it. What thoughts went through your mind as you read the score?"

Once assured that the student wanted a true evaluation, Rossini said with a smile, "You were anxious to produce a masterpiece. And I couldn't dispel this thought from my mind as I made my way through the manuscript, 'How much greater a masterpiece we should have had, if you had died, and Beethoven had written the funeral march.' There is no reaching such a master."

And that is the answer to our complaints that God does not do our will. "There is no reaching such a master." How much better if He writes the score, and we play it! For then our lives, and the answers to our prayers, will be masterpieces!

Psalm 86

CITY OF GOD

How high a boast, city of God, is made for thee, | Mine it is to reckon the folk of Egypt, of Babylon, too, among my citizens! |

Philistines, Tyrians, Ethiopians, all must claim Sion as their birth-place; | None was ever born, the proverb shall run, | that did not take his birth from her; | it was the most High, none other, that founded her.

LIKE IT OR NOT, every creature is destined for the city of God, and takes his origin from it. If, abusing the freedom that God has given us, we become His enemies, we nevertheless owe our existence to Him, and are, worthy or unworthy, citizens of the city of God.

In a stricter sense, we are only His citizens when we share His life, when we carry Him about within ourselves. Then we are incorporated into the heavenly city, destined for eternal fulfillment. Then we have risen above this earthly, corruptible city of the flesh.

It was this comparison of Scripture which inspired St. Augustine's great work. "The city of God we speak of," he writes, "is the same to which testimony is borne by that Scripture which excels all the writings of all nations by its divine authority, and has brought under its influence all kinds of minds, and this not by a casual intellectual movement, but obviously by an express providential arrangement. For there it is written, 'Glorious things are spoken of thee, O city of God. . . .' And in another psalm we read, . . . 'There is a river the streams whereof shall make glad the city of our God, the holy place of the tabernacles of the Most High. God is in the midst of her, she shall not be moved'" (*The City of God,* Book XI).

The City of God on this earth, the heavenly city among men is the one, holy, Catholic, apostolic Church. She is the hope of mankind, the fountain of grace and joy, the spiritual and intellectual mother who, in the famous words of William Gladstone, "has marched for 1900 years at the head of civilization, and has harnessed to her chariot the chief intellectual and material forces of the world. Her art, the art of the world; her genius, the genius of the world; her greatness, her glory, grandeur and majesty have been almost all that in this respect the world has to boast of."

In this day of the secularist's pleasure-search and the Marxist's promises of a paradise on earth, we shall learn again that the City of

God is the one true city for man, not only in heaven, but on earth. "Seek ye first the kingdom of God and His justice, and all these things shall be given you besides," said Jesus. "All these things" are man's earthly needs, not merely a distant joy beyond the grave.

No matter how I view it, Lord, Your Church, Your nation on earth holds, alone and indisputably, the key to happiness. Our heaven is to begin on earth if it is to begin at all. On this St. Augustine insisted when he undertook the Church's "defence against those who prefer their own gods to the Founder of this city." This fortress of the Most High, he says, is "surpassingly glorious, whether we view it as it still lives by faith in this fleeting course of time, and sojourns as a stranger in the midst of the ungodly, or as it shall dwell in the fixed stability of its eternal seat, which it now with patience waits for, expecting until 'righteousness shall return unto judgment,' and it obtain, by virtue of its excellence, final victory and perfect peace" (*The City of God,* Book I).

Psalm 87

TWO LIVES

My life sinks ever closer to the grave; | I count as one of those who go down into the abyss, like one powerless. | As well lie among the dead, men laid low in the grave, | men thou rememberest no longer, cast away, now, from thy protecting hand. . . . | I lie in a prison whence there is no escape, my eyes grow dim with tears. | On thee I call, to thee stretch out my hands, each day that passes. | Not for the dead thy wonderful power is shown; | not for pale shadows to return and give thee thanks.

FROM THE MOMENT we are born, our life begins to shorten. We are always on the way to death. Faced with this clear necessity, our nature objects and rebels; it feels thwarted, for life tends to preserve itself. Even the first act of a new-born child seems a rebellion, for the child begins life with wailing. With this outcry at the beginning, life is on its way to the end.

Life itself is not a democratic institution; we cannot choose the length of our own. God makes the choices concerning life's beginning and end, reminding us at those important moments that we were made to do His Will, not our own. It was His Will that caused us to receive life; it is His Will that keeps this frail creation in existence.

Beyond that, it is true, He gives us freedom. Just what fabric we will make of our life is in our own hands; but the end is like the beginning: we are back in the hands of God—and this, indeed, is the real beginning.

The curtain, at last, is really open, and our second life dawns, the true life we could not find on earth. For even if the eager materialists, after centuries of scientific progress, could convince their fellowmen that they were to live to the age of ninety-five, what would those few years be, compared with the second life? The earth would yet ring from east to west with cries of despair, if men thought they were created for the first life alone.

We were saved from this cry, and from much of the psalmist's gloom, by the advent of Christ. And curiously, He was the one man who came into this world to die, not to live. Against even the good men of this world—His disciples and friends—he kept insisting that dying was His purpose in life.

Christ is the glorification of death. His death was the birth of real life. In the Preface of Easter, the Church rejoices with Him "who by dying has brought our death to naught, and by rising again has restored us to life."

In Christ, St. Augustine could say with joy that although a man begins to die the moment he is born, he also begins to live the moment he dies.

In Christ the saintly René Bazin could say, "Death does not exist, even for a moment—all we have is two lives."

We can agree with the psalmist, Lord, that it is "not for pale shadows to return and give thee thanks." For we know in Christ that God's "wonderful power" is "not shown for the dead," but for the living, those who have gained the second life.

Psalm 88

THE PARADOX OF HAPPINESS

Happy is the people that knows well the shout of praise, / that lives, Lord, in the smile of thy protection! / Evermore they take pride in thy name, / rejoice over thy just dealings. / What else but thy glory inspires their strength? / What else but thy favor bids us lift our heads?

THESE BOASTFUL WORDS of the Hebrew writer are coupled (in the same psalm) with long descriptions of the sufferings the same people have endured "in the smile of God's protection." Whatever the psalmist's uncertainties may have been regarding God's rescue of his people, however dim his vision may have been those long years before the coming of Christ, we Christians should know and feel deeply in ourselves this paradox. Our only real strength is in seeing our weakness, but seeing it lifted up in God's glory. Our only boast is bowing our heads in shame, but seeing them lifted up by His favor.

Every true Christian feels deeply the joy and the pain of this paradox; it is in a real sense the greatest blessing of his life. He would not have life without suffering—it was the school of Christ; it is the school of Christians. Still less would the Christian want life without Christ; and Christ is a living sacrifice.

Yet how many who call themselves Christians have hardly passed a day in this school of Christ. Their lives at home, in school, in business, in pleasure are far from the truths He revealed so clearly. When they are young, a "good time" is their goal, they spend themselves, their abilities and energies in a whirl of activities in search of "fun." As they grow older, their goal and chief desire is "money," their heaviest worry is "money." Surveys and advertisements keep reminding them that having the latest in comfort, gadgetry, and smart-looking baubles is their aim.

Typical of the "better" and "more serious" among our youth was the industrious young man who, unlike many of his frivolous classmates, was working hard to win a scholarship and college.

"What do you intend to become?" I asked him.

"I want to go into law school and become a lawyer and make good money," he said, proud of having reached a decision about his life, a serious decision.

"What then?" I pursued.

"Why, then," he assured me, "I can buy a fine big house for my family, and eventually retire."

I was pleased to see him looking so far ahead, so I continued, "What then?"

"Then I'll do all the things I didn't have time for when I was at my job—hobbies—"

"And then?"

"Then?" He was amused. "Some day I suppose I'll get old and die."

"And then?" I continued.

"It's funny," he replied thoughtfully. "Nobody has ever asked me that!"

Are we Americans, so eager for success, blind to that one great paradox in which is concealed all genuine success? "He who loses his life shall find it."

Psalm 89

BROKEN ARCS

For us thy timely mercies, for us abiding happiness and content; / happiness that shall atone for the time when thou didst afflict us, / for the long years of ill fortune. / Let these eyes see thy purpose accomplished.

THE ANCIENT HEBREW looked hopefully to two lives on earth, the second a reward for the sufferings borne in the first. The second was "happiness that shall atone . . . for the long years of ill fortune." This was his prayer, this was his consolation, his interpretation of God's purpose. Though his vision was earthly, though he did not have a clear idea of man's immortality and the resurrection, his concept was correct. Suffering and misfortune are, in God's purpose, a "first life" to prepare us for a second. The first life, which we know as our earthly years in this world, is a school.

We learn to desire and enjoy Heaven by being without it for a time. We appreciate heat when we come inside after being out in the cold. We value light after being left in the darkness. A summer of drought has taught us to appreciate rain.

Yes, even our mistakes have taught us the value of being right, of having a just conscience.

When we begin our second, eternal life, the injustices of this world have taught us the perfect justice of Heaven. The quick passing of our earthly days has brought us to love the endless joy of God.

Only in this way is life worthwhile. There is no real despair, no real regret, when we see the direction of the first life toward the second.

Our many love songs express this hope and this direction. "Forever and ever," we sing. "Never leave me, say you'll always be mine," we croon, and not in vain.

All on earth that left us dissatisfied, aching, hoping, begging—all this, writes Robert Browning, shall be corrected:

There shall never be one lost good! What was, shall live as before;
The evil is null, is naught, is silence implying sound;
What was good shall be good, with, for evil, so much good more;
On the earth the broken arcs; in the heaven a perfect round.

All we have willed or hoped or dreamed of good shall exist;
Not its semblance, but itself; no beauty, nor good, nor power
Whose voice has gone forth, but each survives for the melodist
When eternity affirms the conception of an hour.
The high that proved too high, the heroic for earth too hard,
The passion that left the ground to lose itself in the sky,
Are music sent up to God by the lover and the bard.
Enough that he heard it once; we shall hear it by and by.

And what is our failure here but a triumph's evidence
For the fullness of the days? Have we withered or agonized?
Why else was the pause prolonged but that singing might issue thence?
Why rushed the discords in, but that harmony should be prized?

(Abt Vogler, ll. 69–80)

Psalm 90

I CANNOT RISE

*Content if thou be to live with the most High for thy defence, /
under his Almighty shadow abiding still, / him thy refuge, him thy*

stronghold thou mayst call, / thy own God, in whom is all thy trust. / He it is will rescue thee from every treacherous lure, every destroying plague.

WE SPEAK of our times as "critical, perilous, more complicated" than those of the past; and we suspect that such expressions have been used many centuries before us. Since Adam's fall mankind has always faced frightful errors, destruction and madness. These spectres have become the material of life's adventures. They are blessings, too, intended to drive us to shelter and safety, to the "rescue" and "stronghold" of which the psalmist writes.

So deep, so penetrating is the tragedy of those who do not find this "stronghold" when they need it, that it puzzles and overwhelms "saner" people, people whose problems are smaller at the moment.

The tragedy of an empty life is too large for most of us to understand. Ordinarily we manage to survive with small, selfish aims, with enough success and satisfaction to compensate for our failures. Many even survive on the pleasure they derive from complaining, scolding, and criticising. But if we are confronted by the very goal of life itself, if a very great sacrifice is suddenly thrust upon us—are we prepared for it, Lord?

How often we hear of those who are not! We read, for example, of a high school student who committed suicide. His popularity rating was excellent: president of his class, winner of honors and awards, captain of the football team, idol of the girls—what more could a high school boy want?

What more could he want! God forgive our blindness. In desperation he took his life. It was not the aftermath of a quarrel, not the mad backwash of a painful humiliation, no particular setback or defeat, no death in the family or among friends that might have accounted for depressing grief. At first there was no explanation at all. But there was no existing report on the state of his soul. No one was able to say whether he could break away from himself and his little world.

No one, that is, but himself. He left the usual suicide note, the brief, much-repeated cliché: "I no longer have anything to live for. I cannot rise out of my despair."

Not all the health in the world, the talents, the popularity, the money, the friends—none of them were worth living for. The young man was right—except that he stopped too soon. "I cannot rise—" Was he right in this, too? There was no true happiness in the goods he possessed. Was there no rising above them?

"I cannot rise—" Even this, his last desperate cry, was true and genuine. I myself cannot rise—but God can raise me up, as surely as He has raised up all His saints who gave up this world.

Lord, if I live for a world above and beyond material goods, yes, above and beyond myself and my plans, I shall not be defeated by the deepest danger of despair.

Psalm 91

NO IMAGINATION

How magnificent is thy creation, Lord, / how unfathomable are thy purposes! / And still, too dull to learn, too slow to grasp his lesson, / the wrong-doer goes on in his busy wickedness. / Still he thrives, makes a brave show like the grass in spring, / yet is he doomed to perish eternally. . . .

IF WE HAVE SEEN an untouched landscape—hills, rivers, trees and flowers—and then a devastated battlefield, we have seen the contrast between the beauty of God's creation and the ugliness of man's sin, man's work against God's. But the destruction of what was once beautiful is nowhere more appalling than in the ruin of a human soul.

We may well wonder how the world has survived the infections with which man has polluted it, the depravities, the lies, the betrayals, the injustices! "Behold how the innocent are murdered, and no man stops to consider," said the ancient prophet. How many millions of times had he to repeat that cry through the centuries, in every nation, on every continent. The prophets themselves, the chosen people, men, women, children of greatest holiness and charity, the most beautiful of God's creatures were most often victims marked for slaughter, victims to teach and prepare fallen man for his crime of crimes—the rejection of Innocence itself, the murder of the Son of Man. How magnificent was this creation, He the head of humanity, the "first-born of every creature." Their crime was a horror to make the very stars scream, to turn back the sun, to darken the earth, a horror to stop all crime forever.

But "still, too dull to learn, too slow to grasp his lesson, the wrong-doer goes on in his busy wickedness." An ever-greater army of bloodied martyrs marches behind the Son of Man, its ranks swollen year by year, its number legion in our own century.

"Must then a Christ perish in torment in every age to save those that have no imagination?" asks the spirit of Cauchon in Shaw's *Joan of Arc.*

Indeed, thousands of Christs have perished in every age, and millions in our own age, "and still, too dull to learn, too slow to grasp his lesson, the wrong-doer goes on in his busy wickedness. Still he thrives, makes a brave show like the grass in spring; yet is he doomed to perish eternally."

Psalm 92

THE WONDERS OF WATER

Loud the rivers echo, Lord, / loud the rivers echo, crashing down in flood. / Magnificent the roar of eddying waters; / magnificent the sea's rage; / magnificent above these, the Lord reigns in

*heaven. | How faithful, Lord, are thy promises! | Holy is thy
house, and must needs be holy until the end of time.*

HOLY SCRIPTURE, and specifically the Book of Psalms, makes
countless references to the marvels of the beauty and power and
pleasure of water. And often, as in this psalm, water is seen as the
symbol of God's beauty and holiness. Its use in both Old and New
Testaments for spiritual purification is not hard to understand.

The Church often refers to the mysterious purposes of God in
creating water, and does so at great length in her baptismal service
on Holy Saturday. That part of the Easter liturgy begins with the
very first book of Moses, Genesis:

"Darkness covered the abyss, and the spirit of God was stirring
above the waters." And again, after separating the light from darkness, God said, "Let the waters abound with life."

In the second prophetic lesson we hear that water has not only a
life-giving power and bears living creatures in it, but it has an
awesome destructive power:

"Then the Lord told Moses, 'Stretch out your hand over the
sea, that the water may flow back upon the Egyptians, upon their
chariots and their charioteers'. . . . When Israel saw the Egyptians
lying dead on the seashore and beheld the great power that the Lord
had shown against the Egyptians, they feared the Lord and believed in Him and in His servant Moses."

Awed by God's wonders with the waters of the Red Sea, the
Church then prays, "For that which the power of Your right hand
did for one People, in freeing them from Egyptian bondage, You
accomplish now for the salvation of all men by the waters of re-
birth."

Finally, one of the finest examples of liturgical beauty, poetic
power and imagery, of prayerful love and perception is the Preface
during which the Baptismal Water and the Easter Holy Water are
blessed. The priest sings of the magnificence of God's creation of
water, of its spiritual meaning, and of the sanctifying powers God
has given water in His plan for our purification and re-birth:

"O God, even at the beginning of the world, Your Spirit stirred the water that it might conceive the power of hallowing. Through water, O God, You washed away the crimes of a guilty world, and You prefigure the means of regeneration in the torrent of the flood: for the selfsame substance worked mysteriously both the death of vice and a new beginning of virtue. . . .

"May this, Your creature, Lord, be holy and faultless, free from every assault of the enemy, and cleansed by the casting out of all things evil. May it be a living fountain, a water that regenerates, a purifying stream: that all who are washed by this saving bath will through the working of the Holy Spirit within them receive the grace of perfect pardon.

"Therefore, O creature water, I bless you by the living God, by the true God, by the holy God, by that God whose Word in the beginning separated you from the dry land, and whose Spirit stirred you.

"He made you flow forth from paradise, commanding you to water all the earth with your four rivers. In the desert He changed your bitterness into a sweet draught, and brought you from the rock to quench His people's thirst.

"I bless you likewise through Jesus Christ His only Son, our Lord, who for a wondrous sign changed you in Cana of Galilee by His almighty power into wine. He walked upon you dry-shod and was baptized in you by John in the Jordan. He brought you forth with blood from His side, and commanded His disciples that they baptize in you all believers, saying: "Go, teach all nations, baptizing them in the Name of the Father, and of the Son, and of the Holy Spirit."

"While we are now fulfilling this command, O almighty God, mercifully be present to us; graciously send Your breath.

"Bless this clear water with Your breath, O Lord, that not only will it cleanse men's bodies by its usual power, but may also cleanse men's souls."

Then in the solemn, thrice-repeated blessing, the Church asks the Holy Spirit to come down to the font, and give the water His power to regenerate men with the life of grace.

"Here may every stain of sin be washed away; here may that nature created to Your image and remade to its Maker's honor be cleansed from all its former squalor. May every man who enters this sacrament of regeneration be born again in a new childhood of true innocence."

Psalm 93

JUST FOR THE RECORD

And they think, The Lord will never see it, / the God of Israel pays no heed. / Pay heed, rather, yourselves, dull hearts that count among my people; / fools, learn your lesson ere it is too late. / Is he deaf, the God who implanted hearing in us; / is he blind, the God who gave us eyes to see? / He who gives nations their schooling, who taught man all that man knows, / will he not call you to account?

HAVE YOU EVER watched people prepare to make a permanent disc recording? Especially if the disc is to be commercialized, to "make sales," it must be perfect. All possible flaws must be prevented; strange noises must be shut out, instruments must be perfectly tuned, singers and speakers must be in excellent form and well prepared—because people will hear it, and judge!

Because people will judge! Poor, human, faltering, deficient judges, burdened with errors enough of their own! So much fuss, so much care and concern, because people will judge.

Then what of the discs we are cutting daily for God? God, the all-knowing, the all-perfect, the all-seeing judge—has He not recorded every word, every thought of ours? When He comes to judge us, will He not play it all back for us then? Will not every word and action be recorded by Him, ready for all to hear? Will we not hear all the secrets uttered in dark corners, will we not hear the true story concealed by every lie? Are we, Lord, like the "dull hearts" and "fools" to whom the psalmist speaks? "Is he deaf, the God who implanted hearing in us?" he asks. "Is he blind, the God who gave us eyes to see?"

It is in the hidden crevices of his mind, in the secret corners of his heart that a man is defiled. God sees the true man, not the "front-man," not the pretense, and that is why Christ ridiculed the hypocrites, and warned His followers against them. "Beware of the leaven of the Pharisees, which is hypocrisy," He said. "There is nothing concealed that will not be disclosed, and nothing hidden that will not be made known. For what you have said in darkness will be said in the light; and what you have whispered in the inner chambers will be preached on the housetops" (Luke 12:2).

"Just for the record," we say, when we want a pleasant truth known about ourselves. "Just for the record," we may add, is true of everything we say or think or do. "The record" has a way of finding the public ear, even when we are most anxious to conceal it. "All things are seen," wrote St. Augustine, "and seen by those the culprit least suspects." But just to make sure no one would imagine that a single act of man goes unrecorded, the Saint concluded, "But supposing that the crime remains hidden from the sight of men, what can he do to conceal it from the all-seeing eye of God, from whom nothing is hidden?" (*Rule,* 3, 20).

Psalm 94

WHAT IS WRONG?

Your fathers put me to the test, challenged me, / as if they lacked proof of my power, for forty years together; / from that generation I turned away in loathing; / These, I said, are ever wayward hearts, / these have never learned to obey me. / And I took an oath in anger, / They shall never attain my rest.

IT HAS BECOME TRITE to accuse modern novels and short stories of too much preoccupation with sin. This is "realism," we are informed, "facing modern problems." Authors seem like contestants in a race to shock readers with the evils men can do, with the horrible dangers to which men are exposed, with the blood-stirring traps into which betrayers lead their victims.

There is danger here, Lord, that we will thus become "lovers of darkness rather than light." Our television, our movies, and our cheap novels will lead us blindly into a false delight in wickedness. The evils dramatized before our weakened imaginations will cause us to think "we're not so bad after all," simply because we avoid the grislier crimes.

Is it, Lord, because we have forgotten what the perfect man is that we descend to a kind of pseudo-condemnation of the very imperfect man? Are we satisfied to think, "the worst evils should not be tolerated, crime should not be encouraged"? If so, we shall never have the strength to pursue the real goal: "I must know what the perfect man is, I must live in his presence, I must make him walk at my side, I must labor without rest to reach the ideal of the perfect man."

Little good it does me to shake my head piously at the lies people tell, the political games they play; to join the indignant outcry against public scandals, to grow increasingly cynical about my neighbor's motives—while seeking always my own "best interests."

God indeed condemned the "ever wayward hearts" of His people, but not without having given them a clear statement of the ideal they were to attain. He had instructed them thoroughly on justice and mercy, on true worship and reverence, on hospitality and charity. He had told these people often enough that through them He wished to bless all the nations of the earth, that from them salvation would come, from them the Savior of mankind would arise.

And when He came, what had happened to the ideal of the sacred writings? Had the thundering prophecies of Moses, Isaias, Jeremias been heeded? Did Israel at last serve its God, was it prepared for its redemption?

But there is no need for us to bemoan the rejection of Christ by the very people to whom He had been given, by the very nation which was to hold this divine ideal before the world.

There is no need, because on us has fallen this responsibility. To all appearances, we have failed. We cry out against abuses, but what is corrected? We say it is high time for a reform, for a return to solid Christian principles, but time passes and the opportunity passes. What is really wrong, that we are not able to correct what we say is wrong?

"What is wrong," writes Chesterton, "is that we do not ask what is right." The very clear ideal of Christ is not at all clear in our minds.

Psalm 95

A SONG FOR CHRISTMAS

Sing to the Lord, and bless his name; | never cease to bear record of his power to save. | Publish his glory among the heathen; | his wonderful acts for all the world to hear. | How great is the Lord, how worthy of honor! | What other god is to be feared as he? | They are but fancied gods the heathen call divine; | the Lord, not they, made the heavens.

THIS PSALM, used by the Church in celebrating the feast of Christmas (in the Divine Office and the Offertory of Midnight Mass), is like the Christmas song of the angels, the *Gloria*. For it reveals the true spirit of Christmas, Christ's true purpose in coming. He comes to give glory to *God,* the true God, not any fancied gods: not to human power, to armies, to slaughter, to intrigue; not to the false glitter of empire, royalty, political machinery, or diplomatic maneuvers. He comes simply to glorify God, His Father, because God alone has the "power to save," He alone is "worthy of honor," He, and no one else, "made the heavens."

The psalm continues: "Tribes of the heathen, make your offering to the Lord, an offering to the Lord of glory and homage, an offering of glory to the Lord's name." Everyone, every human being— sage or silly, lovable or laughable, or that pleasing combination of all elements which people call "nice"—every man praises, blesses, "makes offering," brings "glory and homage" to some god. The question is, what is it that he adores? To what god does he sacrifice? Even if he claims to reverence nothing, to give glory to no one, he has given convincing proof that he adores himself.

The psalmist, however, adores in the Catholic way. He does not thank "science," he does not praise "nature" merely for itself. He finds these abstractions too dull, too lifeless, far too dissatisfying. He finds in the beauty of this world the adorable personality of its Maker and Master. He finds even more: he sees how the world has failed its Maker, how it has gone astray. But the Lord, most worthy of honor, brings back love even to "the tribes of the heathen." Here, indeed, he has foreseen the true spirit of Christmas; he has written us a Christmas song so full of Christian joy, of gratitude and love, that it has seldom been equalled.

"Before the Lord's presence let the whole earth bow in reverence," he sings. "Tell the heathen, The Lord is king now, he has put the world in order, never to be thrown into confusion more."

"He has put the world in order," by shocking us all in the manner of his coming. The world expected a dazzling spectacle, exterior pomp and might, because it forgot that true power lay in the love of God. "He has put the world in order," by despising externals, by emptying himself and becoming an infant, born like an outcast, working like a son of the poorest, living like a vagabond. For in such a life there was nothing to spoil the purity of His selfless love, of His total dedication to "setting the world in order."

He made Christmas an intimate, family feast, because He made Himself so small. We awaited the crash of cymbals and the blast of trumpets, the thunder of His armies and the cry of His judgment —and He surprised us. Messengers, angels, were sent to tell us, "You will not find Him in the palaces of kings, you will not find Him courting Caesar's favors, or in long conference with the dictators of this world; you will find Him wrapped in swaddling clothes, laid in a manger for animals, because there is no room for Him in the inn."

And if you ask, "Why has He chosen so wretched a place for His birth, so humble an occupation for His youth, so simple a life for His public career, so sorrowful and painful a way of redemption?" you will be answered in the Epistle of the Christmas Mass, that Christ came to teach us to "forego worldly appetites, and to live, in this present world, a life of order, of justice, of holiness. We were to look forward, blessed in our hope, to the day when there will be a new dawn of glory, the glory of the great God, the glory of our Saviour Jesus Christ; who gave himself for us, to ransom us from all our guilt."

There is the secret of His mysterious coming: "He gave himself for us." If in our ignorance, in our darkened intelligence we failed to distinguish what in this world is truly important, and what is small and mean and unprofitable and even dangerous and destructive, we have now no more excuse. We have the clear example of Jesus Christ, perfect man, Son of God; and He insisted that His example was to be our pattern of life.

You overturned the false standards of this world, Jesus, conquering the evils of pride with Your manly humility: "If I glorify myself, my glory is nothing," You said. "It is God who judges." You said it is not good fortune that gives a man value, but the good works that he does: "By their fruits you shall know them." You said it is not wealth, health, honor, or pleasure that gives a man value: "Blessed are they who suffer persecution for justice's sake for theirs is the kingdom of heaven."

Is it any wonder that the psalmist prophesies: "The Lord is king now, he has put the world in order, never to be thrown into confusion more!" In the new order of Christ, truth was restored.

Psalm 96

THE SPIRIT OF CHRISTMAS

In the flash of His lightning, how shines the world revealed, / how earth trembles at the sight! / The hills melt like wax at the presence of the Lord; / his presence, whom all the earth obeys. . . . / Shame upon the men that worship carved images, and make their

boast of false gods! / him only all the powers of heaven, prostrate,
adore.

SHAME TO US, Lord, who have made so many false gods of the
glorious feast of Your birth! The Roman martyrs, the persecuted
Christians of the catacombs, knew more of the true Christmas
spirit than our modern tinsel-hangers and gift-wrappers, who might
more honestly wish us a "Merry Merchandise" than a "Merry
Christmas."

It was not without meaning that these heroic Christians of Rome
inscribed their Christmas message in the catacombs, where it remains today for us to read: "He who would understand the spirit
of the Birthday of Christ the Lord, must give in the spirit of Christ
the Lord." He gave; gave everything, gave His very self. There is
the secret of happiness, the secret of freedom, the secret of Christmas. And unless we give back to him, we have no true Christmas,
no true freedom, no true happiness. He who does not give but only
takes, selfishly wrapped up in himself, must necessarily wither and
dry; he cannot grow by feeding on himself, for thus he becomes
smaller and smaller. God gave us this universe to grow in, to ex-
pand ourselves by giving to others. Only when we give ourselves
back to God, to our neighbor, only then is there room for happiness.
This was the conquest of the Christians in the catacombs: they
were feared and hated, but they gave love. They were unjustly persecuted, but they brought the gift of conversion and redemption.
They were happy, because they had found life; and so they grew, ex-
panded, and conquered the world, not by the sword but by the
tree of life, the Cross. They knew the joy of Christmas, because
they "gave in the spirit of Christ the Lord."

It is with this true Christian joy that the psalmist's heart overflows as he sings, "The Lord reigns as king; let earth be glad of
it. . . . Dawn of hope for the innocent, dawn of gladness for honest
hearts!" Christ's own people, arrogant and selfish, will reject Him.
But nature itself will proclaim Him: "The fields, and all the burden
they bear, full of expectancy; no tree in the forest but will rejoice

to greet its Lord's coming" (Psalm 95:12). We are reminded here of the tree from which its Lord would reign: the tree of the Cross. Even in that deep sorrow, the tree could rejoice because it had conquered the world; it was the tree of life and resurrection.

He comes, silently in the night, hidden in a cave, in weak human form, the infant Christ. "O wonderful exchange!" the Church exclaims. God becomes man that we might become gods. He joins our human family, that we might join His Divine Family. He takes the form of a slave, that we might be free men forever. "He comes to rule the earth," sings the psalmist, "brings the world justice, to every race of men its promised award," the award of redemption from sin and all its evils, the award of everlasting life in the Family of God.

What contrast between the joy of God and the joys of this world! "In the flash of His lightning, how shines the world revealed, how earth trembles at the sight!" Earth trembles at its own shame, earth trembles at its nothingness before the infinite beauty of God. Yet His coming, all the beauty of His humanity, all the perfection of His life was but a flash of lightning, a brief instant of revelation. Our vision of His glory is yet to come.

Psalm 97

BALANCE

In God's honor let all the earth keep holiday; | let all be mirth and rejoicing and festal melody! | Praise the Lord with the harp and psaltery's music; | with trumpets of metal, and the music of the braying horn! | Keep holiday in the presence of the Lord, our King; | the sea astir, and all that the sea holds, | the world astir, and all that dwell on it; | the rivers echoing their applause, | the hills, too, rejoicing to see the Lord come.

A GENUINE CHRISTIAN must strike a happy balance between joy and sorrow—or, one might say, between gaiety and seriousness. "Rejoice with the rejoicing, sorrow with the sorrowing," writes St. Paul. And You, Lord Jesus, kept a perfect balance between these apparently conflicting emotions. The Psalms, too, taken as a book, contain a remarkable balance between these opposing moods. And this, Psalm 97, is jubilant.

Too often Christians think the spiritual life is shrouded in an aura of sombre gloom. This seems quite far from the gay psalms that speak of "mirth" and "festal melody," of "keeping holiday" with "braying horn" and "echoing applause." In fact, one of the most important "virtues" of the friends of God is a genuine sense of humor. In his *Memoirs* Thomas Hood insists, "The sense of humor is the just balance of all the faculties of man, the best security against the pride of knowledge and the conceits of the imagination, the strongest inducement to submit with a wise and pious patience to the vicissitudes of human existence." In other words, pride is dispelled by a true sense of humor, and laughter opens the door to humility. Not, of course, a sneer, but a sincere, honest chuckle.

The ever-observant G. K. Chesterton explains that "laughing lays itself open to criticism, is innocent and unguarded, has the sort of humanity which has always something of humility. . . . Laughter has something in it in common with the ancient winds of faith and inspiration; it unfreezes pride and unwinds secrecy; it makes men forget themselves in the presence of something greater than themselves; something (as the common phrase goes about a joke) that they cannot resist."

It is interesting to note that the great authors who speak of humor so often praise it as the one great remedy against pride. Carlyle, Thackeray, Thomas Hood, and Chesterton are in agreement with St. Thomas Aquinas on this point. Humor is a deep and true remedy of soul. "In human affairs whatever is against reason is a sin," St. Thomas writes in his *Summa Theologica*. "Now it is against reason for a man to be burdensome to others, by offering no pleasure to others, and by hindering their enjoyment. . . . A man who is without mirth, not only is lacking in playful speech, but is also burdensome to others."

This release from serious employment is essential to our good mental and physical health, not to mention the spiritual health and remedy we have considered. "I pray thee, spare thyself at times," wrote St. Augustine some 1500 years ago, "for it becomes a wise man sometimes to relax the high pressure of his attention to work." Quoting and commenting on this advice, St. Thomas Aquinas remarks, "This relaxation of the mind from work consists in playful words or deeds."

For whether the mind or the muscles work, man's power is limited, and both become weary. In this recognition of my weakness is the seed of a great virtue, humility. The most necessary of virtues, in a sense, if I consider the catastrophes unleashed by pride. Catastrophes that have spanned history from the damnation of Lucifer and the fall of Adam and Eve to the tyrannies and slave-camps and betrayals of the twentieth century.

Lord, teach me to know my limits. Teach me to temper my very serious importance with some very un-serious laughter at my errors and my weakness. In fact, give me the patience and the understanding to "make merry" over them, for they will lead me to "keep holiday," by growing out of my self-love, "rejoicing to see the Lord come."

Psalm 98

THROUGH THE DOOR

Remember Moses and Aaron, and all those priests of his, | Samuel and those others who called on his name. . . . | And Thou, O

Lord our God, didst listen to them, / and they found thee a God of
pardon; / yet every fault of theirs thou wert quick to punish.

THROUGHOUT HISTORY, the priest has been man's mediator with
God. In every religion, in every nation, men have looked to the
priests for instruction in the ways of the spirit. Men, creatures who
can understand their own excellence and purpose, have always
searched for their Creator. If in the abuse of their freedom nations
and generations came to be called godless, their failures and frus-
trations yet led them back to their Maker.

They cried out to the door-keepers of heaven, who on earth
were their priests. The door must be opened, that they might re-
discover the author of their hopes, the fountain of a lost glory. If
the priests were not found wanting, the people recovered their
godliness.

The priests of God's chosen nation were particularly important.
Theirs was a triple dignity. They were not only called on by the
simple in the hope of some powerful blessing to deliver them from
evil; they were sought by the intellectuals for knowledge and direction; and they were looked to by men of true faith, God's
favorites, for spiritual guidance and holy example, for an interpretation of divine revelation.

The priest is the doorway; particularly so is the New Testament
priest of Christ. Our Lord Himself said, "I am the door; a man
will find salvation if he makes his way in through Me." Christ is
the High Priest, the world's one perfect priest. But every Catholic
priest has his office by reason of Christ's office. Like Christ, he is our
door to God.

Jesus, You insisted on developing this metaphor of the door.
"The shepherd comes in by the door," You said. Christ comes in by
the priest. "At his coming the door is opened and the sheep hear his
voice." At Mass, when You come down, the priest opens the flood-
gates of grace for us, and we hear Your voice.

There is no other way for us but the sacramental way for which
You established Your priesthood. Therefore You say, "The man

who climbs into the sheepfold by some other way, instead of entering by the door, comes to steal and plunder. Believe Me, it is I who am the door" (John 10).

However worn or scarred, however imperfect, a door is the way in. The priest knows he is the way to Christ, and if he is a real priest he expects to be slammed and kicked like a door. Despite its value, a door is seldom praised, hardly appreciated, roughly treated. For all that, it is a door, it is a vital need, and all must pass through it.

"Be ye lifted up, ye eternal doors, that the King of glory may enter." (Psalm 23).

Psalm 99

A GOOD SPORT

Let the whole earth keep holiday in God's honor; / pay to the Lord the homage of your rejoicing, / appear in his presence with glad hearts. / Learn that it is the Lord, no other, who is God; / his we are, he it was that made us.

How OFTEN I take myself too seriously, Lord. I could be content, at least, if not enthusiastic like the saints, if I truly understood "that it is the Lord, no other, who is God." Then, like the saints, I could afford to be laughed at by men because I am loved by God.

There is something to be said for "the good sport" in parlor or tavern who doesn't mind having a good trick played on him. "I ain't got no pride," he says, as he offers himself to the humorous drama. How fortunate he is, if the statement is true! If he can extend that fortunate spirit from innocent fun to serious duty, if human respect does not keep him from the humiliations demanded

ing God's love really means? Has he discovered no true spiritual joy in us? Have we taught God's love to ourselves? Not to say, have we failed to teach it to the next generation?

It is a warped mind, isn't it, that takes such meticulous care of a child's body, that fears the slightest infection, and smothers him with comforts—too much food, too much fine clothing, too many material rewards. Smothers him—rather, smothers his soul with neglect, crushes his true feelings of love, shuts him out from God's love.

"I don't feel I love God." Forgive us, Lord; we have been asleep. We have slept through our prayers, we have slept through the reading of Scripture, we have slept through the example of the saints, we have slept through the demands of charity. The emptiness of our lives has not awakened us, the boredom and frustration have not stirred us, the daily stroke of death around us has not sobered us, the terrors of materialism and enslavement have not aroused us.

Forgive us, Lord; we and our children have been asleep.

Your disciples were to be known by their love, Lord. Alas, You have come to us, too, to find us asleep. What? Can we not arise and watch one hour with You? Have we learned so little from the example of Your love?

Psalm 101

POWER CONTROL

Drained of strength, like grass the sun scorches, | I leave my food untasted, forgotten; | I am spent with sighing, till my skin clings to my bones. | I am no better than a pelican out in the desert, | an owl on some ruined dwelling; | I keep mournful watch, | lonely as a single sparrow on the house top. . . . | Ashes are all my food, | I drink nothing but what comes to me mingled with my tears; / I shrink before thy vengeful anger, / so low thou hast brought me, who didst once lift me so high.

"At the dam Watchman André Ferraud was worried. During the week steady rains had melted much snow from the peaks, swelled the Reyran River. On the dam marker, water had risen to a higher level than ever before recorded, close to the thin rim of the graceful concrete barrier. . . . At 9 P.M. he heard a sound to freeze the blood: sharp cracking noises. He screamed to his wife, 'Let's get out of here! The dam is breaking!' Desperately they scrambled toward higher ground. Behind them the graceful dam writhed in awesome slow motion and folded into the gorge. A wall of water toppled into the black night.

"The highway work camp vanished before its (thirty) occupants had time to form a notion of what was happening. No man among them survived to tell the tale. The water advanced at a speed of 50 mph at heights of over 100 feet in those places where hills narrowed its path. It was now a churning horror bearing off thousands of tons of earth, trees, boulders, parts of villas and farmhouses, automobiles and human beings" (*Life,* December 14, 1959).

Over three hundred people died there, as the force of high waters broke Malpasset Dam near Frejus, France. How many times in history have men stood horrified at the sight of power unleashed! Controlled by the dam, the huge mass of water was a blessing. Control lost, the water became such a raging destruction that one of the men who saw it come exclaimed, "It's the end of the world."

Nature is a great potential for good and evil, but not half so great as man. Through our free will, our intelligence, our mastery over beast and field, most of this power is in our hands. And countless greater tragedies have come from man's uncontrolled power, than from water or fire or earthquake.

Count the millions of innocent victims—the dead, the suffering, the enslaved—of our age's power-mad dictators. Count them, and shudder at the horror of abused power. God has given to men the power of thinking, of planning, of organizing, of ruling their

own destinies, of procreating their own children, of enriching their
earthly existence with knowledge and love and the production of
good things. But if man loses the mastery over these powers he
suffers—accordingly—deception, riot and bloody revolution, enslavement, sexual abuses and perversions, greed and thievery.

The strong man is master over all his powers. The weak man
is crushed by them. If I have no control over my powers, they
will have control over me. If I am not my own master, I am my
own slave.

Pride, impurity and greed are the enslavers of men. Pride is the
abuse of the sacred self-esteem God gave us when He said, "You
are gods, all of you, and sons of the most High." Impurity is the
abuse of the beautiful creative power God gave us when He said,
"Increase and multiply and fill the earth, and make it yours." And
greed is the abuse of the rights God gave us to the fruit of our
labors, the enjoyment of our arts and sciences, when He told us to
take command of all other creatures on earth.

What remains of man, when he has abused these powers, used
them carelessly or wickedly for the pleasures of the moment? No
more than what was left by the broken dam: a wasteland of mud,
debris, and death. Man in all his nobility is then "drained of
strength, like grass the sun scorches . . . , an owl on some ruined
dwelling . . . , lonely as a single sparrow on the house top."

With what meaning, then, he can say to his own abused power,
"so low thou hast brought me, who didst once lift me so high."

Psalm 102

RESTORED YOUTH

*Bless the Lord, my soul, / remembering all he has done for thee, /
how he pardons all thy sins, heals all thy mortal ills, / rescues thy*

life from deadly peril, / crowns thee with the blessings of his mercy; / how he contents all thy desire for good, / restores thy youth, as the eagle's plumage is restored. . . . / He will not always be finding fault, / his frown does not last forever. . . . / The Lord has a father's pity; / does he not know the stuff of which we are made, / can he forget that we are only dust?

"ALL THINGS," writes Ecclesiastes, "must be done by turns. . . . Now we take life, now we save it; now we are destroying, now building. Weep first, then laugh. . . . silence kept, and silence ended. . . . The stones we have scattered we must bring together anew" (Eccles. 3:3–7).

The psalmist perceives, with no little wisdom, that God tempers His dealings with us according to our weakness; He provides change for our changeable nature; He provides refreshment for our weakness. He "restores our youth, as the eagle's plumage is restored." He gives us seasons of hot weather and cold, days of sunshine and gloom and rain and storm, and He gives us similar psychological seasons.

"It is related of the Blessed John (Apostle)," wrote St. Thomas Aquinas, "that when some people were scandalized on finding him playing together with his disciples, he is said to have told one of them who carried a bow, to shoot an arrow. An when the latter had done this several times, he asked him whether he could do it indefinitely, and the man answered that if he continued doing it, the bow would break. Whence the Blessed John drew the inference that in like manner man's mind would break if its tension were never relaxed."

How many a patient has gone to a specialist to be given sound advice like that! Blessed is the man who is resigned to the seasons of the mind as God created them. If, like St. Paul, the modern apostle ought to be "all things to all men," that he might "gain all men," he must also learn to be all things to himself. The bow that will not bend when it ought to, must eventually break.

It is not difficult to show how a man must be serious in season.

No thinking man or woman is ignorant of the evils that come from not taking our responsibilities seriously. The effects of our spiritual sluggishness are indeed visible. From the greatest crimes to the smallest irksome faults, the wrongs of man are noticeable enough. In arguing about them, we might heartily disagree on causes and solutions, but we all see the evil, that evil which mushrooms around people who are not serious in season.

For most of us it is harder to see the evil of taking everything *too* seriously. We are not so quickly aware that taking ourselves, our importance and our opinions too seriously is evil, a very subtle form of pride. We remark at times that someone "worked himself to death" or "worried himself sick," without taking note of the underlying spiritual failure.

The spirit of man, like the body of man, needs relaxation: rest and renewal. The spirit needs joy: cheerful acceptance of Your Will, Lord. A true, confident, loving attachment to You is a constant refreshment.

"I am not resigned," the saintly Chantal used to say to her old friend. "Resignation is sad. How can one be resigned to the will of God? Does one resign oneself to being loved?" (Georges Bernanos, *Joy,* p. 104).

Psalm 103

LAUGH AND LIVE

From thy high dwelling-place thou dost send rain upon the hills; / thy hand gives earth all her plenty. / Grass must grow for the cattle; / for man, too, she must put forth her shoots, / if he is to bring corn out from her bosom; / if there is to be wine that will rejoice man's heart, / oil to make his face shine, / and bread that will keep man's strength from failing. / Moisture there must be for the forest trees, / for the cedars of Lebanon, trees of the Lord's own planting.

No ONE doubts the material needs of man. Considering the time and place of the psalm's composition, these requests of the author are quite literal. But God's meaning in any of the psalms, as we are assured by all Christian writers from Saints Peter and Paul through St. Augustine to Cardinal Newman, is much fuller than that. If the modern poet can give special brilliance to his art by carrying a meaning on two, three, or more levels at one time, we need not speculate, Lord, whether You might do so, or even whether You did so in fact. Wiser men than ourselves have stressed the metaphoric meanings of Holy Scripture.

What, then, is the food—the corn, wine, oil and bread—and the moisture which You rain on us in such abundance? The psalmist himself says You give them to "rejoice man's heart, . . . to make his face shine, . . . to keep man's strength from failing."

So much for the physical benefits. They are man's refreshment. What further refreshes the heart of man, according to us moderns, if not relief from tension, a break in our serious moods, relaxation from strenuous competition?

"You're too tense—learn to relax," the psychiatrist tells us. "Make use of your sense of humor."

Humor is the wine, the oil, the moisture that softens our fears, oils down the irritations, showers down our over-serious pride and ambition. Humor is like a refreshing spray, to drown worries and cares. Humor, more than the latest beverage, is the "pause that refreshes."

Look for *humor* in the large, library-sized Webster Dictionary, and you take note with a little surprise of the first definition: "Archaic: moisture or vapor." This is derived from the ancient notion of bodily humors, long outdated. Yet in a metaphorical sense (with a real meaning) this is a good definition. A true sense of humor is the moisture-maker of life; it keeps life from becoming hard and dry, from shriveling and dying.

Humor thus becomes the handmaid of humility, for it makes me aware of my limitations and of my foolishness and of my mediocrity. Humor, if rightly taken, will stir my dormant common sense and awaken me to true values. Humor is in many ways more sense than nonsense. Carlyle went so far as to say, "The man who cannot laugh is not only fit for treasons, stratagems, and spoils, but his whole life is already a treason and a stratagem." And the novelist Thackeray added that "people who do not know how to laugh are always pompous and self-conceited."

I have often laughed, Lord, at the strange phobias and superstitions and idolatries of my neighbors. But the truest sense of humor would bring me to a sound, hearty, and remedial laugh at my own phobias and idolatries, my own foolish sentimentalities and mediocrity.

After all, of God's many creatures on earth, only man has the privilege of criticizing his own weakness. It is a joy, for it will lead me to a very real knowledge of the perfection of God. This knowledge is the overtone of wisdom's laughter, not because I accept weakness as my goal, but because in it I discover my native desire for the strength of God, and my own fulfillment in that strength. It is You, my God, who are the "wine that will rejoice man's heart, oil to make his face shine, and bread that will keep man's strength from failing."

Psalms 104 and 105

OF MERCY AND INGRATITUDE

Ever they passed on from country to country, | the guests of king or people; | but he suffered none to harm them; | to kings themselves the warning came; | Lay no hands on them, never hurt

them, / servants anointed and true spokesmen of mine (Psalm
104).

*They believed, then, in his promises, / sang songs, then, in
his honor, / but soon they forgot what he had done, / and could not
wait upon his will. . . . / They made a calf, too, at Horeb, / casting a golden image and worshipping it, / as if they would exchange
the glory that dwelt among them / for the semblance of a bullock
at grass. / So little they remembered the God who had delivered
them . . .* (Psalm 105).

THE STORY CONTAINED in these two psalms is the recurring story
of our ingratitude, the darkness and weakness of our appreciation.
"Remember the marvellous acts he did, his miracles, his sentences
of doom," the psalmist recalls in 104, memories to stir the dullest
heart to gratitude. And what return have we made for the lavish
gifts of God? We "soon forgot," cast our own "golden image" and
worshipped it, foolishly, treacherously "exchanging the glory" that
was ours.

A true picture, Lord, of our appreciation, of our constancy and
perception. If Your love for us were not perfect, were not a total
gift, we should long ago have lost it.

I might have true happiness now, had I responded to Your total
generosity in kind! A generous soul, God-centered and full of
faith, would see the emptiness of the material gain for which our
passions thirst, and thirst in vain. He would learn from experience
how paltry and frustrating is the happiness of "worshipping a
golden image," seeking satisfaction in material goods.

But clinging to matter has warped our imaginations, and we
have convinced ourselves that You are far, that You are hardly real.
And the distant, unattainable material goals seem deceivingly near.
"Come, soul, thou hast goods in plenty laid up for many years to
come; take thy rest now, eat, drink, and make merry" (Luke 12:19).

Thus does greed conquer us, Lord. You are really near, and our

diseased imaginations hardly see You from afar. Wealth and comfort is our reality, seems always in reach. "One more gain," we
tell ourselves, "and I've got all I want."

If I am "lucky" enough to get it, the fire of desire for more is
fanned. "One more gain—" but there is no end. Each new success
becomes more bitter than the last, until finally we are made drunk
with greed.

While ever and again we, Your people, invite punishment and
destruction on ourselves for our ingratitude and covetousness,
Your mercy continues, Your infinite patience pursues us.

If we are praying as we ought, Lord, we are praying daily that
Your mercy will at last conquer our ingratitude, even if it be by
some hard-learned lesson. The starvation of the prodigal son was
not exactly an easy experience, but it did bring him back to his
father's house.

Psalm 106

POOR SOULS THAT WERE THIRSTY

*Some have wandered in parched deserts, / missing the way to
the city that was their home, / hungry and thirsty, so that their
spirits died within them. / So they cried to the Lord in their
trouble, / and he relieved their distress, / guiding them surely to the
place where they should find a home. / Praise they the Lord in his
mercies, / in his wondrous dealings with mortal men; / poor souls
that were thirsty, contented now, / poor souls that were hungry,
satisfied now with all good. /*
*Some lay where darkness overshadowed them, / helpless in bonds
of iron; / their punishment for rebelling against God's decrees, /
for thwarting the will of the most High. / Their hearts bowed down
with sorrow, / none else to aid their faltering steps, / they cried out*

*to the Lord in their trouble, / and he relieved their distress, rescuing
them from darkness, / from the shadows, tearing their chains asunder. / Praise they the Lord in his mercies, / in his wondrous
dealings with mortal men; / the Lord who has shattered the gates of
brass, / riven the bonds of iron.*

THIS, one of the most beautiful psalms, reminds us that the
soul must be cleansed and perfected before it is worthy of final
glory, that in the life of the soul, too, it is "always darkest just
before the dawn."

No saint has written an autobiography without stressing this
fact: the dark night of purification must come, and it is a cleansing
fire that sears and cracks the soul's armor. Rising to the height of
God, you see, is no small matter. Did not the psalmist say, "Lord,
thou hast put us to the proof, tested us as men test silver in the
fire. . . . Our way led through fire and water"? (Psalm 65:10–12).

Yet how little the average Christian is purified in this world! He
leaves this world with how much yet to be cleansed. This school of
purgation beyond the grave, where we may in God's mercy re-
educate and cure our crippled spirits, has never been so well described as by Dante in his *Purgatorio*. When in his meditation he
entered this sacred school, an angel traced on his forehead the marks
of the seven deadly vices, which as yet stained his soul. The angel
said to Dante: "Do thou wash these wounds when thou art within."

Then the great gates of Purgatory opened, and Dante listened
intently for the first sound he might hear. It was mingled music
and voices, and a chorus sang the Te Deum, "We praise Thee, O
God," for thou hast broken the chains of our sins, and hast mercifully relieved us of our filth.

Now at last the souls will learn what they neglected on earth. The
stains of pride are washed away, Dante observes, while the souls
are shown examples of true humility. Foremost among these is
Mary's example: "Behold the handmaid of the Lord: be it done to
me according to thy word."

Here the wrathful untie the knots of anger, and Dante hears the singing of "Blessed are the merciful" and "Rejoice, thou that overcomest."

Here the slothful at last exercise their spirits with true prayer and penance, the envious learn to love and share, the lustful learn reverence and self-conquest. And as he makes his way through these circles of purification, Dante suddenly hears the whole mountain of Purgatory tremble. Then on all sides a great shout of joy arises: "Glory to God in the highest!" The jubilation, he writes, is shared by every suffering soul in that vast realm. It is the expression of universal, unselfish gladness over the deliverance of one soul, cleansed, ready and worthy to rise.

Such is the condition of the unprepared souls. On earth they sought God, and never quite lost Him. But they died weighted down with much imperfection, with too much of this world on their minds. Darkness yet overshadowed them, as the psalmist writes, but in this school of purification, "their hearts bowed down with sorrow, none else to aid their faltering steps, they cried out to the Lord in their trouble, and he relieved their distress, rescuing them from darkness, from the shadows, tearing their chains asunder. Praise they the Lord in his mercies, in his wondrous dealings with mortal men!"

Psalm 107

NO MORE SHADOWS

O God, mount high above the heavens | till thy glory overshadows the whole earth. | Now bring aid to the men thou lovest, | give our prayer answer, and lift up thy right hand to save.

A FITTING PRAYER for the souls in Purgatory, on whom we have meditated. Lord, these are indeed "men thou lovest." But they have come asking admission to Your presence conditionally. They love You, too, and they have no desire to appear before You unworthy. They long to be purified and beautified for that glorious day. They are possessed at last with that self-conscious love of the saints which makes them feel deeply their unworthiness. If every true lover on earth has realized his unworthiness of the beloved, Lord, how much greater is that conviction in your saints! The state of mind in these suffering souls reminds us of that charming story told of St. Perpetua the Martyr. Thrown to the ground by a wild beast in the arena, she stood up again, combed her hair, and straightened up her clothing, because she "didn't want to go to glory unkempt and soiled."

The holy souls know that they have arrived before God with too much of this world still clinging to them. They are fully aware that they cannot yet remain in Your company, Lord, "till thy glory overshadows the whole earth."

St. Catherine of Genoa explains how gladly the departed soul avails itself of this purification. The soul in Purgatory, she writes, is like a freshly cut diamond. It is truly one of God's most beautiful creatures, and being directed toward God, it has not lost its primeval beauty. Yet it is far from perfect. The Divine Artisan must bring it to its full powers by polishing it; this is the process of purification.

These are earthly figures, Lord, but we who use them are earthly men. Our experience has not yet extended beyond this world. We do know that we ourselves would not come before a great earthly personage—king, prince or cardinal—unwashed, improperly dressed, soiled or bleeding. If by accident we arrived in such a condition, we would look for a place to wash and prepare ourselves for the occasion.

What then shall we do to prepare for You, Lord, who know every corner of the mind and heart? Where shall we go to burn away our blemishes? "How didst thou come in here without a wedding garment?" said the Master to his guest in the parable. But death, "coming like a thief in the night," indeed caught us unprepared. We were fortunate in that we were not completely turned away from You—for that, too, has happened during our life-time!

As it is, we have died too soon, we have much yet to learn of You, and much to correct in ourselves. If the best of Saints had to suffer so many things to become worthy of Your rewards, how far we have yet to go! Indeed, there is deep pain, always, before love is real and proved, and the very depth of true love is itself a torture.

It is no wonder, by the very nature of love, that the souls suffer greatly in their desire for union with You, who are all goodness and beauty; and this desire is not yet accomplished. The purification, too, is painful, for the vices were all too firmly rooted. The soul cannot rid itself of them by a mere wish. Years of sin, weakness, and bad habit must be driven out; the crippled good works, the hampered virtues must now be unchained. Selfish, corrupted desires and motives must be separated from the good.

Yet there is joy here, for the soul is liberating itself from darkness—or rather, Lord, You are delivering it. Ignorance, misunderstanding, blindness, prejudice, deception and corruption hinder the souls no longer. The truth has at last become clear—and what pain this alone must be! The scales have fallen from their eyes; they see the true meaning of life, these souls, and in it they know their own selves as never they knew on earth.

Truly, Lord, You have given "aid to the men thou lovest," have answered their prayer, "have lifted up thy right hand to save." When at last "thy glory overshadows" the dross, the earthly matter which yet blemishes men after death, then at last are all shadows removed!

Psalm 108

EXCUSE ME, NOT RESPONSIBLE

Cursing he loved, upon him let the curse fall; / for blessing he cared little, may blessing still pass him by. / Let cursing wrap him about, sink like water into his inmost being, / soak, like oil, into the marrow of his bones!

HERE IS ONE of the strong, virile passages of the psalms which the modern "progressive" reader calls repugnant. This peculiar species, soft-hearted and soft-headed when it comes to sin and vice, will seek out some excuse if not criticism for the "harsh" statements of God in Sacred Scripture.

To sympathize with this mentality, Lord, which finds Your inspired word "too harsh" for modern ears, we must "understand" its position. We must, above all, depart for the time being from our stern, "harsh" acceptance of the principle that man is free and therefore responsible for the choices he makes. What with endless statistics, the ready scapegoats of heredity and environment, the glib equation of freedom with license, the confusion between genuine psychiatry and mollycoddling, the public fuzziness about moral law, the ineffectiveness of modern discipline in home and school—just what do we expect the modern man to think?

From this "modern" viewpoint, which finds hell "too cruel" to believe in, the modern reader is supposed to be embarrassed to hear the inspired word insisting—strongly—that as a man sows, so he must reap.

For that, Lord, is really what Your psalms of curses have to tell us. I may ask myself: do I willfully though subtly reject the law of God or those who teach it? Do I slander and calumniate those who, for all I know, speak God's word and do God's will far better than I? Do I wantonly ignore the way of truth and justice mapped out by God and taught by His Church? If so, is it too much for God to say I have chosen curse upon curse, and I shall have what I have freely chosen?

There is really no problem at all with the so-called psalms of cursing if we accept the simple fact of man's freedom to choose. If free will has any meaning at all (other than that men differ from one another, as do cows, pigs, trees, and stones), then the psalms of cursing are both meaningful and necessary. Evil and man's weakness for evil can hardly be cursed too much if we—sleepy and undiscerning as we are—are to be turned away from it.

Lord, we moderns have been brain-washed into a soft, weak optimism. We have been led to think that when ideal conditions finally exist (as they never will on this earth), there will be no more need to resist temptation or mortify the flesh. If only enough money is spent to build bureaus and sympathize with sin, we shall have paradise regained. If this is true, what a bleak future is ours! Gone will be all adventure and purpose in life. Man will no longer be able to make himself, no, nor even to break himself. Poor victim of top-heavy organization, he will be reduced to an environmental statistic.

What gratitude we owe You, Lord, for the stinging curses You have hurled against evil, and the glorious blessings You have promised those who keep Your law. This alone assures us that a choice is worth making, life is worth living, and death is worth preparing for.

Psalm *109*

ALL BEAUTY WITHIN

To the Master I serve the Lord's promise was given, | Sit here at my right hand while I make thy enemies a footstool under thy feet. . . . | From birth, princely state shall be thine, holy and glorious; | thou art my son, born like dew before the daystar rises. | The Lord has sworn an oath there is no retracting, | Thou art a priest for ever in the line of Melchisedech.

WHO WOULD HAVE THOUGHT IT, as they met a quiet, sun-browned, dark-haired boy on the dusty streets of a miserable small town, that this was he? Who would have guessed it, as he wandered through the market-place to buy a few provisions for his parents and himself, as he traded, dressed in the clothes of the poor, that this was he? Who would have imagined, as they passed his father's workshop, and saw him, a strong young teenager, sweating and straining with a few crude tools, that this was he?

If passers-by had stopped to look closely, or if they had known for what they were looking, they could well have been amazed at the lad's attractive qualities. Had they been searching for it, they would have been impressed by the mystery, the unassuming greatness of this family. There was an air of quiet dignity and perfect composure about them that might have fascinated the more appreciative and cultured Jews, but here at Nazareth it could go on quite undetected.

After all, wasn't it a Galilean proverb that "nothing good had ever come out of Nazareth"? As far as these very crude people could make out, Joseph and Mary and her Son were calm, hard-working people, silent and not foolish. They had managed to stay out of trouble (so far), unlike Nazareth's zealots, swindlers, highway men, beggars, small-time scribes and meddlesome Pharisees. But they were very common people. It was not likely that in such a hidden family there was one to whom God had said, "From birth, princely state shall be thine, holy and glorious; thou art my son, born like dew before the day-star rises."

One story had got back to the townspeople from Jerusalem; it had something to do with the disappearance of the son during the feast days. The fact could be taken as ordinary enough. He had reached the age of legal independence that year, and who wouldn't expect a teenager to try some stunt with his new-found, artificial freedom? He had been well-trained, they knew, but he was nevertheless a boy.

It took his parents three days to find him. They were grief-stricken, as what parents would not be, especially since this was their only son. Yet to all appearances, he was a worthy son, a fine specimen of boy. Any mother from Nazareth, for all her ignorance and suspicion and prejudice, knew of no other time that this boy had openly defied his parents.

In fact, the gossip was that he was in conference with the wisest doctors of the temple, and had astounded them with his brilliance. Perhaps it was only gossip, they thought, since he never sported his intelligence at home. Well, whatever it was, his parents must have disciplined him roundly, since no such incident occurred in his home town.

Redeemer of Israel? What a ridiculous idea! Even if they had known his serious and noble personality, his strong character and physique, where, they could ask, should this boy come by the wisdom and influence? Influence? There was the only key to leadership, and where was his?

King or Messiah? You had to be a mighty keen observer, you had to take notice with a poet's imagination, to be especially attracted to this young man. There were many others like him, after all—but what chance had a Galilean to save the world?

Redeemer of men? Hope of the world? Divine conquerer? What?

This boy? Only if the powers above used their wit to make a huge joke of the idea. Pardon the irreverence, Lord, but the joke would be just what in fact it was: that not with the noise of trumpets and cavalry and mobs would the world be saved, but by some surprise that would catch the world from behind, that would catch men off guard and would unseat the supposed great ones from their thrones forever.

This, indeed, was he of whom the inspired poet-king had written, as he saw one Lord speak to the other, "Sit here at my right hand while I make thy enemies a footstool under thy feet. . . . Thou art a priest for ever in the line of Melchisedech. . . . Thou art to bear rule in the midst of thy enemies."

Champion, everlasting victor, ruler of men, priest for all time, sacrificer and offering, the world's beginning and end—this humble boy of Nazareth. "All his beauty is within," as the psalm says, within—where the root and branches and foliage of beauty have always been.

Psalm 110

WHO EVER LOVED?

Chant we the Lord's wondrous doings, / delight and study of all who love him. / Ever his deeds are high and glorious, faithful he abides to all eternity. . . . / No act but shows him just and faithful; of his decrees there is no relenting. / Perpetual time shall leave them changeless; right and truth are their foundation. . . . / Wise evermore are you who follow it; yours the prize that lasts forever.

HERE IS A COMMON THEME in the Book of Psalms: the eternity of God's love. The faithfulness, the consistence, the unchanging goodness of God towards men.

I accept this fact—as a beautiful by-word. I enjoy hearing it sung or recited poetically against a backdrop of blue lights and soft music.

But in practice, Lord, do I truly accept the fact of Your changeless love for me? Do I understand that in pain as well as pleasure, in failure as well as success, in sorrow as well as joy, Your love for me is unchanged? Too often I measure Your love by my own shifting standards, and I become blinded. No longer are Your "wondrous doings" my "delight and study." Unconsciously, but really, I have begun to blame You for my troubles. I am ignored or hated, I am unappreciated and cast aside, I am misunderstood and falsely accused, and I act as though You have abandoned me.

I would not doubt the constancy of Your generous love, would I, if I remembered the example You set? Have I forgotten how Your Heavenly Father's love brought You to Bethlehem, to dull Nazareth, to ungrateful Jerusalem, to Gethsemane and Calvary? All this because You were ever faithful to His Will!

Who of us have been faithful to You? Have we not often enough ignored or insulted You? Nevertheless, Your love remains constant. We have made ourselves odious, but Your love has not changed.

We only doubt Your love, Lord, because we ourselves have never really loved. We don't really know what love is. We think of it as a hot, fleeting passion which song, movie, and novel flaunt before us. We think, to speak plainly, that selfishness is love.

This is hardly what great men made of love. Far from a romantic evening amid flowers, embraces, and sweet bits of nothing, they thought of love—as did the author of the Canticle—as something "strong as death and hard as hell" (Cant. 8:6).

Far from a passing infatuation, love was a firm direction of will. Love, as Shakespeare saw it, was that overwhelming power in man which made him faithful to death amid the greatest struggle and sacrifice; love was a force of spirit that surpassed all flesh:

> Let me not to the marriage of true minds
> Admit impediments. Love is not love
> Which alters when it alteration finds,

> Or bends with the remover to remove:
> O, no! it is an ever-fixed mark
> That looks on tempests and is never shaken;
> It is the star to every wandering bark,
> Whose worth's unknown, although his height be taken.
> Love's not Time's fool, though rosy lips and cheeks
> Within his bending sickle's compass come;
> Love alters not with his brief hours and weeks,
> But bears it out even to the edge of doom.
> If this be error and upon me proved,
> I never writ, nor no man ever loved.

(Sonnet CXVI)

If man can be so sure of the unshaken, eternal strength of love, what must be God's love for us! A love which can die or weaken with any alteration is no love, says Shakespeare. It is the star which guides us back to truth, when we wander. And like the star, love has a value beyond our knowing; although we can "take his height," we know how high above us is the star. So also we know how high above us is God's love, and our love for him. Such love does not pass with Time's "brief hours and weeks," but faithful as God from whom it comes, love "bears it out even to the edge of doom." No sacrifice is too great for real love.

Love that is worthy of the name will always have this eternal quality. It is born of God, and as the psalmist sings, "Faithful he abides to all eternity." This eternal love became flesh, and in Christ we saw true love. The saints understood this love, lived gloriously in its constancy, carried its bright flame through every trial "to the edge of doom." If their love, "the prize that lasts forever," is not love at its purest and truest, then Shakespeare is right—no man ever loved.

Psalm 111

WISDOM OF THE SAINTS

Good men see a light dawn in darkness; his light, who is merciful, kind and faithful. / It goes well with the man who lends in pity, just and merciful in his dealings. / Length of days shall leave him still unshaken; men will remember the just forever. / No fear shall he have of evil tidings; on the Lord his hope is fixed unchangeably. / Patient his heart remains and steadfast, quietly he waits for the downfall of his enemies.

HERE IS THE WISDOM of the saints, a recurring theme in the psalms, and in all of the inspired Scripture. Who wants wisdom, who wants assurance that life has not deceived him? Who is weak, but desires lasting strength? Who has failed, but strives for the final victory?

Much has been written on man's thirst for success, on his fear of failure, on the despair which failure brings him. Innumerable "success stories" have been published, yet most of them are a surface, a veneer beneath which lies a deeper failure. Many have boasted of making themselves "a name," which in the end is lost or without meaning.

Who sees beyond the illusion of this world's success stories? Who has gained a genuine distaste for "success politics" and the never-satisfying power struggle? Who is tired of "pulling strings" and in the end entangling himself in them? A book of advice has been written for him, the like of which the world has not the discernment to publish.

It is understandable enough that the world will never offer a success story to equal this, for we are dealing here with the Word of

God, as we are dealing with it in Psalm 111. The man whose "hope is fixed unchangeably" on God has no real failure to fear. If he is really true to God, then "patient his heart remains and steadfast, quietly he waits for the downfall of his enemies." Not that he hates his enemies or plans their destruction; but that they are obscured and obliterated by the glory of his success. This book, the genuine success story, is the Book of Wisdom, of the Old Testament:

"How boldly, then, will the just man appear, to meet his old persecutors, that thwarted all his striving! And they, in what craven fear they will cower at the sight of him, amazed at the sudden reversal of his fortunes! Inward remorse will wring a groan from those hearts: 'Why, these were the men we made into a laughing-stock and a by-word! We, poor fools, mistook the life they lived for madness, their death for ignominy; and now they are reckoned as God's own children, now it is among his holy ones that their lot is cast.

". . . Weary it proved, the reckless way of ruin, lonely were the wastes we travelled, who missed the path the Lord meant for us. What advantage has it brought us, all our pomp and pride? How are we the better for our vaunted wealth? Nothing of that but is gone, unsubstantial as a shadow, swift as courier upon his errand. . . .

"Short-lived are all the hopes of the godless, thistle-down in the wind, flying spray before the storm, smoke that whirls away in the breeze. . . . It is the just that will live forever; the Lord has their recompense waiting for them" (Wisdom 5:1–16).

Psalm 112

MIGHTIEST IN THE MIGHTY

The Lord is sovereign king of all the nations; his glory is high above the heavens. / Who is like the Lord our God, so high above

*us, that stoops to regard both heaven and earth, / lifting up the poor
from the dust he lay in, raising the beggar out of his dung-hill, to
find him a place among the princes?*

You CAN ALWAYS identify truly great people by their humility.
Those who have real greatness within, need not fear stooping to the
most lowly. It is the small, petty, puny man that fears humiliation,
that disdains the smell of poverty, that shows annoyance when he
is not given sufficient attention and honor.

The secret of happiness is the secret of genuine humility. It consists of forgetting my own importance, of going out of myself, in
order to remember the importance of others.

How easy this should be, Jesus, when I see Your utter debase-
ment, Your free choice to live in the greatest poverty, ignored by
Your neighbors and later rejected by Your townsmen, who could
not bear to see "the carpenter's son" coming by all this wisdom and
the power to work miracles. "Why begin now?" they meant to say.
"For thirty years he was nothing. He was but a sweating, poorly-
clothed village lad. If he is someone great, he would never have
humbled himself to be born and raised here, in Nazareth, of all
places!"

They missed the very point of Your choice, Lord. You were so
great that You could well afford to empty Yourself. "All the king's
beauty is within," the psalms remind us. He has gone out of himself entirely, has not merely stooped down to lift us "from the dust
we lay in," but has been born and raised a poor child among the
poor.

Even in Your public life, when after thirty hidden years of poverty, You had to tell the world who You were, You accepted no rewards, took no offers of glory, made no display of greatness. Like a
homeless vagabond, You could justly say You had "not a place
to lay Your head." Your home was indeed the universe. You had
no need, no desire to accumulate anything less.

Lord Jesus, You, the "sovereign king of all the nations," with a
"glory high above the heavens," could stoop to "lift the poor from

the dust," to raise the beggar from his stinking dung-hill, and to find glory for these lowly ones "among the princes." You feared no loss of Your excellence by giving of Yourself to all—even to the least loved of men.

Such was Your humility, because of Your infinite superiority. The quality of humility is like the quality of mercy observed by Shakespeare: "it is mightiest in the mighty."

The smaller the man, the greater his pride. The greater the man, the smaller he becomes in his own eyes, since he has gone out of himself to see what he can do for those around him. He soon knows that he has opened the way to unlimited self-sacrifice and heroism, no matter where he is. Of such devotion the world has always more than enough need.

Psalm 113

LONELINESS

Why did you leap up like rams, you mountains, leap up, you hills, like yearling sheep? / Let earth thrill at its Master's presence; it is he that comes, the God of Jacob, / who turned the rock into pools of water, the flint-stone into a springing well. / Not to us, Lord, not to us the glory; let thy name alone be honored.... / Why must the heathen say, Their God deserts them?

WE ARE CREATURES, we have not caused our own being, we cannot stand alone, we are not sufficient to ourselves: these things we know well. The knowledge should at once make us rejoice in our Creator, in whom is all our sufficiency; should make us realize our own limits, our helplessness against powers greater than ourselves.

It was this realization that made the psalmist see the very mountains and hills leap with joy at the thought of their Maker and his plentiful power. In Him we find all cause for joy; we are but the overflow of His plenty.

Why, then, should a Christian ever be lonely? Why, in any case, should he find gloom and despair in such loneliness as comes from the loss of human comforts and human companionship? A Christian cannot lose the best human comfort and the chief human friend.

If I am Christian at all, there is one thing I know: You will never abandon me, Lord God. Even if I should deserve the most wretched loneliness and abandonment, even if it should be a loss of my own making, I shall know You have never left me, You have never removed Your love. I cannot be less certain than the psalmist, who insists that You are always faithful, that Your promise is never broken. It is only this, really, that matters.

If I respond as a creature should to its Creator; if, failing this, I but return to You, no fear can ever conquer me. And soon, in fact, I will welcome earthly loneliness, that I may think the more of You.

"Social life, associations, and amusements are not necessary to happiness," wrote a young mother, "except as a seasoning to the joy you must find within yourself at no expense."

It is certainly true that if I depend on the externals of this world for my happiness, I will not be satisfied very long. And what should my last hour be, if I have found no rest but in creatures? The final horror will be a vast loneliness, a mounting sea of despair. No one will console me then; not my dearest love can accompany me then.

Infinitely wiser for me to have prepared this journey by a life-long friendship, like that written of by Robert Browning in "The Boy and the Angel":

> He did God's will; to him, all one
> If on the earth or in the sun.

Psalm 114

A TYRANT

Return, my soul, where thy peace lies; the Lord has dealt kindly with thee; he has saved my life from peril, banished my tears, kept my feet from falling. Mine to walk at ease, enjoying the Lord's presence, in the land of the living.

EVERY MAN is born a tyrant. He is a slave to greed and vainglory all his life, unless by a miracle of grace the charity of Christ sets him free.

Alas, how often he is disguised in virtuous visage! He appears generous, kind, zealous, deeply religious; he is your most respected friend and patron—until one day you happen to cross a secret path, you happen to find some hidden, earthly tie. You did not suspect, but now you have hit the sensitive nerve. Now you shall feel his wrath.

You have experienced this surprise often enough, living among human beings; you have noticed it most often, perhaps, in yourself. Know yourself, and you know that man is a born tyrant, violently jealous of all that he thinks his own.

There is only one kind of man who cannot be thus invaded: he is that rare creature who has become in the fullest sense "a son of God," as St. John writes. This man has been emptied by charity. There is no more greed, no arrogance or vanity, no false desire, no wall around self. He is attacked, but not disturbed; he is invaded, but not angered; nor indeed is he ever conquered. Such men we call saints, when their struggle to become thus emptied of self begins to produce true effects.

All of us, Lord, are either saints or slaves. Slaves indeed, though we act like tyrants. We cannot tolerate our neighbors' invasion of our "personal" (very greedy) aspirations. They must bow to our wishes; they are not free to cross our self-planned path to comfort or vanity. Irascible and domineering, we are in no real sense free; we are self-enslaved.

Who is free, but he whom Christ has emptied, he from whom Christ has taken all tyranny? Such a man's path cannot be crossed, for the path is not straight, is not rigid or unbending. It is forever elusive, forever winding this way and that, as the breath of the Spirit prompts it. It follows a mysterious route: the Will of Christ. When you try to cut off this path, when you attack it, it bends for you; it makes room, it strikes out in a new direction, and every new detour hastens it more surely to its goal. "Charity seeks not its own."

"Return, my soul, where thy peace lies; the Lord has dealt kindly with thee," sings the psalmist. Such unworldly peace is for those who "are born, not of the flesh, nor of blood, nor of the will of man, but of God."

Psalm 115

WHAT CAN I GIVE YOU?

The Lord's mercies have never failed me; what return shall I make to him? / I will take the cup that is pledge of my deliverance, and invoke the name of the Lord upon it; / I will pay the Lord my vows in the presence of all his people. . . . / Thou hast broken the chains that bound me; I will sacrifice in thy honor, and call on the name of the Lord. / Before a throng of worshippers I will pay the Lord my vows, here in the courts of the Lord's house, here, Jerusalem, in thy heart.

"WHAT CAN I GIVE YOU?" say the lover to his beloved. "What can we give them?" say the parents, thinking of their well-loved children. "What can we give him?" ask the children, grateful to their hard-working father.

Gifts are symbols of love and friendship, given to members of our own family and to our own circle of friends. Gifts are connected with celebrations—birthdays, anniversaries, feast days like Christmas and Easter. Gifts are signs of gratitude; they are given because we owe something to the receiver.

For all of these three reasons, men have always wanted gifts for God. Pagans threw their precious jewelry into the sea, as a gift for the gods. The Hebrews worshipped God as a spirit, and their gifts literally rose to heaven in smoke. The burnt offerings were set aside for God by their removal from the use of men.

These gifts for God were given like gifts to men, for even if sacrifice was made to God out of fear rather than love, its purpose was to turn fear into love, to bring God's love and friendship to man. The gifts were often made on religious feast days, and they were made by reason of man's conviction that he owed much to God: "The Lord's mercies have never failed me; what return shall I make to him?" asks the psalmist.

Heroic sacrifices were made by pagans, in order to win divine favor. Before the Trojan War, the Greek general Agamemnon sacrificed his most beloved daughter, Iphegenia, on the altar of Artemis. Among pagans, as among the Hebrews, the best was reserved for a divine offering. God Himself asked Abraham to make the supreme gift, to test his faith and love. When He saw that Abraham did not hesitate to offer what he loved most, his son Isaac, He stayed Abraham's hand, and commanded him to offer a ram instead.

The Indians of the new world felt strongly the need of sacrifice. Such was the Aztecs' frightening custom of offering living human hearts to appease the Great Spirit when he was angered by sin. Cortez left us a detailed description of this painful ceremony. Fourteen of his soldiers were victims in the temple of Montezuma in one day, while he watched helplessly from afar. Whatever the abuses of these sacrifices were—whether among savages or among the civilized Romans—the idea itself was natural to man.

Gifts were made to God for a good harvest, as atonement for sin, and to avert calamities. In Jerusalem the smoke arose in the temple from morning to night, and on some feast days even at midnight. The bloody offerings of the pagans and the burnt offerings of the Jews recognized this fact: it is the essential ceremony of religion to give something to God. And throughout history, religions without this notion and this action have had a deep-felt emptiness about them.

Our gift to God is the Mass, a perfect gift because He Himself has provided it for us. If, as St. James writes, "every perfect gift descends from the Father of lights," there is no more perfect gift than Himself, descending Himself in His human nature.

We who are "the sons of God" must ask, "What can we give Him?" We feel impelled to offer our love and friendship in some concrete way, we want to celebrate His feasts as we celebrate our own, we owe Him all that we are and all the good we have, and we desire some real expression of our gratitude.

Catholics find the Holy Sacrifice of the Mass a joyous fulfillment of these deepest desires. The Mass is our gift, perfect in every way, for it is Christ, God-made-man. He is truly *our* gift, for He has joined the human family, taking the full nature of man. Yet He is a totally worthy gift, because from all eternity He has belonged to the divine family, the ever-Blessed Trinity. In a spirit of truest, deepest joy, we begin the Mass with the psalmist, "I will go up to the altar of God, to God, the giver of youth and happiness." It is no wonder that through the Church's history of persecutions, sorrows, and struggles, a slogan grew that is never forgotten: "It is the Mass that matters." It is the Mass that answers best the psalmist's question, "What shall I return to the Lord for all He has done for me?"

Psalm 116

WHY LIVE?

Praise the Lord, all you Gentiles, let all the nations of the world do him honor. | Abundant has his mercy been towards us; the Lord remains faithful to his word for ever.

MAN WAS MADE for the praise of God. Any man who thinks of God at all knows how "abundant has his mercy been towards us." He sees, too, in God's mercies on earth that He "remains faithful to his word for ever," that eternal happiness is a reality.

One day when Hilaire Belloc was to speak at a special program in an American city, he was briefly interviewed by the conductor of the orchestra. Among the questions was this: "Mr. Belloc, why have you chosen to write both history and poetry?"

To which Mr. Belloc answered, "For the same reason that you conduct the orchestra, sir—to gain heaven."

Unfortunately, people are staggered by such an answer; they are not expecting it. Which is to say, they are not thinking of it, and that is the tragedy.

How often do we stop to think, Lord, that a life which does not praise God is a life wasted? No tragedy can be so great: a long sickness is not as sad, a painful death is not as pitiful, as a life empty of God. Really, Lord, if we are Christians at all, what does it matter whether we are rich or poor, healthy or sick, remembered or forgotten, exalted or humiliated—so long as our actions are praising You? Until we feel this truth intimately, until it is the central fact of our life, how are we better than pagan?

The famous musician, Bruno Walter, had conducted the New

York Philharmonic Symphony Orchestra in an afternoon of Anton Bruckner's music. At intermission time he was asked by interviewers, "Which do you think is the best of Bruckner's musical compositions?"

Bruno Walter answered, "His *Te Deum,* of course."

"What is the greatness that you see or feel in Bruckner's *Te Deum?*" they asked.

"It is so Catholic," he answered.

Somewhat puzzled, they asked, "What do you mean?"

"Well," said the great conductor, "it *belongs* in the Church: it is Bruckner's whole life. It is sincere praise of God; it was his whole effort, like the birds singing in the morning. All he ever wanted to do with his music was praise God."

Such music, indeed, is "Catholic" and "belongs in the Church." If Bruno Walter's judgment is the actual fact about Bruckner, then here was a musician who had caught the spirit of the saints.

If You can say of my work, Lord, "it is sincere praise of God," then my purpose in life is accomplished. Then I have arrived at the perfect joy of the psalmist who cried out, "Praise the Lord, all you nations. . . . Abundant has his mercy been towards us."

Psalm 117

THE RESURRECTION PSALM

Alleluia! Give thanks to the Lord; the Lord is gracious, his mercy endures for ever. . . . / The very stone which the builders rejected has become the chief stone at the corner; this is the Lord's doing, and it is marvellous in our eyes. / This day is a holiday of the Lord's own choosing; greet this day with rejoicing, greet this day with triumph!

THIS IS THE JOYOUS Resurrection hymn of the Church, which we hear at the Easter Vigil Service on Holy Saturday evening, and in every Mass during Easter week. It is a song of suffering turned into triumph; and that is the theme of Holy Week, the theme of Christ's life on earth, the theme of every Christian's life on earth.

Jesus applied this psalm to Himself, when speaking of His day of suffering and of victory. It was in the third year of His public life, most probably in the last week or two before His death and resurrection. The Pharisees had already shown their hatred of Jesus openly, and sought a way to capture Him and have Him executed. They were held back only by fear; Christ was as yet too popular with the people; they would have to discredit Him first, or else catch Him secretly and have Him done away with before the public found out about it.

Meanwhile Jesus taught openly in the temple and on the streets, still trying to make the people understand that He was truly the promised Redeemer and the Son of God. One morning in the temple court the Pharisees openly attacked Jesus by demanding that He tell them where He got His authority. Jesus promised to tell them, if they would answer *His* question: "Where did John the Baptist get his authority?" This the Pharisees were too cowardly to answer; Jesus had cornered them. If they said that John's authority was from God, Jesus would answer, "Then why did you refuse to believe him?" If they said it was not from God, the people would stone them for slandering John. So they said, "We don't know."

Jesus was not satisfied with this hypocritical answer. If they were cowards, He was not: He would make His point very clear. He pursued the question of His authority by telling His enemies a story which unveiled their sin. The owner of a vineyard had sent messengers to his employees, demanding that they pay him what they owed from the revenue of his vineyard. When the wicked servants killed his messengers, he sent his own son, saying to himself, "Surely they will reverence my own son." But he soon received the shocking news that the workers had killed his son, too. What was he to do?

The Pharisees, many of whom owned their own vineyards and demanded revenues aplenty, did not hesitate to say that these workers should be executed, and the vineyard should be given to others who would pay their debts on time. "You are right," said Jesus. "Have you never read these words in the scriptures: 'The very stone which the builders rejected has become the chief stone at the corner; this is the Lord's doing, and it is marvellous in our eyes'?" Commenting on this prophecy from Psalm 117, Jesus told the Pharisees plainly: "I tell you, then, that the kingdom of God will be taken away from you, and given to a people which yields the revenues that belong to it" (Matt. 21:33-46).

In this paradox explained by the Son of God Himself, the Church rejoices. This is the joy of resurrection: Christ is rejected by those who owed Him most and should have loved Him most. But even in this awful betrayal, He is not defeated. In this greatest of man's crimes lies also his greatest cause to rejoice: the Son of God's eternal victory over death, and the foundation of His Church. Not "the gates of hell," all forces of evil combined, will ever destroy this victory.

Lord Jesus, You had come to build the city of God among men. You had chosen a race to be Your builders. But in their pride and ignorance and by their false standards, their leaders lost sight of the very corner-stone. They rejected You, because they did not know of what the city of God is built.

What of us, Lord? You know well enough how their faults are our faults, how much like their false standards are ours, and what poor builders of the city of God we have become!

They drove You out of the city—called the "holy city" by themselves!—and crucified You as an enemy. But not all the evil of man can prevail against the mercy of God. The rejected stone has become the corner-stone of all history. The centuries of history itself are numbered from the year of Your birth. You are the foundation and the walls and the pillars and the tower and the altar of Your Church, for You are the Church and we are Your members. Truly, this greatest reversal, this greatest surprise in history "is the Lord's doing, and it is marvellous in our eyes."

Psalm *117, b*

DAY OF TRIUMPH

They cut me off from every way of escape, but see, in the power of the Lord I crush them! / They swarm about me like bees, their fury blazes up like fire among thorns, but see, in the power of the Lord I crush them! / . . . The homes of the just echo, now, with glad cries of victory; the power of the Lord has triumphed. . . . / I am reprieved from death, to live on and proclaim what the Lord has done for me.

THE PHARISEES, as the psalm says, had "cut him off from every way of escape," and in doing so, they had forced Jesus onto the road of His supreme victory—so it seemed. But He had chosen this road from the beginning.

It is no wonder that throughout the week of Our Lord's resurrection, the Church sings in every Mass and in every hour of the Divine Office, "This is the day which the Lord has made; let us rejoice in it, let us triumph in it." The incredible has truly taken place. We see before our eyes a fact of which we might have dreamed at best: that a man could come to this world, could take upon himself all the sorrows and miseries that man has known, could take these awful burdens upon his own shoulders, and could make of them at once the world's greatest joy; that a man could come, and accepting what to the world seems the most humiliating defeat, could turn it into history's greatest victory.

For this reason the Church chose Sunday, instead of the traditional Sabbath of the Old Law, as the Lord's Day. Sunday was the "day which the Lord made." It was a day "to rejoice, to triumph in" forever. It was the day that turned all tears of bitterness into tears of laughter and happiness. It was the day promised by God in the Apocalypse, the day on which "God will wipe away every tear" from the eyes of His people, "and there will be no more death, or mourning, or cries of distress, no more sorrow; those old things have passed away. And he who sat on the throne said, Behold, I make all things new. . . . I am Alpha, I am Omega, the beginning of all things, and their end; those who are thirsty shall drink—it is my free gift—out of the spring whose water is life. Who wins the victory? He shall have his share in this; I will be his God, and he shall be my son" (Apoc. 21:4–7).

This is the Church's victory song: "Christ is risen; all things are set right." The world has no such glory to offer. What the world offers is very brief, very passing, very uncertain. What the Church offers remains forever, cannot be lost by treachery, deception, ill-fortune or accident. It depends entirely on the will of man as conformed to the Will of God, on man's well-grounded hope in Christ. Not the weathering of time or the woes of tragedy can change this assurance of victory. Whoever hopes in Christ and firmly wills to share the victory of Christ, is assured of it in advance.

If there is suffering or sorrow, there is the example of Christ: His suffering and sorrow. If there is apparent defeat or failure, there is Christ's assurance that when we live united to Him there is no such thing as defeat or failure. Not only the Resurrection on Easter morning, but the Cross itself is victory. The Cross is suffering united to victory, and the Resurrection is joy united to victory.

You could not have risen from the dead, Lord Jesus, had You not first died. You could not have conquered the evils of this world, had You not faced them, had You not met them and fought with them. There is no victory without struggle; this is the Christian's consolation and inspiration in the face of evils and temptations. He cannot be called a winner, if he has not come out ahead of an opposing force after a struggle with it.

He hopes to come before his Lord like a warrior who has endured much, who has suffered so many things, who has overcome such great difficulties, that his love and his loyalty cannot be doubted.

"I would do it for you again, any time," said a dying soldier to his captain on the battlefield. He had risked his life; he had lost it—but he had already given his life willingly. The risk itself was proof of his loyalty. The true Christian will do as much for Christ: but there is really no risk. Whatever happens, victory is his. Nevertheless the tasks undertaken are proof of his loyalty.

"The homes of the just echo, now, with glad cries of victory; the power of the Lord has triumphed." Psalm 117 is the Church's joyous Easter song; for now every one of us can sing with the psalmist, "I am reprieved from death, to live on and proclaim what the Lord has done for me. The Lord has chastened me, chastened me indeed, but he would not doom me to die."

No, our death is no longer a sentence of doom. It is now only the road to resurrection; it is now only the beginning of life. "I am the resurrection and the life," You assured us. "He who believes in me, though he is dead, shall live on, and whoever has life, and has faith in me, to all eternity cannot die" (John 11:25-26).

These words were confirmed by Your own resurrection; if You could die, and then raise Yourself to life by Your own power, surely You could raise us to life. Sun, moon, and stars rejoice! He is risen, and we shall rise! Mountains, forests, and rivers, rejoice at the Lord's coming! He is risen, and we shall rise! For this He was born; for this we are born, and live, and die—for the "day which the Lord has made—the day of His resurrection, and ours."

Psalm *118*

DIVINE LAW

Ah, blessed they, who pass through life's journey unstained, who follow the law of the Lord! | Ah, blessed they, who cherish his decrees, Make him the whole quest of their hearts!

OURS MIGHT very well come to be called the lawless century. The unfortunate people crushed under the Communist heel must certainly come to think of law as a whip wielded by lawless men. Communist "law" is a cloak for the outrageous betrayal of human dignity and freedom. In the free nations, just laws have been abused so much by unjust men that true law is a confused concept, and most of us nod our heads solemnly to statements like that of Goldsmith: "Laws grind the poor, and rich men rule the law." Perhaps in no country has true law come to be so disregarded and disrespected as in our own, where the free play of false doctrines has done so much harm. Our youth, like too many of their elders, look upon law as the disagreeable enemy of "freedom," while the "law of God" is ignored or ridiculed by money-makers and pleasure-seekers.

Yet the divine decrees cannot go unheeded without inevitable ruin. When the law of God is not "the whole quest of their hearts," peoples and nations experience the progressive loss of good order, justice, peace and freedom.

There is no hope for man but in the law of God. If ever this should have been clear to man, it should have been clear to us today. The fearsome spectacle of murdered millions, of enslaved people, of the appalling slaughter of nations and of their just hopes —this terror should have awakened us to an unprecedented reverence for the law of God.

Instead, Lord, it has left the majority of men colder and weaker than ever. They go on, selfish and unheeding, unsympathetic, unconcerned, unthinking.

There is little worldly consolation for him who, like St. James, "has looked carefully into the perfect law of liberty and has remained in it" (James 1:25). Like the prophets of all centuries and like the psalmist, he soon knows the ultimate vanity of the ways of men. This temptation conquered, he will act from principle, not from expediency. His keen perception of the lasting truth of God's law will ever increase: "Comfort this earthly exile; do not refuse me the knowledge of thy will. . . . Expound, Lord, thy whole bidding to me; faithfully I will keep it. Enlighten me, to scan thy law closely, and keep true to it with all my heart. . . . Eyes have I none for vain phantoms; let me find life in following thy ways. . . . Freely shall my feet tread, if thy will is all my quest" (Psalm 118).

All human life is permeated with a crying need for divine law. Nations have brought catastrophes on themselves by ignoring God's decrees, and rare is the individual who has not experienced the price of lawlessness.

Lord, as I review every failure of my life, every cause of unhappiness and unrest, every dark hour of the past that I would sooner forget and not repeat, I see that adherence to Your law would have saved me. From every defeat I have suffered, Your commandments would have rescued me.

"All went well with them," said Achior of the Hebrews, "so long as no sin of theirs offended his eye, the God that is an enemy to all wrong. . . . There was no beating down such a people as this, save when they forsook the worship of the Lord their God; only when they worshipped some god other than himself, their own God, would he let them be plundered, and slaughtered, and treated with insult. Even then, did they but repent of their revolt from his allegiance, the God of heaven would give them strength to resist their assailants" (Judith 5:21, 17–19).

Psalm 119

TREACHEROUS TONGUES

Lord, have pity and deliver me from the treacherous lips, the perjured tongue. / Perjurer, he will give thee all thy deserts and more; sharp arrows from a warrior's bow, Blazing faggots of broom.

Suppose I call up an old friend one day, and after the usual greetings and small talk I ask him what he's doing for a living.

"I make my living on minor injuries," he answers.

"I suppose you operate a kind of first-aid station?" I ask, not yet alarmed.

"No, I don't repair the injuries. I give them," he replies, undisturbed.

"You *give* them?" I am puzzled, but only for a moment. "You vaccinate people? You give vitamin shots? You feed people intravenously?" I venture.

Now he is laughing at what he calls my ignorance. "Your guesses are missing me on every side," he says goodnaturedly. "The fact is, I carry a good number of painful pins and needles with me wherever I go, and when I come across someone I know, I take a good jab at him. I get a great kick out of the injuries I can inflict daily. It's pretty much an all-day hobby, and I live well on it."

With that he hangs up the phone, and I am left to wonder. If he wasn't fooling me, that's one friend I can do without. I don't think I'll be seeing more of him—but how can it be? How can anyone make it his day-to-day job to injure others?

"Yes, it can be, and it is!" I say to myself after a moment's thought. "How many of us live—and think we live well—on the injury we do to others." Wasn't it St. James who wrote, "The tongue is a tiny part of our body, and yet what power it can boast!" Sadly he observed that "no human being has ever found out how to tame the tongue; a pest that is never allayed, all deadly poison" (James 3:5, 8).

The shame of making a fat living by injuring others—yet that is what we attempt with our tongues! Harm enough is done by speaking too freely of the well-known and proven faults of others, but when real malice is at work with suspicion, hearsay, or slander —then, indeed, the "perjured tongues" are like "sharp arrows from a warrior's bow, blazing faggots of broom," and the wretched soul makes its living by doing others injury.

Slander, writes Shakespeare, is like a knife

Whose edge is sharper than the sword, whose tongue
Outvenoms all the worms of Nile, whose breath
Rides on the posting winds and doth belie
All corners of the world: kings, queens and states,
Maids, matrons, nay the secrets of the grave
This viperous slander enters.

                                                    (*Cymbeline*, III, 4)

Psalm *120*

AT THE SUMMIT

I lift up my eyes to the hills, to find deliverance; from the Lord deliverance comes to me, the Lord who made heaven and earth. / Never will he who guards thee allow thy foot to stumble; never fall asleep at his post!

THIS IS A PRAYER of the suffering, a prayer that might well be directed at us by the enslaved peoples of our world who look—though they have looked vainly for years—for deliverance.

We have looked, too, and vainly, for deliverance of our brethren from the godless tyranny that holds them in chains. We have "lifted up our eyes" to "the summit" where conferences were to bring peace to the world. We have found only treachery and greed and betrayal from those who understand "peace" in terms of a subjugated, enslaved, beaten world, where dwells a race no longer human, where God is long ago forgotten.

To this hill, "the summit," we have lifted up our eyes in vain, because God was not there to meet us. Instead, many were there who would "allow our feet to stumble," or who "fell asleep at their posts."

We have learned from these failures, as we have learned for

centuries, that man without God will always fail. We have experienced many conferences of our own, with "important people" whose help we sought, whose promises we believed, conferences with employers, superiors, associates or friends. We have placed our confidence in these people, and later we were betrayed or forgotten. This was to teach us that there is no hope from man when God is not there.

There is but one summit to which we can come with trust, without fear of deception, with no chance of double-dealing, no danger of a trap—and that summit is God. There we shall meet true justice, perfect trust, final peace and triumph. If this summit is well prepared for, on our side, there shall be no wrecker and no wreckage.

Men of the age of "reason" and "enlightenment" who could so easily dispense with God, even when they believed in His existence, must have come at last to see how little reason and enlightenment there is in man, unless he fears God and keeps His commandments. To this summit we must always come, first and last; we have nothing to hope from any other. If God has departed, then justice, order, peace, reason, and humanity itself have departed. "It is the Lord that guards thee, the Lord that stands at thy right hand to give thee shelter. The sun's rays by day, the moon's by night, shall have no power to hurt thee. The Lord will guard thee from all evil; the Lord will protect thee in danger. The Lord will protect thy journeying and thy homecoming, henceforth and for ever" (Psalm 120:5-8).

Psalm 121

THE ROYAL RACE

Welcome sound, when I heard them saying, We will go into the Lord's house! / Within thy gates, Jerusalem, our feet stand at last; Jerusalem, built as a city should be built that is one in fellowship.

"I WAS OLD when I was brought to work in this royal household. I had spent a healthy youth, I had grown strong and sturdy, I was well-fed. I felt honored, in a way, when I was uprooted, taken away from all that was dear to me, my parents, my kinsmen, my home, my native country. I, after all, was destined to serve at a palace, to fill a regal post far above what my countrymen could ever boast of.

"I became the royal mediator. Everything had to be done through me. No one ever entered His Majesty's presence without my knowledge; no official act was completed without my courtesies. Through me all nobility entered the court, those born into the regal race as well as those who later obtained the privilege. I was the way to the throne. I saw them brought to the King to obtain his favors; I showed them into the royal presence, where by his signature and seal they were granted perpetual freedom, irrevocable royal privilege.

"I opened the way for these privileged ones, this gracious nobility, as they returned again and again to enjoy audience with the great one, to accept his gifts, to take advantage of his lavish generosity.

"I approved their entry into the palace when they were knighted by him, were anointed with sweet-smelling oil, renewed their vows of allegiance, received new gifts to honor their noble rank.

"I was on hand like an honor guard, as they entered in jubilant, solemn wedding procession; I saw these spoiled children, these happy subjects smothered in privileges, receiving the king's blessing anew. I stood by as they walked out, carting off his gifts; I shuddered to think how those precious things would be set aside to soil, to wear out, to decay—all by neglect and insolence.

"Was I envious? No, not really. I was sad. Sadder yet when at length I saw these privileged ones carried past me again, in funeral procession, carried into his presence, still honored by him, mourned by him and his court, sung to, prayed for, wept over. Never did king console bereaved families as did he.

"Year after year I saw these families of the nobility, saw them come to me, and through me to His Majesty; saw them, infants, children, knighted soldiers, young lovers, parents proudly bringing their children to him, young and old laying their troubles and sorrows before him. Never did he reject any of them.

"I saw much of this privileged race of the court, and I tell you, they are unworthy, all of them.

"Unworthy and ungrateful. Negligent and ignorant. Not the best of them understand the immeasurable superiority of their privileges.

"I know. I came from a land where it was not so. No such joys were ours. We had a certain kind of native happiness, you might say. We were attached to our homeland, we grew, lived well, and flourished. But I could never have returned to that land, once I had taken my important post at his palace.

"Well, at last I must confess, I did envy this race; it was a holy envy that made me burn with indignation to see these people blind to their exalted nobility, and to the infinitely gracious qualities of their king. No other race ever enjoyed such privileges nor served such a king. Of this I am sure: they never gave him the honor and love he deserved.

"They never knew—none of them, poor wretches—what manner of king was this. They are gone now, most of them. I saw their bodies carried past me to the grave. But their king remains; it is only right that he should. I'm here, too, and expect to be for a long time. And I confess, I'll never know what made these people so blind. . . .

"Pardon me for not introducing myself. I was a sturdy oak tree in the forest. Uprooted, I took up a new post—in fact, a door-post. I became door-post and door of a Catholic church. Yes, I am the door of the Church. Now you understand why I moan as I do.

"I was like the gate spoken of in Psalm 121. I was the way to Jerusalem, the city of God on earth, 'built as a city should be built.' It was indeed a 'welcome sound, when I heard them saying, We will go into the Lord's house.' If only they had understood the great joy of it!"

Psalm 122

WAITING FOR HIS MERCY

Unto thee I lift up my eyes, unto thee, who dwellest in the heavens. | See how the eyes of servants are fixed on the hands of their masters, the eyes of a maid on the hand of her mistress! | Our eyes, too, are fixed on the Lord our God, waiting for him to show mercy on us.

IF, AS THE PSALMIST indicates, our eyes are fixed on the hands of our Master, waiting for His mercy, we have seen every proof of that mercy in the Son of God made man.

All Your life, Jesus, You continued to give up all that You had a right to, because You came to serve us—although we should have served You instead. It was not enough, Lord, that You should empty Yourself and be born poor, although You are the Creator, the Ruler and Owner of the world.

Nor was it enough that the king who should have given up his throne to You was seeking to kill You instead.

It was not enough, either, that You hid Yourself from Your own people, who had been instructed by their prophets to love You with

all their heart and soul, all their mind and strength. They thought
nothing of You, silent, hidden young man of Nazareth, dressed in
the coarse robe of the poor, skin darkened by the sun and by the
sands of the streets. Your beauty and brilliance were hidden: "How
should we recognize that face?" Isaias asked. "How should we take
any account of him, a man so despised?" (53:3).

"The carpenter's son," they called You. How could such a one
come by any wisdom, honor, or dignity? When at last You showed
Yourself the Son of God, the people began to follow You, but the
rulers turned against You.

Your band of disciples, it is true, watched Your every movement
and at least after Your resurrection they remembered Your words
and Your example. But when the hour of Your great sacrifice had
come—what were they doing? At Your last supper with them they
quarreled about who should be the greatest of them in the kingdom,
thus showing that they had not grasped Your example of humility,
they had not understood Your lesson of unselfish love.

But You forgave them, and at table You consecrated bread and
wine into Your Body and Blood, a gift to Your friends as long as
the world would last. This, too, they did not understand; none gave
themselves to You in return a few hours later, when Your hour had
come in the garden of Gethsemane. "Then all His disciples left
Him and fled."

All Your life had been sacrificed for Your creatures. What works
of charity You had done! And when Your hour of sorrow had
come, who of them were there to comfort You? A few of Your
most faithful ones came and stood with Your Mother under the
cross, when You were about to die. Mary, Your humble mother, was
all but alone to share Your sorrow with You.

The third day, Sunday morning, You arose from the dead, so that
the world would know that the man it had forsaken was indeed its
God.

Should You not have rejected Your people, then, who had murdered You out of hatred and envy, or who had done nothing to
show their gratitude? Could You not justly abandon Your apostles

and disciples who had abandoned You in Your sufferings? Should You not reject us, who continue to commit these crimes against Your creatures, in whom You dwell? "I am Jesus, whom you persecute. . . . What you have done to the least of these, My brethren, you have done to Me."

Yet on the day of Your resurrection You came to Your disciples—You came to us all, gave us the kiss of peace. To those who had abandoned You, You gave joy by Your glorious presence, made them Your choice ambassadors, promised to be with them and their successors "all days, even to the end of the world." Thus You have treated Your ungrateful creatures for centuries.

Who would not "lift his eyes" to such an infinitely selfless Master? Who would not "fix their eyes" on You, Lord, "waiting for Your mercy," knowing he had not long to wait?

Psalm 123

TIDE AND SNARE

It seemed as if the tide must have sucked us down, the torrent closed above us; closed above us the waters that ran so high. | Blessed be the Lord, who has not let us fall a prey to those ravening mouths! | Safe, like a bird rescued from the fowler's snare; the snare is broken and we are safe! | Such help is ours, the Lord's help, that made heaven and earth.

THE TIDE which threatens to engulf us, the snare from which we must be rescued is our own sinful self. No need to look for any other, when we know too well the story of our self-inflicted suffering! Most of our vices come equipped with automatic punishments. Sleepless nights, headaches and nausea—the aftermath of willful worries. Willful, because we refuse to remove the selfishness from which these worries stem.

Enmity, rancor, vehement criticism. The inward torments of jealousy, fear of losing our own importance; of envy, fear of others' progress; of outright hatred, blindness to others' good; gnawing desire, eagerness for worldly goals difficult to attain; terror at the thought of failure, fear of insult, humiliation, defeat, ridicule.

Not only do the self-imposed punishments of these vices bring deep mental disturbance; they are often sources of physical pain. Body and soul gradually sink into a state of sickness for which the cure is hard, and from which the patient too often cannot rise.

Life offers us pain enough and troubles aplenty, God knows, without the help of our vices. Lord Jesus, You never experienced the torture of hurt pride, corroding greed, needling envy, or frustrated desire. Yet Your whole life was sacrifice, and You redeemed us through bitter agony. Your pain was real and heroic; ours is fired by imagination and petty self-love. How ashamed ought we be at how much we suffer for unworthy causes! It is not *what* we endure, but *why,* that makes us great or small. And we are nearly always much too small.

Yet in the inscrutable mystery of pain, in Your infinite wisdom and mercy, is there not room for genuine reparation even in self-inflicted punishment? Is there not reparation at least so long as we struggle against the unworthy cause, not immediately able to remove it? Is our own weakness not "a sting of the flesh" through which we might find You, and then find ourselves?

Behold how low we have fallen, Jesus, and there is in ourselves no rescue from the tide of our petty vices. No rescue, but in throwing ourselves at Your feet. We have sinned, all of us. We have all need of the glory of God. Your truth, Your greatness in selfless love shall rescue us at least from the snare.

Psalm 124

THOSE WHO TRUST

Those who trust in the Lord are strong as Mount Sion itself, that
stands unmoved for ever. | The hills protect Jerusalem; so the Lord
protects his people, now and for ever.

HE WAS SLEEPING. Bound with two chains, watched by "four files
of soldiers," he was sleeping. On the last dreadful night before
his execution, he was sleeping.

Lord, You love people who can sleep like that, because You love
people who trust You like that! No wonder You loved Peter. Peter
was the hope of the newborn Church; the newborn Church had to
suffer and to trust and to overcome. From Peter the newborn
Church learned how to trust You.

Everybody was fearfully praying for Peter; the Church was
weak without him. Herod intended to murder Peter in the morning. Kings, princes, dictators—all seem to go in for murder of the
innocents. After centuries of "civilization" they haven't changed
much, except for the worse.

But Peter was sleeping. "Those who trust in the Lord are strong
as Mount Sion itself." In the arms of God, a condemned man can
sleep.

Peter had no way of knowing whether God intended to spare his
life. The whole Church was praying for him. Clearly he remembered Jesus saying, "Will not God avenge His elect, who cry to Him
day and night? I tell you, He will avenge them quickly." But he
also remembered Your saying, Lord, "They will persecute you and
put you to death for My sake."

Which was it now? Was it the end? Perhaps. But God could still do what He pleased.

All the same, Peter must have been surprised at what You chose to do. When You sent an angel to wake Peter, to snap his chains, to break jail with him, Peter must have been greatly surprised. You have a way of surprising Your friends at times like that, Lord.

Perhaps You would surprise us oftener, too, if we trusted You as Peter did. We forget that more than the Almighty Creator, You are our personal, loving Father.

You are my Father, Lord, in the most real and beautiful sense of that word. You know me completely, everything that I am, everything that I need—far better than I know it myself. This is the reality of "divine providence" which we tend to think of as such a cold, impersonal force. The truth You came to reveal, Lord Jesus, was the intimate, personal, face-to-face contact of love which God our Father has with each of us.

It is because of this infinite yet warm and touching love of God that "those who trust in the Lord are strong as Mount Sion itself, that stands unmoved for ever."

Psalm 125

SCHOOL OF ANGUISH

Deliver us, Lord, from our bondage; our withered hopes, Lord, like some desert water-course renew! / The men who are sowing in tears will reap, one day, with joy. Mournful enough they go, but with seed to scatter; / trust me, they will come back rejoicing, as they carry their sheaves with them.

OUR LIFE is a school, a school of anguish in which we prepare for eternal glory, a school of trials in which we must learn to conform our wills perfectly with the will of our Creator. If anything is written in nature and in revelation, this surely is. If anything is made clear by Your example, Jesus, it is this: we are born that we might at last submit ourselves with joy to the mysterious will of a loving father, Your Heavenly Father. Of Your example St. Paul writes: "Son of God though He was, He learned obedience in the school of suffering."

We are all placed in this school, and no man escapes doing its work. If he utterly fails to accept the divine will, he must yet obey it in the eternal loss, the emptiness of hell, where he must of necessity abide by his choice—his choice to reject the boundless happiness of God.

If a man conforms himself perfectly on earth with Your heavenly plan, he will soon learn that only "passing through fire and water," as the Scripture warns us, shall we at last reach "the place of refreshment." He will soon learn that he must sow the seeds of eternal hope in tears, in pain, even in bitterness, until at last the seed has sprung up into eternal life. He will cry to You often, in the anguished tones of the psalmist, "Deliver us, Lord, from our bondage!"

Most of us reject this perfect conformity, because it must do violence to our languid flesh. Yet we fear God enough to seek His will in most things; we do not entirely turn away from Him. Nevertheless, Lord, we insult You day by day, taking back piece by piece what we have promised (and even vowed) to give You. At every bend in the road we again fall short of what we have pledged.

Then death comes, like a thief in the night. How much remains undone! How much distance we have left to cover! How long before our understanding and will approach perfection! When we were young, our mothers used to tell us, "You have so very much to learn yet." Now we are at the end of life, and there is yet so very much to learn.

But in Your mercy You have provided us a place of purgation. This school of humility and love will be our hope and strength beyond death, our consolation and preparation for final perfection.

What gratitude we owe You, Lord, for this school which Dante in his *Purgatorio* calls "the Mount where Justice searches us," where "God ordains our debt should be repaid" (Cant. iii, 3; x, 108). Here there will be no wasted tears, here "mournful enough they go, but with seed to scatter; trust me, they will come back rejoicing, as they carry their sheaves with them."

Psalm 126

UNLESS THE LORD . . .

Vain is the builder's toil, if the house is not of the Lord's building; / vainly the guard keeps watch, if the city has not the Lord for its guardian.

Of all the psalms, perhaps this one has prophesied the most; this one has forecast in clearest terms the great catastrophes of history—falling empires, ruined cities, heaped corpses, broken families, love turned against itself.

The psalm assures us that a nation, a city, a family where God is not enthroned bears within itself the seeds of its own destruction. History has no clearer lesson to teach.

Nothing on earth has been so cleverly organized, so intelligently planned, so disposed in good will that it could endure, if God was not its beginning, its end, its reason for existing.

Egypt, Assyria, Greece, and Rome in ancient times learned this lesson. If emperors' tombs could speak to us, what other truth would they find worth the telling? "You look upon us as antiques of a dim past," they would tell us, "but there is one quiet message we bear, and that should be no secret, for your own prophets and writers have told you: All is vain that is not of God; all is vanity but to serve Him."

Lord, if I may allow "politics" to mix into meditation just for today's lesson, I may read this psalm as a note to the modern world. . . .

"You toil much, you great scientific builders, you great psychiatric advisors, you great intellectual speech-makers—but have you noticed lately that your toil is in vain?

"You have wasted untold hours, days, months, years, on 'disarmament.' You would save the world for Freedom, then abuse that freedom.

"You have appointed committees and established investigations until I fear you may run out of men, but do you now, on this account, feel safe? Have your problems approached solution? Or have your countrymen circumvented your probes and monitors until you yourselves have doubted their value?

"You are men of good will, you 'seek the solutions'—no one doubts that!—but are you pleased with the results?

"You talk of moving forward and onward, and you do seem to be moving somewhere and somehow, but where are you arriving?

"I am but an ancient psalm, scribbled by a poet now long dead, sung to a lyre now long buried in the dust. I have no great claim to your 'modern' ear—unless you have been thinking lately. Have you? Do you really believe that your world is closer to heaven than the world of my day? Or have you felt alarmed of late, as King David felt alarmed at the pagans of his day?

"That, you see, is why he sang: 'Vain is the builder's toil, if the house is not of the Lord's building; vainly the guards keep watch, if the city has not the Lord for its guardian.'"

Psalm 127

MY PARTING ADVICE

Blessed thou art, if thou dost fear the Lord, and follow his paths! . . . / Thy wife shall be fruitful as a vine, in the heart of thy home, the children round thy table sturdy as olive-branches. . . . / Mayest thou live to see thy children's children, and peace resting upon Israel.

A FATHER growing old and wise in experience should have much to teach his son. What should he hope especially that the young man will learn?

The aging Polonius advised his son Laertes:

"Give every man thy ear, but few thy voice;
   Take each man's censure, but reserve thy judgment. . . .
This above all, to thine own self be true
And it must follow, as the night the day,
Thou canst not then be false to any man."

(Hamlet, I, 3)

It was advice good enough, for all that, but vague enough and general enough to offend no listener and to call for no discussion. It was worthy of the windy Polonius.

The elder Tobias had far more to give his son, words of direction that reached to the young man's innermost life:

"Do thou, while thou hast life, think ever upon God, nor lend thyself to any sinful design, nor leave the commandments of the Lord our God unfulfilled. Use thy wealth in giving of alms; never turn thy back on any man who is in need, and the Lord, in thy own need, will have eyes for thee. . . . Alms-deeds were ever a sovereign way of escape from guilt and death, a bar against the soul's passage into darkness; none has less to fear when he stands before the most high God than he who does them" (Tobias 4:6–12).

Tobias counselled his son in all the natural virtues, concluding, "Fear we but God, shun guilt, and do the good we can, blessings shall be ours in abundance."

Polonius advised his son to cherish a high reputation among men; Tobias bade his son treasure a high reputation with God. "Live well, do good," they told their sons, "and you shall be rewarded."

Noble advice from noble men; we approve, we applaud, we admire. . . .

Then we hear the counsel given by a mother to her seven sons, in the Book of Machabees:

"Into this womb you came," she told them, "who know how? Not I quickened, not I the breath of live gave you, nor fashioned the bodies of you one by one! Man's birth, and the origin of all things, he devised who is the whole world's Maker; and shall he not mercifully give the breath of life back to you, that for his law's sake hold your lives so cheap?" (II Machabees 7:22–23).

Live well, please men and please God? More than that, says this courageous mother, give up your life gladly, sacrifice everything and die well, that you may not lose eternal life.

This, indeed, was the best advice of all. It was no question of whether she would inspire her young sons to view the world optimistically or bitterly. Above the realistic warnings against men's betrayals and injustices, men's greediness and ingratitude, the world's brief and passing successes, its coldness and man's loneliness—above these tragic truths of life, this great mother saw as a prophet the white light of the risen Christ. "This world, its frame and figure, shall pass away, my sons, but your immortal spirits shall remain. And God has promised to restore your bodies, glorified and strengthened to fit your heroic souls, which suffered and perfected themselves in these bodies. This, after all, is the one necessary advice."

Psalm 128

WHICH IS HARDER?

Sore have they beset me even from my youth . . . but never once
outmatched me. / I bent my back to the oppressor, and long was
the furrow ere the plough turned; / but the Lord proved faithful,
and cut the bonds of tyranny asunder.

FOR THOSE who have experienced it, Lord, no prayer gives greater
joy than this, the prayer of victory over temptation.

"Sore have they beset me even from my youth." What man or
woman has not suffered the sting of temptation? And who of us
has not been weak, has not fallen, has not suffered remorse for our
weakness? Who does not know the pain of regret, and how much
worse is the wound of the sin than the pleasure of the weakness?

So easy to slander, so hard to repair the harm done.

So easy to condemn in anger, so hard to apologize.

So easy to rage over our injured pride, so hard to humble ourselves and confess the wrong.

So easy to add injury to envy, so hard to recover the lost friend.

So easy to give way to the flesh, so hard to recover reverence and
self-respect. So hard to justify our disgust at the vulgarities of others,
when we have so often been more guilty.

So easy to neglect good example to the young, so hard to "understand" their actions later.

Alas, when we look back at our lives, Lord Jesus, how much easier
it would have been to overcome temptation than to face the inevitable results of our sins! What pain is like the pain over wasted
opportunity, uncontrolled passion, lost friends? What sickness is
like the sickness of weak will, undeveloped virtue, decayed self-

esteem? How late, Lord, when at last we learn that no earthly triumph would have brought joy like that of conquering temptation.

The athlete who trains his body experiences both pain and pleasure. There is pain, especially in the first exercises of the season, when the muscles that have been idle must resume their work. There is the burden of the daily push and pull, the natural tedium that accompanies oft-repeated exercise. The young contestant must run farther than the weakened body pleases; his limbs will be stiff and sore for a few days. But this, he says, is very little compared with the pleasure of feeling his reawakened strength, of sensing the new health and vigor as it grows with him. He will soon forget the pains, when each day the weights become easier to lift, the track is easier to run, and every physical effort diminishes.

The joy of the spiritual athlete is no less. Indeed, Lord, much of our human joy would be lost, if we had no temptation to conquer. The spiritual life would seem dull indeed if it cost us nothing, if it did not bring us the glory of battle and of victory.

What saint would care to pray, "Sore have temptations beset me from my youth," if he could not at once add, "but never once have they outmatched me"?

What saint could rejoice in saying, "I bent my back to the oppressor," if he could not add, "but the Lord proved faithful, and cut the bonds of tyranny asunder"?

On the other hand, who could boast of "never being outmatched" if no temptation ever tried to "outmatch" him; or who rejoice that the Lord had rescued him from tyranny, if there were no tyrants that the "Lord had proved faithful" against, if there were no world, no flesh, no devil which first were "unfaithful"?

Psalm 129

PENANCE

Out of the depths I cry to thee, O Lord; Master, listen to my voice; let but thy ears be attentive to the voice that calls on thee for pardon.

As HE BEGAN the tract on *Penance* in moral theology class, a certain professor defined, "Penance: a most beautiful virtue which many people think they have and do not."

Not too scientific, Lord, but very much to the point. To recite "An Act of Contrition" is a pure external; to *mean* it is quite another matter.

"Out of the depths have I cried. . . ." It is one step toward the real virtue of penance to realize the depths into which I have fallen. I have debased myself. Not that I can degrade or injure God, who is all perfection; but that He loves me eternally, and wishes to raise me up.

"Out of the depths have I cried. . . ." Spoiling my own nature does reflect on God, in whose image I was created. I am an ungrateful son who has ruined himself, thus rejecting his Father's gifts and making light of His love.

"Out of the depths. . . ." So low have I fallen, because I set myself up so high. Unsatisfied to be Your child, Lord, I tried to make myself a god—and how low this god has fallen! I have needed little time to find the cause of my fall: for as I began to examine my conscience, I thought of the capital sins, the seven vices. The first is pride: so much and in so many ways have I sinned by pride, that I have not yet made my way to the second vice.

Pride caused my fits of unjust anger, whereby I offended those I ought to love. Pride was the seed of my insults and injuries.

Pride caused me to be silent, when I should have corrected those for whom I am responsible: I feared criticism.

Pride poisoned my tongue, when I spoke evil against my neighbor. Pride would not let me forget injuries done, not the smallest accidental slight.

Pride caused my most humiliating sins, because by overconfidence I did not beware of temptation or know my weaknesses. Pride caused me to ignore my own sinfulness to complain of others.

"If thou, Lord, wilt keep record of our iniquities," says the psalm, "Master, who has strength to bear it?"

I am glad to have You forget my sins, Lord, but do I forget those of my neighbor? Oh, how exact is my record, how accurate my memory! Every unkind word, every forgetful omission, every oversight—all is carefully noted in my "black book." No one escapes.

If no one escapes, Lord, how shall I escape? Where shall I find pardon? For as I forgive, so shall I be forgiven. If so, Lord, how great must my mercy become!

Psalm 130

BLACK THREAD THROUGH
THE BLAZE

Lord, my heart is not lifted up, my eyes not raised from the earth; / my mind does not dwell on high things, on marvels that are beyond my reach.

THIS PSALM expresses the author's trust in God, a confidence he proves by not setting his mind or his heart on things too far above his reach.

The point is well taken: do not desire favors or marvels beyond your reach, and you will be spared disappointment. There is truer happiness in lowliness.

But a further meaning can be found here: a complaint that the mind of man is slow to rise above this world of material things. If heaven is "a marvel beyond my reach," I am not helped by dwelling on it so little.

How much greater I could become, Lord, if my eyes were but "raised from the earth"! How small my complaints, my quarrels and envies would become! How genuine and healthy my charity would be! I would see, like Robert Browning, that

> No work begun shall ever pause for death!
> Love will be helpful to me more and more
> In the coming course, the new path I must tread.
> (*The Ring and the Book*)

This same great poet has compared the darkness of this world with the glory of the next by calling it "this black thread through the blaze." ("An Epistle.") Eternity and heaven, great and beyond our reach as they are, surround the earth, cover it on every side, and stoop down to it. Indeed, when we least suspect, God and the angels who tremble in reverence before Him are at our side, and see in our souls a beauty and a power which we ignore.

If we could once see, as Lazarus saw, the other, the eternal side of life, why, then we would see how "the small becomes the dreadful and immense!" (Browning, "Mr. Sludge the Medium.")

Once we leave this puny earth, this weak, uncertain life, this "black thread through the blaze," how truly we will say then, with the psalmist, "A child's thoughts were all my soul knew."

If then I recall, Lord, that in spite of my witless folly, my ignorance of Your true glory, if yet I serve You because I trust Your word, what joy! Blinded I was, "my eyes not raised from the earth" and its foolishness, but hardly knowing, much less understanding the "vast orb of glory on either side that meager thread," I was yet led to it by Your grace.

Could I then die again, I would die of shock in finding what I might have lost by my ignorance.

Psalm 131

THE SECRET OF HAPPINESS

Never will I come beneath the roof of my house, or climb up into the bed that is strewn for me; / never shall these eyes have sleep, these eye-lids close, until I have found the Lord a home, the great God of Jacob a dwelling-place.

DAVID IN THIS PSALM describes his years of suffering, fighting the heathen, striving vainly to rally his people to a respect for divine law, laboring unceasingly at the impossible task of finding a place fit to use for honoring God and a people fit to do Him the honor. Were these years lost, because others failed to measure up to David's nobility, because in their duplicity they rejected him and revolted against him?

Was he a failure because his wife Michol reviled him and laughed him to scorn for dancing before the ark of God, and because his son Absalom led a traitorous attack against him?

How many of us, Lord, would have given up in despair, completely ignorant of the happiness we had really found? For David's songs are full of love and happiness—and with very good reason!

No worldly success or scheme or popularity or financial gain has the power to make us happy. Whatever is not the work of unselfish love is not the work of happiness. That is why Turgenev could write, "The key to the whole of life is to be able to put oneself in the second place." This is the secret of David's happiness. Once he had learned the painful lesson of sin, he found his true place in life. Though he was king of a privileged race, his was second place, a very definite second place he himself had chosen.

Once he had learned through God's punishment that his place in life was not to receive but to give, he was prepared for genuine happiness, and no calamity could ever destroy the deep joy of his spirit.

The foundation of his happiness was a constant, self-effacing love for his God, and the foundation of his love was an unwavering confidence. He no longer doubted that the Almighty's love never fails, that He chastens and corrects for our good, that in His Will is all our joy and peace.

This is why the saints had such deep, unselfish concern for the good of their fellowmen. This is why they were yet filled with joy and tenderness in their bitterest trials. The secret of happiness was theirs, not merely its splendid theory, but its true practice.

"He who would rejoice in the spirit of Christ the Lord must *give himself* in the spirit of Christ the Lord."

That spirit, Lord Jesus, was the thirst which made You say, "There is a baptism I must needs be baptized with, and how impatient am I for its accomplishment!" Your desire for death, selfless as it was, deep and great as life itself, was Your secret of happiness.

Psalm 132

CHRISTIAN UNITY

Gracious the sight, and full of comfort, where brethren dwell united. . . . / It is as if dew like the dews of Hermon were falling

on this hill of Sion; here, where the Lord grants benediction and
life everlastingly.

UNITY IN LOVE has always been a thing of beauty to man. Most
beautiful of all is God's union of love, love for our neighbor as
ourselves, rooted in Christ: it is called the Communion of Saints.

In this Communion, most of all, "brethren dwell united," and
have the deepest reason for unity, the mystical body of Christ,
"where the Lord grants benediction and life everlastingly."

It was You Yourself, Jesus, who showed us how truly united we
were as Christians when You said, "I am the vine, you are the
branches. . . . He who abides in me, and I in him, bears much fruit:
for without Me you can do nothing." It was here, at Your eucharistic
supper with Your disciples, that You taught true unity in love: "By
this shall all men know you are My disciples: that you have love
for one another" (John 15:4-5 and 13: 35).

Of this unity among men which You came to bring, Your disciples could then say, as St. Paul wrote, "Let us grow up in every
respect in love and bring about union with Christ who is the head.
The whole body is dependent on him. Harmoniously joined and
knit together, it derives its energy in the measure each part needs
only through contact with the source of supply. In this way the
body grows and builds itself up through love" (Ephesians 4:15-16).

The Communion of Saints, "when brethren dwell united,"—the
glorious saints in heaven, the souls being purified in purgatory, the
souls struggling on earth—is one of the most beautiful mysteries
of the Church and of mankind. So intimately and so profitably does
it bind us with our fellowmen that we are constantly helping one
another, even when we take no thought of it.

If I say a prayer for a suffering soul in purgatory, I cannot know
whether that soul needs it, or is already worthy of heaven. Yet, my
prayer is never lost. You know well, Lord, as head of this body,
what member stands in need of my help, and what member deserves it. And some day, united with them in heaven, I will be
thanked for my charity by people I have never known on earth. I

will be amazed at how much my prayers and good works have accomplished. Who knows what calamities have been averted, what sinners have been converted, by the prayer of an innocent child?

"Faith, hope, and charity remain: but the greatest of these is charity." And indeed, its effects reach into eternity, to God Himself, from whom it takes its origin, and through God, to all "His least brethren," many of whom we may never see on this earth. This is the true and final unity for which we were created.

Psalm 133

A SONG IN THE NIGHT

V. *Come, then, praise the Lord, all you that are the Lord's servants; / you that wait on the Lord's house at midnight, lift up your hands towards the sanctuary and bless the Lord. R. May the Lord who dwells in Sion bless thee, the Lord who made heaven and earth.*

COMMENTATORS are quite agreed that this psalm was a formal greeting to the priests who came to keep the night vigil in the temple; colloquially, a word of encouragement to the night shift.

Those who came to the temple at night to pray, came with a duty in many ways enviable. The night—who has not experienced this?—had much to commend it for fervent prayer. It was generally cool and pleasant, peace had descended, the darkness and silence had shut out distraction. What could bring the soul nearer to God than these sacred hours, when the noise of worldly activity had finally ceased, when the harsh realities of business and labor, of worry and sin seemed at last conquered?

It is not surprising that the Church continued the Hebrew custom of night prayer, assigning the hour of Compline to the darkness after sundown, and the longest canonical hour of prayer, Matins, to a night hour.

How many saints, burdened with daily cares in schools, hospitals, parishes, in serving their neighbor, reserved these quiet night hours for their soul's refreshment, alone with God! Thus they atoned, Lord, by their genuine love for You, who so often "spent the night in the prayer of God," for those who abused the sacredness of night.

For how many of Your creatures, Lord, has the night been a time of darkness supreme, of unbridled passion, of unleashed hatred, revenge, betrayal, and murder! "And it was night." With this awful note of gloom begins the account of Your own betrayal, Jesus, by Judas, and by the leaders of the people. How much evil has the night covered! How truly these quiet hours have become symbols of ignorance, deception, foul deeds, secret sins.

Yet to Your saints, "all things are clean," and to the pure the night hours are the purest, unsurpassed in their beauty, in the great silence that speaks volumes.

For the night hours the Church chose psalms that begged God to save us from evil, from the horrors and terrors of darkness, as in Psalm 90. Yet she has never forgotten the beauty and glory of the night: *Deus dedit carmen in nocte:* God poured out a song in the night (Job 35:10). And so for these same night watches, Psalm 133 was chosen, that we might praise God in the night: "You that wait on the Lord's house at midnight, lift up your hands toward the sanctuary and bless the Lord."

Psalm 134

IDOLS TO FEED

What are the idols of the heathen but silver and gold, gods which the hands of men have fashioned? / They have mouths, and yet are silent; eyes they have, and yet are sightless; ears they have, and want all hearing, never a breath have they in their mouths. / Such the end of all who make them, such the reward of all who trust them.

NEVERTHELESS, LORD, the heathen continues to build his gods, to fashion his dreams, to labor all his life for them.

"Idols of silver and gold": money, expensive possessions, comforts, "the good life," good looks, good time, flattering friends, self-importance, prestige, externals over which worldly men boast, "gods which the hands of men have fashioned." Gods which the psalmist calls silent, sightless, deaf, lifeless. "And those who make these gods," he adds, "become like them; those who trust in these gods shall one day be as empty as they."

They have mouths to be fed, they grow fat at a great expense, they demand all our time and effort, the very strength of our soul. They tend more and more to devour us—while yet never opening those mouths to teach us, to console us, or assure us of happiness. If they could speak, how they would ridicule us, as did the false gods of *Everyman* in the medieval play. One after the other, these dear friends of his life abandoned him. None would promise to accompany him to the grave. Friends and kinsmen abandoned him when first this journey was mentioned. Said *Fellowship:*

> No! Nothing could even tempt me;
> Not a foot will I go. Had you but tarried here,

> Never would I leave. But since you go,
> God speed you on your solitary journey!

And *Kindred* added:

> Go with you? Is that what you wish?
> No, Everyman; why, to fast for five long years
> On bread and water were better fare!

There were better friends, higher gods, such as Knowledge, Beauty, Strength, and Discretion, who promised to stay on when all others had abandoned. But when they caught sight of his grave, the conversation quickly changed:

Beauty: I've changed my mind. Adieu, my worthy friend,
I've just remembered that I've other work to do.

Everyman: Where are you going, Beauty?

Beauty: Peace! I will not hear you,
Will not look behind for any price.

Everyman: Alas! Wherein can I place my trust?

Strength: I'm sorry, Everyman, but I must leave you, too.
I do not like this game at all.

Everyman: Will you also forsake me now? Dear friend,
You said that you would stay with me forever.

Strength: Well, I have brought you far enough.
It seems to me that you are old enough
To go upon a trifle like a pilgrimage alone.
It was a mistake for me to come....

Discretion: Everyman, I must follow Strength and leave you.

Everyman: For love of God, show pity! Come and see the grave
In which I must lonely lie, if all desert me thus!

Discretion: That would be *too* close! Farewell, my friend!

So "Everyman"—every one of us— is at the last as silent, sightless, deaf and lifeless as the false gods we worshipped. . . .

Unless before that time we found the true God, and with Him, true life.

Psalm 135

MERCY AND WISDOM

Eternal the mercy that remembers us in our affliction, eternal the mercy that rescues us from our enemies, eternal the mercy that gives all living things their food. / Give thanks to the God of heaven, his mercy is eternal.

THE PSALMIST, child of a nation that had suffered continuous oppression, fear, famine, and war, knew what that nation owed God for rescuing it time and again from these evils. It is, nevertheless, a tribute to that nation's faith that these trials had not made its people bitter or resentful. There were yet faithful souls who saw God's infinite mercy even in their sorrows. They never doubted that, in the end, God's eternal love would be manifest.

There is herein a confidence that every good Christian possesses. No danger, no evil or catastrophe, however great and fearsome, shall ever leave him doubting "the God of heaven, whose mercy is eternal."

But what of us who have been showered with too many material blessings? Can such a psalm have any meaning for us? Yes, the same meaning, in the reverse sense. If we are true to life's realities, if we honestly desire to please God, we may say that God's "eternal mercy remembers us in our affliction," the affliction of too much worldliness, the affliction of lukewarmness, the affliction of too little faith—and here, as well, we find "eternal the mercy that rescues us from our enemies."

If by now we have seen in the psalms, and through them in the teachings of the Savior they proclaim, if we have seen herein God's way with man, God's mysterious, loving manner of saving us, we can now see "eternal mercy" in the afflictions God sends us, as well as in the respite He sends when these trials threaten to overwhelm us.

"Eternal the mercy that gives all living things their food," but if the spirit of man is to be nourished and sustained, it must receive its due proportion of bitter food. The very consecrated spiritual food which the Church offers us is, in truth, the Body of Christ broken for us in sacrifice, the Blood of Christ offered us from the bitter pain of the Cross.

For all these mercies—the scourge, nail, and thorn as well as the wine of joy, the crown of victory, and sceptre of peace—we "give thanks to the God of heaven, his mercy is eternal," extending from time into eternity in an unending marvel of wisdom.

Psalm 136

PILGRIMS AND STRANGERS

We sat down by the streams of Babylon and wept there, remembering Sion. / Willow-trees grow there, and on these we hung up our harps when the men who took us prisoner cried out for a song.... What, should we sing the Lord's song in a strange land? / Jerusalem, if I forget thee, perish the skill of my right hand! Let my tongue stick fast to the roof of my mouth if I cease to remember thee, if I love not Jerusalem dearer than heart's content!

THOSE WHO ACCOMPLISH real good in the eternal records of God are seldom those who see the results of their work. The psalmist understands, here, the obligation to go on doing good despite all apparent failure and the bitterest opposition.

It is so much easier to see failure, loss, and corruption—easier to see the results of our neglect than the results of our faithful service. Failures have scandalized and ruined many who began well.

Despair is never far from those who set out to do good; the temptation is always present: "What? Should we sing the Lord's song in a strange land?"

"Yes, Lord," we must answer. "For we are here pilgrims and strangers." We should not expect to see the results of the good we do, Lord. How many great men ever did? But we dare not on that account give up. Too many have shrugged their shoulders, have lost their zeal and fallen into spiritual decay, because they found no palpable effects of their efforts.

You Yourself warned us, Jesus, that because the world is heaped with scandals, "the charity of many shall grow cold."

But You never asked that we see results. You Yourself did not stay in this world to witness the results of Your work. It was enough that You had done Your Father's Will, that You had not lost an ounce of Your charity, that Your Father in heaven would see the results, and You would send another Paraclete to complete the work You had begun.

Why can we not learn the lesson contained in this psalm: it is not our earthly success but our perseverance in love that counts. If the lives of the saints teach us anything, it is surely this: Love to the end, and remember, results will come in God's good time, not in ours.

Psalm 137

PERSEVERANCE

Though affliction surround my path, thou dost preserve me; / it is thy power that confronts my enemies' malice, thy right hand that rescues me. / My purposes the Lord will yet speed; thy mercy, Lord, endures forever. . . .

LIFE IS FULL of entanglements, bitter coldness, shocking revelations. We come out of an innocent youth one day into a jolting world of reality. It is then, more than in our childhood, that we are in real need of help. And where shall we turn? Suspicion has replaced confidence, pride has replaced the humility which made it easy to be helped; and when at last we bring ourselves to ask, the hoped-for charity has paled, the promises have collapsed—no one seems willing to sacrifice anything for us.

It is easy to become embittered and resentful, easy to resort to selfish tactics. "No one helps me—I will help no one; I made my own way—why can't he make his?" Happiness flees with these revengeful thoughts; when we clutch so firmly the little we have, more good is lost than gained.

A true, noble heart does not become embittered, no matter what bitterness the world serves it. A true, noble heart might, however, learn its lesson. Perseverance in genuine goodness is too great a work for man's own power. It is a gift direct from God. Many, too, "followed Jesus, but He did not trust Himself to them, for He knew what was in man" (John 2:24–25).

If our confidence in human helps to human success has not been exaggerated, if our hopes were built on more than human props, our trust will recover and happiness will not be lost.

Perseverance is a habit, a virtue. Its nature is not to fail when human resources fail. It is the work of a truly Christian perseverance to remind me, Lord, "though affliction surround my path, thou dost preserve me. . . . My purposes the Lord will yet speed; thy mercy, Lord endures forever."

One of the most powerful and beautiful prayers for perseverance ever composed is that of the Papal blessing given *"urbi et orbi,"* to the city and to the world, by a newly elected Pope:

> In virtue of the prayers and merits
> of Blessed Mary ever Virgin,
> of Blessed Michael the Archangel,
> of Blessed John the Baptist,
> of the holy apostles Peter and Paul,
> and of all the saints,
> may almighty God have mercy on you,
> and after all your sins have been forgiven,
> may Jesus Christ lead you into eternal life. Amen.
> May the almighty and merciful God grant you
> forgiveness, absolution, and remission of all your sins,
> a sufficient time for true and fruitful penance, a heart always pliant,
> reformation of your life, grace and consolation of the Holy Spirit,
> and final perseverance in good works. Amen.
> And may the blessing of almighty God, the Father and the Son
> and the Holy Spirit, descend upon you and remain forever. Amen.

Psalm 138

I CANNOT DESCRIBE IT

Such wisdom as thine is far beyond my reach, no thought of mine can attain it. . . . / Of my soul thou hast full knowledge, and this mortal frame had no mysteries for thee, | who didst contrive it in secret, devise its pattern, there in the dark recesses of the earth. | All my acts thy eyes have seen, all are set down already in thy record. . . . A riddle, O my God, thy dealings with me, so vast their scope! | As well count the sand, as try to fathom them; and, were that skill mine, thy own being still confronts me.

THE THINGS most important to us are the most difficult to discuss. We can argue for hours on meaningless details. We can describe and explain them undisturbed—except perhaps for a vague sense of frustration, a conviction that we have been wasting time. It was not really that important to us.

Is it not well, after all, that we reserve silence for our most intimate thoughts? Mere words cheapen them. Those who give utterance to their most sacred desires and their highest hopes are in danger of being taken lightly. Perhaps it is pride and envy that will not sympathize with it; perhaps it is fear and shyness that cannot give it proper utterance; but perhaps most often it is simply that the inexpressible should not have been expressed.

Many of life's mysteries confront us in this way, and it is well that they do. It is well that "thy dealings with me," Lord, are "a riddle," that I may "as well count the sand, as try to fathom them." By understanding this in my innermost heart, I may at last develop a genuine humility.

I may, by this same understanding, develop true reverence for my neighbor. We who attempt the higher forms of charity must know this reverence well, Lord. When a noble young man, for instance, is in very deep distress, we do not help him by demanding that he explain in clear detail what is wrong. It is a kind of inhuman torture, which might repel him from seeking help forever. But if in our charity we understand his thoughts without his need to explain, if we can point toward the right solution without demanding a painful confession, we may see his face brighten with appreciation. If we can give expression to his feelings in such a way that he knows we feel it with him, we have made a friend, or rather, have made ourselves friends, and the inexpressible has been safeguarded. A young man's fear of expressing certain interior things may often be a blessing: it preserves his respect for them; it saves him from abusing them or ignoring them.

Man's highest ideals and greatest loves need this quality of mystery and silence. It is well that the things most precious to us "are beyond our reach," so that "no thought of ours can attain it." We are not blessed in glibly thinking we can explain away our own intuitions, not to mention what presumption it is to claim that we understand the innermost motives and aspirations of others.

To think, Lord, that I know exactly what is wrong or what troubles everyone else, and that I can set everyone right by a statement of my imperial judgment is indeed a brazen, naive species of pride. If I can say with the psalmist in regard to myself, "A riddle, O my God, thy dealings with me, so vast their scope"— and this is something I do like to say:—shall I find reason to respect less the mysteries of Your dealings with my neighbor?

You gave me a mind with which to judge, it is true; but it is not right for me to elect myself to the "highest" court, interpreting the innermost conscience of my neighbor—no, not even if he be much younger than I. It is a kind of immodesty; that interior chamber You have veiled from me. Let me know the soul of my neighbor as a treasure-house of god-like mystery. Let me reverence it as I reverence my own. Let no soul be lost or harmed or embittered by my rash irreverence.

Let me know "the tender love of Christian brotherhood, that kind of trembling from mercy and fear which seizes, in the presence of another soul, a soul marked with the love of God" (Jacques Maritain, *Quelques pages sur Léon Bloy*).

Psalm *139*

THE NEGLECTED COMMANDMENT

Rescue me, Lord, from human malice, save me from the lovers of oppression, / always plotting treachery in their hearts, always at their quarrelling, / tongues sharp as the tongues of serpents, lips that hide the poison of adders.

MANY TIMES King David in the psalms refers to the sins against what today we call the neglected commandment: "Thou shalt not slander thy neighbor."

It is not enough to explain these frequent references in terms of the special sufferings of David himself. Nor should we be satisfied by recognizing these experiences as our own. For since the psalms are Your inspired work, Lord, it is clear that You wished to give us clear and repeated warnings against "lips that hide the poison of adders," and "tongues sharp as the tongues of serpents."

It is little consolation to apologize and explain that most of our unjust criticism is done without thinking or without realizing the harmful consequences. No one is ever genuinely consoled by assuring himself that he acted without thinking—unless, indeed, he has the insolence to excuse himself for not thinking.

For when we stop to reflect upon the offences committed by our tongues, Lord, we are confronted by a long parade of petty vices—pride, envy, revenge, impatience, sloth—every form of selfishness from inflated ambition to thwarted passion. Not only has the tongue gotten out of control: the virtues of which it ought to be the instrument of expression have decayed, if ever they were strong.

"It is what comes out of a man's mouth that defiles him, not what goes in," You said, Lord.

If we consider the harm done by this "plotted treachery in our hearts," Lord, we shall be appalled at the evils our tongues can multiply. There is, first and most obvious, the harm done to those whose sins and faults we reveal: the lost reputation, the lost right to what all men—strong and weak, noble and wretched, courageous and cowardly—all hold most dear: some measure of respect and honor, friends to sympathize with and trust them, to sorrow with them and rejoice with them. To be robbed of these goods by venomous tongues is an immeasurable loss, an evil whose extent can literally not be measured. Enough to say that it eventually destroys the victim's hope of reforming himself.

Macbeth, who had long ago silenced his own conscience, who seemed no longer able to shudder at his bloody deeds, was not yet too cold to mourn the tragedy of lost reputation:

> I have lived long enough: my way of life
> Is fall'n into the sere, the yellow leaf;
> And that which should accompany old age,
> As honour, love, obedience, troops of friends,
> I must not look to have; but, in their stead,
> Curses, not loud but deep, mouth-honour, breath,
> Which the poor heart would fain deny, and dare not.
>
> *(Macbeth, V, 3)*

Good men and women instinctively feel the cowardly method employed by the slanderer. His victims are knifed in the back, with no chance to defend themselves. It is in no way a fair fight.

Better persons realize, too, the harm done to the speaker himself. Not only has he added sins against charity to his list, not only has he revealed his state of mind, but he has further deteriorated his condition. He has further blinded himself to his own faults, has convinced himself, "I'm not as bad as. . . ," has cut down the hope of ever conquering his own vices.

And there is yet, most subtle of all, the harm done to all who hear the slander or detraction, an evil that can only be guessed at by the best of men, the most careful, the most discerning. Who shall measure the extent of the poison, the hardly perceptible moral deterioration which such talk must finally bring about? Who can determine what scandal is actually effected? Who can read the souls of those listening, who can observe the fading good intentions, the falling off from efforts towards stronger virtue, the dim shadows of evil that becloud—however slightly—the sight of God and His goodness, the ideal toward which every soul must constantly work?

You alone know the full measure of evils, Lord, but can I not be among these latter discerning souls, whom I have dared to call "the best" among the listeners—those who have in fact no desire to listen, or who listen with fear, and pray to avert the yet unknown consequences of each slander?

Might it not be that sins against the eighth commandment have done more than any other sin to corrupt a whole society, to corrode nations, and bring misery to cities, towns, and families? Does not this sin constantly cut away the respect and reverence which men should have for goodness and virtue, and the charitable esteem in which we should hold our fellowman?

"Man He created to His own image and likeness." Behold, Lord, how we have disfigured the image in one another! "Rescue me, Lord, from human malice, save me from the lovers of oppression. . . ." Let me never be numbered among them!

Psalm 140

TRUE FRIENDS

Lord, set a guard on my mouth, post a sentry before my lips; / do not turn my heart towards thoughts of evil, and deeds of treachery; / never let me take part with the wrong-doers, and share

*the banquet with them. / Rather let some just man deal me heavy
blows; this shall be his kindness to me; / reprove me, and it shall
be balm poured over me; such unction never will this head refuse.*

THREE TRUTHS are contained in this part of the psalm. First, that
I cannot resist temptation without Your grace, Lord. It was neither
mere rhetoric nor cowardice that prompted the psalmist to turn
to You rather than himself. It is only You, Lord, who can keep my
heart from evil. I am too well acquainted with myself to think
otherwise.

Second, that even good men can be very trying to my patience,
that even friends can injure me—willingly or unwillingly—and at
that I should not be surprised. This possibility and this fact is
based simply on the limitations of men. Who could foretell, even
with effort, how every word and every act will affect me? Not
even I myself!

But with a fair measure of humility and common sense, I can
profit and learn much if "some just man deal me heavy blows."
How can the psalmist call such an offense "his kindness to me"?
Clearly, Lord, we are in many ways like the world of plants. Trees,
hedges, flowers must be pruned if they are to produce their best
foliage. And there is no human being who does not need seasonal
pruning. Do we not know from the biographies of men and women
that the best of them soon corrupt when their power is not curbed,
when they are not surrounded by good people who discover their
weaknesses, who sometimes "deal them heavy blows" to make them
wise and prudent?

Have I so little confidence in You, Lord, that I refuse to see
Your hand, Your Fatherly concern for me in these "blows"? If
so, let me listen to wise men, who have commented on this, the
third truth contained in the psalm: the reproof of a friend is
valuable, and should prompt me to love him the more.

"A faithful friend is the medicine of life and immortality," writes
Ecclesiastes (6:16). How shall he be medicine, if there is no disease
to cure, no strength to give?

"Friendship was given us by nature as the helper of virtue, not as a comrade of vice," wrote Cicero, "because virtue cannot attain her highest aims unattended, but only in union and fellowship with another" (*De Amicitia,* n. 82). How shall there be pure virtue, if vice is not pointed out and curbed?

Like all of Your creatures, Your gifts, Your tokens of divine love, Lord, You have given us friends to bring us to heaven:

> Friendship, peculiar boon of Heav'n,
>   The noble mind's delight and pride,
> To men and angels only giv'n,
> To all the lower world denied.
>   (Samuel Johnson, *Friendship*)

Psalm *141*

CHALLENGE AND CONQUEST

I look to the right of me, and find none to take my part; / all hope of escape is cut off from me, none is concerned for my safety. / To thee, Lord, I cry, claiming thee for my only refuge, all that is left me in this world of living men.

EVERY HERO who has lived long in the minds of men has been able to say this prayer with King David. Every victory worth singing has followed a painful struggle. It is the very nature of our life on earth.

Great men always had great obstacles to overcome—so great, in fact, that at times they failed. Caesar had his wars of conquest, then was defeated himself because he had not overcome all obstacles: his enemies in the senate. Alexander the Great had an empire to conquer, and conquered it, then died young, himself conquered by his weakness for drink.

Our own national heroes, Washington and Lincoln, could often say with David, "All hope of escape is cut off from me; I find none to take my part." These very impossibilities were, in a sense, the cause of their greatness.

Life has more than enough struggle and enough impossibility for all of us. The millions of saints have proven that. There is no end of adventure, battle, and conquest for any man or woman who will accept the challenge. Thanks to You, Lord, there will always be another unique saint, like a Joan of Arc, a Thomas More, a Vincent de Paul, a Francis Xavier, or a Thérèse of Lisieux.

It is in the very blood of humankind to thrill at the sight of a struggle, a difficult enemy to be vanquished. What boy has not come alive at the story-book heroes—Jim Hawkins' struggle and victory in *Treasure Island,* or the trials and temptations of Ben Hur, Robinson Crusoe, Robin Hood, Huckleberry Finn, Oliver Twist? Every good story has a war for the hero to wage, great tests for him to undergo, great strength to muster for the supreme crisis, because he *is* a heroic figure.

From the bloody, crude efforts of Beowulf, to the more cultured, subtle trials of Hamlet and the sublime, spiritual struggle of Chantal in Bernanos' *Joy,* mankind has always seen the need for conflict, and men and women alike have grown strong and noble by the challenge. It does not matter that these heroes suffered death at the hands of the enemy: their heroism has already made them immortal.

St. James points out this truth in his epistle; he tells us that the immortals of the Old Testament—Abraham, Jacob, Joseph in Egypt, Moses, Elias, Job, Judith, Esther, David, Jeremias, and all the prophets—all these great men and women, these heroic people prove that "only through great trials shall we enter the kingdom of God."

All great men suffered many things before they achieved their victory; when there were not great enemies from without, there was always the great enemy within: sloth, weariness, the desire for an easier life, discouragement, the temptation to rest here and proceed no further. Such must have been the trials of explorers like Marco Polo and Magellan; of scientists like Galileo, the Curies, Pasteur; the great poets like Dante, Shakespeare, Keats and Browning. All were wearied with labor before their tasks were accomplished.

But the greatest example of all is that of Jesus Christ, and the complete and perfect sacrifice He made, the example of perfection He gave once for all, the great and inhuman sufferings he underwent before the day of His great victory: the redemption of the world and His own Resurrection from the dead.

There is no better remedy for the fear and discouragement that comes to me when nothing "is left to me in this world of living men," than to recall, from the lives of all men worth remembering, that before Easter Sunday there must always be Good Friday.

Psalm 142

A THIRST UNQUENCHED

What man is there living that can stand guiltless in thy presence? | See how my enemies plot against my life, how they have abased me in the dust, set me down in dark places, like the long-forgotten dead! | My spirits are crushed within me, my heart is cowed. And my mind goes back to past days; | I think of all thou didst once, dwell on the proofs thou gavest of thy power. | To thee I spread out my hands in prayer, for thee my soul thirsts, like a land parched with drought.

No FALL, LORD, is as fearful and as bitter as the fall of those You once had raised to the greatest heights. David, who in so many ways deserved the greatest glory, now had been "abased in the dust," and had learned "how his enemies plotted against his life." But he had the humility to know that he had sinned, too, had deserved punishment: "What man is there living that can stand guiltless in thy presence?" And never did he abandon You or complain against You, as having dealt unjustly with him. Like a true, faithful lover, he sued for Your mercy, by reminding You— and reminding himself—of days past, of days in which the clear signs of Your generosity, of Your lavish favors surrounded him: "My mind goes back to past days; I think of all thou didst once, dwell on the proofs thou gavest of thy power." Like a true, noble heart, rather than rebel or blame You for his present suffering, he thirsts for Your return, pleads with You to make known Your presence again.

Lord, make me true, humble, and loyal as this servant of Yours. When my days of suffering come, whatever the source of pain may be, keep all bitterness out of my heart. Remove far from me any rancor or sourness of attitude. For these things only increase the pain and make the cross unprofitable to me, when I ought to know that in Your mercy You gave me the cross to save me.

Let there be no other thirst in my heart but to embrace such a cross, even to seek it, that my love might be exercised. "For thee my soul thirsts," Lord, not for revenge, or hatred, or pride in human recognition.

Most tragic are those whose thirst for earthly power and pleasure turns to bitterness within them. These untrue ambitions must at last poison us, since they were not made to be our true nourishment—much less to be our saturation. The darkness and the "crushed spirits" that these worldly reverses bring were meant to be our warning, our signal that another way to safety must be taken.

There is no other way, my Lord, than that pointed out by St. Augustine: "Our hearts are restless until they rest in Thee." My thirst for true refreshment must ever be unquenched. I must accept nothing untrue, which would only in the end poison me, turning all to bitterness and despair. With David, my thirst must be single and constant: "Do not turn thy face away from me," Lord, "and leave me like one sunk in the abyss. . . . Thou art my God" (and nothing and no one less can be so), "teach me to do thy will; let thy gracious spirit lead me, safe ground under my feet."

Psalm *143*

STRONG FOR BATTLE

Blessed be the Lord, my refuge, who makes these hands strong for battle, these fingers skilled in fight; | the Lord who pities me and grants me safety, who shelters me and sets me at liberty, | who protects me and gives me confidence. . . . And is not the people happy, that has the Lord for its God?

BLESSED IS THE MAN, indeed, who thanks God for making him "strong for battle" and "skilled in fight." Such a man understands the purpose for which God has placed him on this earth. "No rest on earth; there is peace enough in heaven," has been the battle cry of the saints.

Here is something of vital importance that we moderns must learn, Lord. We tend to deceive ourselves. We have the latest comforts, and we have the mistaken notion that they are going to bring us happiness. We forget that life is a battle, and happiness is won only by "skill in battle." We like the easy life: eating, sleeping, and being entertained. We know well enough that the easy life has never produced a great man. But what too many of us forget is that the easy life has never even brought *happiness*. That softness and living for a good time has never produced heroes, every one knows. That softness also produces very unhappy men, almost every one forgets.

But there comes a day—and it cannot come too soon for our own good—when we must face life as it really is. It is a period of trial; it is the time in which God tests us, to see what we are worth.

God has given us freedom; but He does not force happiness upon us against our own will. Greatness will never come floating into my lap, Lord, while I am having a good time. If I want nobility, I myself must make the necessary sacrifices. Greatness only comes with hard work; greatness has to be earned, every square inch of it.

Have we really, Lord, fallen into the old materialistic error of the ancients that earthly goods in abundance are the sure sign of God's blessing on a nation and its people? Has our thinking advanced so little in three thousand years?

And do the lives of Your great saints, Jesus, bear out such a supposition? Were the saints not, and shall they not always be, the people most blessed by God? And have any of them been raised to the altars and called blessed by men because they boasted of the greatest material comforts? Can we even *imagine* a saint seated deep in a soft chair, relaxed and grown fat on the money he's made and the gadgets he's installed to insure every comfort and the precautions he's taken to remain *undisturbed*?

And finally, my Lord, is this the picture we Christians get of *Your* life, which—we would be first to insist—is the "true pattern of life for all the faithful"? *Regnavit a ligno Deus*—"Our God reigns from the Cross," the Church tells us repeatedly in the liturgy. But nowhere are we told that this glorious throne of Yours was the latest in design for comfort and convenience.

Psalm *144*

I GET SO BORED

And shall I not extol thee, my God, my king; shall I not bless thy name for ever and for evermore? | Blessing shall be thine, day after day; for ever and for evermore praised be thy name.

GOD IS TO BE PRAISED without interruption, without change, without end. A fine thought in word and in writing, the modern reader agrees. But in work? There are the Trappists, the Carthusians, the Poor Clares—the chosen cloistered souls; let them take up the endless praise of God. Not us—we're entirely too busy.

We're really not as busy as that, and we know it. We have time for everything else. We have more leisure than any generation the world has seen. We have endless time for parties, sports, entertainments, gossip, and mere idleness.

It's not the time that really bothers us, Lord. It's our peculiar modern fear of boredom. We can't sit still and think of life's meaning. It frightens us; we dread the thought of a quiet hour. Even in our activities, we must be constantly entertained. We complain sarcastically of having attended another "*bored* meeting"—to which, however, we ourselves contributed nothing.

Our children imitate us with great success. They hate school, grumble about boring classes, long to get away from the awful silence and the obligation to think! "Let's do something different today. Life gets so boring," we are told.

What is real boredom? Merely repeating an action regularly? Hardly. We eat and sleep, wash, dress, and primp ourselves, and never seem to tire of these common things. Some have defined boredom as "getting sick of doing nothing." Or better, it is "weariness of doing nothing worthwhile."

Surely the greatest remedy for boredom is serious, worthwhile work. I could not sincerely become bored if I knew that my day's work had really given praise to God. If I spent another day trying to inflate my own importance and striving to saturate myself with the world's pleasures, most likely I have failed in both and have finished another day sick of myself and of the world.

If I am waiting for others to make my life interesting and exciting, Lord, if I am willfully bored, I deserve all the feeling of emptiness that accompanies it; for I am, in fact, empty. If I can think of nothing better to do with my leisure than sleep or watch television indiscriminately or stand on street corners and stare at the world going by, I am empty. If I am incapable of rescuing myself from boredom because I am a flitting butterfly, never content more than five minutes, then, Lord, You have only one consolation for me.

You can say to my problem: "Well, child, if ever you begin to make yourself useful to others, you won't be bored anymore. If ever you begin to practice the rudiments of charity, life will become interesting. If ever you really learn what it means to love God and your neighbor, if ever you begin 'to bless My Name for ever and evermore' in reality, life will be anything but boring. Your problem then will be, not having enough hours each day to accomplish the good you desire to do.

"But if you continue to yawn away your life waiting for pleasures to come, if you keep dragging your feet going nowhere, life will be a bore, and when you die, nobody will really be able to say they miss you. The people we miss when they're gone, you see, are those who with their love of God and neighbor, with their persistent generosity, have made life happier for everyone around them."

Psalm 145

MAN-MADE MONOTONY

*Praise the Lord, my soul; while life lasts, I will praise the Lord; /
of him, my God, shall my songs be while I am here to sing them.*

"Now what could be more monotonous than that?" asks the
modern listener—if he's at all listening.

"Spend my life praising the Lord? A routine of psalms and
hymns? What do you take me for?" says the modern Christian.

He is thinking of sad angels on fleecy clouds, plucking inadequate
musical instruments: child-sized harps, lutes, brass trumpets, and
even banjos! Praising God like these sorrowful creatures in pale-
colored gowns which he sees on cheap Christmas and Easter
cards? It seems too much punishment for a man to take.

Well, if he took the time to investigate, he could very easily dispel those false notions of heaven and the praise of God. There is
very much he could do to find his way to the living God with the
reason God gave him—not to mention the wealth of a virile and
vigorous Catholic writing from the Church Fathers to our own
lively contemporaries. Least of all things are the living God and
His saints dull or uninteresting, least of all are they sentimental or
flossy. This the modern Christian can learn quickly enough, if he
has the least desire.

But too often this fear of the non-existent religious boredom is a
cloak. The real fear is not the fear of boredom or of a sugary
mentality. Quite the contrary! He fears the very vigor of God's demands, the pains of the Christian's endless battle, the strain of developing a Christ-like will power. He is like a boy who says he
does not like football because it requires no skill, when really he

inwardly fears getting hurt, or being humiliated by stronger and more skillful players.

Too many of us, Lord, who pretend to fear the "boredom" of religion, the "monotony" of praising You "while life lasts," too many of us simply want to do nothing. We falsely term "boring" the very things that would deliver us from the greater boredom we desire. We fear all things that might compel us to do something worthwhile—because these great works always demand some sacrifice from us.

The danger we are in, Lord, is very great. Doing nothing is a first-class form of selfishness. And selfishness is the principal element of sin. Utterly bored with ourselves and the little we accomplish, and afraid of the effort or the self-effacement or the ridicule we might suffer if we rise out of our lethargy, we will turn to some form of sin as a way of getting something done. We call it "getting the fun out of life," we call it "living only once." In other words, we are so self-centered that when we do rise from sleep, we act in a selfish way.

Take any sin you choose—gossip, stealing, cheating, neglect of duty, anger, impurity—they are all forms of selfishness. It is the people who cannot get interested in doing good out of pure love of God and neighbor who fall into these snares.

People who are charitable, generous, patient, thoughtful of others, eager to work for Christ—such people have no time for sins. Nor do they have the selfishness that causes sin. To praise the Lord while life lasts, to make Him the subject of all their hopes—this is a constant joy to them. They find endless work to be done in praise of God; every creature leads them to Him; every talent is spent for Him; they have no time for boredom.

Psalm *146*

GRATITUDE FOR LIFE

Strike up, then, in thanksgiving to the Lord, with the harp's music praise our God; | the God who curtains heaven with cloud, and lays up a store of rain for the earth, | who clothes the mountain-sides with grass, with corn for man's need. . . .

AT FIRST THOUGHT, gratitude seems to be something we give away, a kind of return we make for favors received. Thus the psalmist asked, "What return shall I make to the Lord for all He has given me?"

But to the psalmist, as to the poet, there are

> Two kinds of gratitude: the sudden kind
> We feel for what we take, the large kind
> We feel for what we give.

Our larger thanks should be for the larger gratitude—what we give in appreciating God, creation, ourselves; the joy of recognizing what we have, what we are, what is constantly being given us. While it is true that all who have done us genuine good deserve something of ourselves in return, we really do not give anything away in being thankful.

Truly, Lord, this is the mystery of giving. That gratitude we feel for what we have given, as well as for what others have given, that gratitude we cannot give away. It is rooted in the heart, where it remains, the secret of all happiness.

Without gratitude, no one could ever be truly happy. That is why the Church has given so much of the text of the Mass to thanksgiving. Our whole life ought to be a miniature of the Mass, just as Christians are to be miniature Christs.

And therefore it is we, not You, Lord, who suffer from our lack of gratitude. When You showed sadness at the ingratitude of the nine lepers, You were not feeling sorry for Yourself. You were distressed at the loss suffered by the nine men themselves, who had missed the greater happiness of the one grateful Samaritan. The true blessing of the miracle was the joyous, thankful heart of the receiver, and this greater grace the nine others had rejected.

What You said, Jesus, was not "Why have the nine not returned to thank me," but "Has no one been found to give glory to God except this stranger?" That glory is an interior quality of heart.

Psalm 147

NOT GIVEN TO ALL

Praise the Lord, Jerusalem; Sion, exalt thy God! / He it is . . . that makes thy land a land of peace, and gives thee full ears of wheat to sustain thee. . . . / This is the God who makes his word known to Jacob, gives Israel ruling and decree. / Not such his dealings with any other nation; nowhere else the revelation of his will. Alleluia.

BOASTING this may be called, but justified boasting. This, the chosen people of God, had been honored above all the nations of the world. To no other race had He revealed Himself, directly and intimately. These people were indeed His favorites, a fact proven by countless messages and miracles, and by promises beyond the highest hopes of the heathen.

Yet when we read the whole account of God's chosen ones, we may rightly ask which is the stronger: the just pride or the just

complaint? Which do we hear oftener, Lord: that these are indeed
Your people, or that they have strayed far from You? "This
people honors me with their lips, but their heart is far from me."

Numberless the complaints, Lord Jesus, immeasurable the sorrow You felt for this people, so privileged, so blessed, and so ignorant of what they had received. Throughout the psalms, throughout the prophecies, throughout Your public life, Lord, I have
heard Your complaints. From Isaias as from Yourself, I have
heard the story of the chosen vineyard, the garden of Your divine
delight. I have heard how You expected to find fruit, and found
only thorns. "What then shall the Master of that vineyard do?"
You asked. And those very people who knew no gratitude answered,
condemned themselves out of their own mouth: "He shall take the
vineyard away, and give it to others, who will yield the fruits thereof
in due season."

Let us take warning, then, Lord, while we have time. We, like
those people whom You once rejected, "eat the same prophetic food,
and drink the same prophetic drink, and are nourished by the
same prophetic rock, the rock that is Christ." Must it be said of us,
too, that "with most of them, God was ill pleased"? (I Cor. 10:4-5).

How much we ourselves feel the slightest ingratitude, Lord. Those
who have received any special favor from us are expected to pay for
it dearly. And truly, the ingratitude of our fellowman is painful:

> Blow, blow, thou winter wind,
> Thou are not so unkind
> As man's ingratitude. . . .
> Freeze, freeze, thou bitter sky,
> Thou dost not bite so nigh
> As benefits forgot.
> (*As You Like It,* II, 7)

It is good for me, Lord, to feel deeply this callousness of my
friends, of those to whom I have given much. For in this pain I
shall learn the pain I myself have caused. In their thanklessness I

see the image and quality of my own gratitude. In the hurt I feel, I learn the pain I have caused others.

Whenever again I look down upon someone who has returned me evil for good, Lord, let me say in all truth: "There is the image of myself. There is what I do to You, day after day, my Lord, in return for the graces You have lavished on me. There go I, my Lord. What I despise in him is what I myself have done too often to count.

"Then, at least, my Lord, I can forgive him. Then perhaps You will say, 'He is not entirely ungrateful, after all. He remembers his own falls, and now repents.' Forgive us our offences, Lord, as we forgive those who offend us."

Psalm 148

A NAME AS NO OTHER

All you kings and peoples of the world, all you that are princes and judges on earth; young men and maids, old men and boys together; / let them all give praise to the Lord's name. His name is exalted as no other, his praise reaches beyond heaven and earth. . . .

WHEN WE ARE GIVEN a name in infancy, no one can foretell what that name may some day mean. Nor can our family name predict what value, what grace or disgrace, it may some day merit in our hands.

But the name that is "exalted as no other" was given to a child a thousand years before his birth. And every name he was given in the prophecies that followed was significant: they were names that none other on earth could ever merit.

He was called the Messiah, "he who is to be sent." Already in the Book of Genesis we hear of him: "Juda shall not want a branch from his stem, a prince drawn from his stock, until the day when he comes who is to be sent to us, he, the hope of the nations" (Genesis 49:10).

He was called the Christ, the Anointed One. A king, a leader, chosen and sacred. Caiaphas said to Him, "I adjure thee, by the living God, that thou tell us if thou be the Christ, the Son of the living God."

Many of the names by which he is known were given him by his prophet Isaias, some seven hundred years before his birth: "For our sakes a child is born, to our race a son is given, whose shoulder will bear the sceptre of princely power. What name shall be given him? Peerless among counsellors, the mighty God, Father of the world to come, the Prince of peace. Ever wider shall his dominion spread, endlessly at peace; he will sit on David's kingly throne [son of David], to give it lasting foundations of justice and right; so tenderly he loves us, the Lord of hosts" (Isaias 9:6–7).

And so, seven centuries before his coming, the world already knew his name. Isaias himself had taken his name, the Hebrew "Yeshaya," God the Savior, in accordance with his own message, "God himself shall come and save us." From this same prophecy, this same hope for a Savior, we have the name *Yeshu,* Jesus, Savior.

When, in due time, his birth was announced to Joseph, the angel told the husband of Mary what the child's name would be, and why that name would be given him:

"Joseph, son of David, do not be afraid to take to thee Mary thy wife, for it is by the power of the Holy Spirit that she has conceived this child. And she will bear a son, whom thou shalt call Jesus, for he is to save his people from their sins" (Matt. 1:20–21).

This is the name of Him whose name, as the psalmist sings, "is exalted as no other," whose "praise reaches beyond heaven and earth." These are almost the very words used by St. Paul in speaking of Jesus' death on the cross: "That is why God has raised him to such a height, given him that name which is greater than any other name; so that everything in heaven and on earth and under the earth must bend the knee before the name of Jesus" (Phil. 2:9–10).

This is that name of which St. Peter said, "Salvation is not to be found elsewhere; this alone of all the names under heaven has been appointed to men as the one by which we must needs be saved" (Acts 4:12).

This name, most dear to every true Hebrew in hope and anticipation, in desire and longing, is most dear to every true Christian, in joy and fulfillment. The name of Jesus is, in the words of St. Bernard, "honey to the mouth, music to the ear, a shout of gladness in the heart. . . . Behold with the dawning of that name every cloud scatters and clear day returns. Has anyone fallen into sin, and does he run despairingly towards the toils of death? If he but invokes the name of Life, will not life be renewed within him?" (Sermon 15 on the Canticles).

Few have written so beautifully as St. Bernard on this divine name. Meditating on the Canticle's praise of the beloved's name, this saint writes: "Not without reason does the Holy Spirit compare the name of the Bridegroom to oil, when he inspires the bride to say to the Bridegroom: Thy name is as oil poured out. For oil gives light, it nourishes, it anoints. It kindles fire; it renews the flesh; it assuages pain. It is light, food, medicine. See how like to this is the name of the true Bridegroom. It is light when it is preached; it is food in meditation; it is balm and healing when it is invoked for aid."

Psalm 149

TOWARD VICTORY

Still the Lord shows favor to his people, still he relieves the oppressed, and grants them victory. / In triumph let thy faithful servants rejoice, rejoice and take their rest.

No ONE desires suffering or humiliation for its own sake. It is for the sake of the final victory, the triumph in which we at last "rejoice and take our rest" that we bear all things, suffer all, hope and persevere, strive faithfully to the end.

Only when our eyes are constantly on this final goal, when our whole inspiration is from the final victory, only then are we truly happy. No one really wants happiness today only, at the loss of tomorrow and ever after. The greater joy is the joy of anticipation, the assurance that the best is yet to come.

Sometimes this anticipation appears in the form of prudence or wisdom rather than enthusiasm or emotion, but in those who truly love God, the anticipation is always present nonetheless.

Raskolnikov the murderer, in Dostoyevsky's *Crime and Punishment,* is saved by meeting such a soul in Sonia. Reminding Sonia of how the evil Luzhin might have sent her to prison, innocent or not, he asks her, "Imagine, Sonia, that you had known all Luzhin's intentions beforehand. Known, that is, for a fact, that they would be the ruin of Katerina Ivanovna and the children and yourself thrown in—since you don't count yourself for anything. . . . Well, if suddenly it all depended on your decision whether he or they should go on living, that is whether Luzhin should go on living and doing wicked things, or Katerina should die? How would you decide which of them was to die? I ask you?"

What he wanted was her agreement that all evil-doers ought to be exterminated. But she answered what we would expect of one who truly loved God, and looked forward to His triumph:

"But I can't know the Divine Providence. . . . And why do you ask what can't be answered? What's the use of such foolish questions? How could it happen that it should depend on my decision —who has made me a judge to decide who is to live and who is not to live?"

St. Augustine speaks of this anticipation of the just when commenting upon the psalms. "Why does God allow evil men to live on doing evil?" For the sake of their conversion, he concludes, or to exercise the good men. Strength must be made stronger, virtue must be exercised. "Would to God, then, that they who persecute us would be converted and persecuted with us." Such a statement seems to be folly—and it is. It is the folly of the just, who know that always and ever "the Lord relieves the oppressed, and grants them victory." It is the folly of the just, who know that he who is humble must be humbled, he who loves must love unto death, he who is holy can be yet holier. He who has God's favor, must have it yet more. Love bears with the beloved, clings to him, "even to the edge of doom." No rest now; eternity is long enough. To this eternity all true happiness looks.

There is, to be sure, some measure of happiness in reminiscing. We can, to some extent, relive the happiness of days long gone. But if a new and deeper appreciation has not replaced it, if the cause of happiness is not greater in us now than it was, there is really only sadness in the memory of yesterday's joys.

That is why my heart and mind must be ever set on the day of triumph, Lord. That is how I can find genuine happiness in today's burdens and sorrows. If I am faithful in these trials, I am schooled with the saints. Their constant and superior happiness was that of the psalmist, who in viewing the course of his life saw there always the Lord who ever and everywhere "relieves the oppressed and grants them victory," who always and in all ways makes sure that "in triumph his faithful servants rejoice, rejoice and take their rest."

There can be no unhappiness for men of this attitude.

Psalm 150

THE GRAND FINALE

Praise God in his sanctuary, praise him on his sovereign throne. /
Praise him for his noble acts, praise him for his surpassing greatness.

IT IS presumed that the Book of Psalms has opened for us the way to true happiness in God. If anything has become clear throughout these psalm-meditations, it must be that the end for which we are created is joy in God, and all things on earth, bitter or sweet, are meant to lead us to God.

It remains for us to rejoice in this unfolding revelation. If we have caught the spirit of the psalms, we are fully prepared, like the saints, to make melody in our hearts to God.

After the struggle, the victory; and after the victory, the feast and song. In books, on stage and screen, when the struggle ends, the story is over. We see no more; the characters fade into memory. It is the end. It seems not in the nature of this world to tell us more.

Not so, fortunately, is real life. The second life, the day of triumph, is an eternal day, with no new conflict to mar its joy. There is activity aplenty, but no more danger, no fear of loss or failure. And it is not the end—but the beginning.

What remains, then, but the grand finale, which is at once the grand opening, too—the trumpeting of silver clarion, the joyous dance of the tambour, the majestic crash of the cymbal. "Rejoice! God has been found, and we are saved. Alleluia! praise God!"

> Praise him with the bray of the trumpet,
> Praise him with harp and zither.
> Praise him with the tambour and the dance,
> Praise him with the music of string and of reed,
> Praise him with the clang of the cymbals,
> The cymbals that ring merrily.
> All creatures that breath have,
> Praise the Lord. Alleluia.